GOVERNING
UNDER
STRESS

GOVERNING
UNDER
STRESS

The Implementation of Obama's
Economic Stimulus Program

TIMOTHY J. CONLAN, PAUL L. POSNER,
and PRISCILLA M. REGAN, Editors

Georgetown University Press
Washington, DC

Library of Congress Cataloging-in-Publication Data

Names: Conlan, Timothy J., editor. | Posner, Paul L., editor. | Regan, Priscilla M., editor.
Title: Governing under stress : the implementation of Obama's economic stimulus program / Timothy J. Conlan, Paul L. Posner, and Priscilla M. Regan, editors.
Other titles: Public management and change.
Description: Georgetown University Press : Washington, DC, 2017. | Series: Public management and change series | Includes bibliographical references and index.
Identifiers: LCCN 2016007100 (print) | LCCN 2016008597 (ebook) | ISBN 9781626163690 (hc : alk. paper) | ISBN 9781626163706 (pb : alk. paper) | ISBN 9781626163713 (eb)
Subjects: LCSH: United States. American Recovery and Reinvestment Act of 2009. | United States—Economic policy—2009– | Economic development—United States. | Economic stabilization—United States. | Federal aid—United States. | Political planning—United States.
Classification: LCC HC106.84 .G677 2017 (print) | LCC HC106.84 (ebook) | DDC 338.973—dc23
LC record available at http://lccn.loc.gov/2016007100

♾ This book is printed on acid-free paper meeting the requirements of the American National Standard for Permanence in Paper for Printed Library Materials.

18 17   9 8 7 6 5 4 3 2   First printing

Printed in the United States of America

Cover design by Rebecca Lown. Cover image adapted from ARRA logo.

CONTENTS

ILLUSTRATIONS

Figures

Tables

PREFACE

This volume chronicles an episode in our national policy experience that warrants a book-length treatment. The American Recovery and Reinvestment Act (the Recovery Act, or ARRA) constituted a public action that conventional wisdom said could not be accomplished in our seemingly gridlocked policy process. Yet, in the wake of the most significant financial crisis in postwar America, policymakers responded by enacting a stimulus whose magnitude was among the largest undertaken by the nations belonging to the Organization for Economic Cooperation and Development, helping to pull the US economy out of the ditch of recession. The many programs and subsidies that composed the stimulus provided a laboratory for analyses of policy formation and implementation.

What most intrigued the authors contributing to this volume was the widespread reliance by the national government on a highly decentralized array of networks to actually deliver stimulus programs and dollars. Unlike the New Deal, Obama's stimulus did not prompt the creation of new federal bureaucracies and employees but rather engaged a wide range of third parties across the states, local governments, nonprofits, and for-profit firms as the program's implementers. As such, ARRA represented the culmination of broader trends in the nation's governance that had been building during the postwar years.

Those of us teaching in George Mason University's Master of Public Administration (MPA) program had decided several years before to transform the program to place the study of "third-party governance" at the core of our curriculum. We strongly felt that students going into public service either within or engaged with government needed better grounding and skills in orchestrating and managing the shared governance networks that had become the new norm for American public administration at all levels.

Our faculty collectively came to realize that the extant scholarship in public administration had not delivered the research needed to inform the study of these increasingly pervasive governance models. We saw within the Recovery Act an opportunity to build a deep, rich, and empirically based understanding of emerging practices in this relatively uncharted world of shared governance.

It is unusual, perhaps even extraordinary, to find a group of seven colleagues in the same academic program who agree on anything, let alone are able to work together collaboratively for several years on a book project like this one. Thus, first and foremost, this book is a testament to the collegiality of the George Mason MPA program faculty.

We also benefited from the able support of many of George Mason's MPA research assistants. These students helped with data collection and in managing an extraordinarily complex undertaking involving the assembly of numerous documents, databases, and interviews. The following students were the key contributors: Brett Doyle, Tim Higashi, Ashley Raphael, Danielle Rainwater, Dana Kaasik, Shelley Bradley, Asif Shahan, and Emily Connolly. Additionally, Janice Cohen and Carrie Drummond provided extensive administrative support during this project, and Carrie played a critical role in editing early versions of many chapters.

This research would not have been possible without the generous funding support and encouragement of the Smith Richardson Foundation. Its support was essential for us to undertake the fieldwork in both Washington and the states that make this research so well grounded and credible. Its funding also enabled the preparation of a research report, *The Implementation of the Recovery Act: Networks Under Stress*, prepared under the auspices of the Centers on the Public Service at George Mason University. We are particularly thankful to Mark Steinmeyer of the Smith Richardson Foundation for his insight and patience in working with us for several years to complete this project.

Several portions of this book have been presented earlier as conference papers or presentations, including "Implementation and Shared Governance in the US Intergovernmental System: Lessons from the American Recovery and Reinvestment Act," which was recognized in 2013 with the Deil Wright Award for Best Paper by the American Political Science Association's Section on Federalism and Intergovernmental Relations. In the process, we have benefited from the comments, critiques, and suggestions of many reviewers and colleagues, and we wish to thank them all.

We also want to thank the people at Georgetown University Press for their encouragement and support. Beryl Radin, who edits the Georgetown Press series Public Management and Change and is a good friend and colleague to many of us, was instrumental in supporting the publication of this work. Given her insights on public administration and the federal system, we were gratified that she felt this project rose to sufficient importance to warrant publication. We are also grateful for the patient advice and support of

Don Jacobs, the press's managing editor. He and his capable staff, including our editor Alfred Imhoff, took a draft and turned it into a highly polished and professional book that will help generate broad interest in our message. We are also thankful for the thoughtful and detailed comments of the anonymous reviewers who examined the manuscript.

We also want to thank the many public officials and others who made themselves available for interviews. We were fortunate to have access to top officials at both federal and state levels of government, and we benefited greatly from the insights and documents that these officials provided. We also benefited from the views of other analysts and observers of the Recovery Act, some of whom we brought together at George Mason University for a workshop in December 2012.

Finally, the authors wish to collectively thank our spouses and significant others who patiently stood by us as we were sometimes overconsumed by the research and writing for this project.

We dedicate this book to the George Mason MPA program. The faculty and students of this program provided the inspiration, impetus, and support for the completion of this project.

ABBREVIATIONS

ARRA   American Recovery and Reinvestment Act
BIP   Broadband Initiatives Program
BTOP   Broadband Technology Opportunity Program
CBO   Congressional Budget Office
CDE   community development entity
CDFI Fund   Community Development Financial Institutions Fund
            (of the US Treasury)
DOE   US Department of Energy
DOT   US Department of Transportation
ED   US Department of Education
FAHP   Federal-Aid Highway Program
FCC   Federal Communications Commission
FHWA   Federal Highway Administration
GAO   US Government Accountability Office
IG   inspector general
IRS   Internal Revenue Service
MOE   maintenance of effort
NMTC   New Markets Tax Credit
OIG   Office of Inspector General
OMB   Office of Management and Budget
PTC   Production Tax Credit
RAT Board   Recovery Accountability and Transparency Board
RTTT   Race to the Top
RUS   Rural Utilities Service
SDOT   state departments of transportation
SFSF   State Fiscal Stabilization Fund
TARP   Troubled Asset Relief Program
WAP   Weatherization Assistance Program

1

Managing the Great Recession

A STRESS TEST FOR MODERN GOVERNANCE

Timothy J. Conlan, Paul L. Posner, and Priscilla M. Regan

ON FEBRUARY 17, 2009, President Barack Obama signed the American Recovery and Reinvestment Act (the Recovery Act, or ARRA) into law. This enormous piece of legislation was one of the most important legislative achievements of Obama's presidency, and—at $787 billion—it was by far the largest and most sophisticated piece of countercyclical, antirecession policy since the 1930s. In brief, the program provided an infusion of $275 billion in additional grant-in-aid funds to state and local governments, another $288 billion to citizens and corporations in the form of tax cuts, and a remaining $224 billion in a mix of federal spending for purposes such as enhanced information technology systems in health care, clean energy production and transmission, and improvements to federal facilities and infrastructure. Among the more than ninety different federal aid programs that received additional funds under the Recovery Act were a mix of highly flexible grants to the states; additional money for existing aid programs in education, social services, and infrastructure; and new grant programs designed to stimulate innovative programs at the state and local levels.

Though hotly debated in Congress before its enactment and widely discussed in the media during its first year, the Recovery Act has attracted less scholarly attention than warranted given the initiative's size, scope, and significance. To be sure, a number of economists have examined its macroeconomic effects and have produced varying, but mostly positive, estimates of its effects on economic growth and employment.[1] A handful of other studies have sought to examine some elements of its impact on state and local finances or individual policy domains such as energy and education.[2] But these efforts have left serious gaps in our understanding of this sweeping legislation, including several theoretical puzzles raised by ARRA's implementation. This is most unfortunate. A central argument of this book is that the implementation of ARRA is uniquely informative about how large federal programs can be effectively implemented and held accountable in an era of indirect and networked governance, about how our political and governmental institutions respond to large doses of fiscal shock therapy, and about the wide discrepancy between public perceptions of governmental performance and realities on the ground.

For example, take the issue of disparate perceptions. A widely held public perception has been that ARRA was a colossal failure. A 2010 poll by the Pew Research Center found that nearly two-thirds of the responding public believed that the stimulus program failed to improve the nation's employment situation, whereas only 33 percent believed that it helped.[3] In contrast, 97 percent of economists polled by the Initiative on Global Markets at the University of Chicago believed that the stimulus initiative reduced unemployment. Moreover, two-thirds of economists believed that ARRA's economic benefits outweighed the costs of funding the program, in taxes and borrowing, whereas only 5 percent believed the costs outweighed the benefits.[4]

What explains this discrepancy in public and expert assessments? No doubt it is due in part to economists' greater knowledge of macroeconomic theory in general and to specific estimates produced by economic models of the stimulus act's effects. But the public's negative assessment of the Recovery Act was also a product of pervasive mistrust in the efficacy of government that has grown during the past several decades, fueled by unrelenting partisan attacks on the program and anecdotal media stories during and after its enactment. According to one survey, nearly half the public reported hearing mostly negative things about the stimulus program in news reporting.[5] During the summer of 2009, as the first round of stimulus funds were being spent or obligated, examples of negative news stories proliferated. A $3.4 million project in Florida to create "turtle crossings" under a busy highway received considerable, though often inaccurate, attention in the media.[6] So did improvements at a lightly used border crossing in Montana.[7] Many of these stories emanated from a collection of so-called wasteful stimulus projects collected and publicized by Senator Tom Coburn (R-OK), an iconoclastic but very conservative skeptic about most forms of government spending.

Indeed, in a program of this size, widespread waste and complexity were universally expected—by the media, which established crack investigation teams designed to root out the waste, which they assumed would be forthcoming;[8] by public interest advocates, who encouraged citizen investigations designed to "crowdsource" problems;[9] and by the Obama administration it-self, which feared negative political fallout from fraud and waste and thus built an unprecedented system of accountability and transparency into the program.[10]

However, there is surprisingly little evidence of widespread waste, fraud, and mismanagement in the Recovery Act programs. As a *USA Today* retro-spective on the program put it, "The financial losses under the 2009 Recov-ery Act have been just a fraction of what the government expected."[11] For example, in 2009 members of Congress were concerned that the Recovery Act might lose as much as $55 billion to waste and fraud, based on an esti-mate by the Association of Certified Fraud Examiners that 7 percent of funds are lost to fraud and waste in a typical program.[12] Yet after five years of audits and investigations, auditors for the Recovery and Transparency Board found only $57 million in fraudulent spending, or just 0.007 percent of the total stimulus, despite ARRA's unprecedented scope and pace of implementa-tion.[13] Consequently, ARRA is absent from Paul Light's inventory of forty-one government programs experiencing significant failures between 2001 and 2014.[14]

Indeed, many of the cases that initially seemed to be credible reports of waste or fraud in stimulus programs did not stand up on closer scrutiny, as in the case of the Florida turtle crossing project. In other cases, the Obama administration vigorously disputed the critics' characterizations of projects as wasteful or ineffective.[15] Similarly, a Mercatus Center report in 2009, which claimed that the Obama administration was selectively steering stim-ulus funds to congressional districts represented by Democrats, received considerable media attention.[16] As the political blogger Nate Silver observed, however, this report was fatally flawed. It failed to account for the fact that virtually all the congressional districts that received the most stimulus funds encompassed state capitals. As Silver noted, "A lot of stimulus funds are dis-tributed to state agencies, which are then responsible for allocating and ad-ministering the funds to the presumed benefit of citizens throughout the state."[17] It just so happened that state capitals were more likely to be repre-sented by Democrats than other, often less urbanized, areas. A subse-quent, more sophisticated reanalysis of the data by two political scientists vindicated Silver's critique. A paper by Jeffery Lazarus and Jason Reifler concluded that "these findings indicate that stimulus funds are being distrib-uted largely according to the criteria set out in the legislation. Once a House district's ability to substantively claim stimulus money is controlled for, its member's party is no longer a significant predictor of the level of funding it receives."[18]

Theoretical Perspectives on the Recovery
Act's Implementation

Even if the public rhetoric surrounding the Recovery Act was misguided or exaggerated, serious puzzles remain for both scholars and public administrators. For example, the existing political science literature on policy implementation has traditionally been pessimistic about the performance of new, large-scale federal initiatives. This was certainly true of early studies by scholars such as Martha Derthick, Jeffrey Pressman, and Aaron Wildavsky. Their research efforts into the New-Town In-Town initiative of the late 1960s and the Economic Development Administration's urban areas grants were motivated by a desire to understand why both programs were colossal failures.[19] Later research attempted to identify factors associated with the potential for successful implementation, while still conceding that "effective implementation of major programs . . . is exceedingly difficult."[20] And such problems remain. One can easily fast forward to contemporary research on more recent programs such as No Child Left Behind and find a comparable concern with why major federal programs fail to deliver on their promises.[21]

Moreover, the core findings of such implementation research make the design of the Recovery Act read like a virtual manual of what *not* to do. The literature consistently argues that factors such as program complexity, multiple layers of administration, rushed implementation, and ambiguous statutory instructions all tend to undermine effective program implementation. Yet the Recovery Act seemingly violated each and every one of these precepts.

For example, one context in which implementation research has found potential for successful implementation has been in programs that were given long periods of time to err, evolve, and improve. For example, this was a key finding of Michael Kirst and Richard Jung's analysis of the Elementary and Secondary Education Act's Title I program for disadvantaged children.[22] Similar results were later replicated across a number of programs in research conducted by Paul Peterson, Barry Rabe, and Ken Wong, who emphasized the contributions that professionalization, learning, and coalition building could make in gradually improving program implementation over time.[23] Yet, here as elsewhere, the Recovery Act appears to be precisely the type of large-scale, short-term initiative that should have been destined, based on this literature, for a rocky beginning and a short and unhappy life.

To make matters even worse, much of ARRA was implemented through techniques of indirect governance and complex intergovernmental networks. These approaches pose uniquely difficult challenges for both accountability and performance in federal programs. The heavy reliance on indirect tools of governance, such as grants and tax expenditures, and nonhierarchical networks of federal agencies, state and local governments, nonprofit organizations, and private-sector companies sharply differentiated ARRA from the last great experiment with countercyclical spending during the New Deal, which was implemented primarily through direct channels of federal administration.[24]

An impressive but nascent body of scholarship has begun to emerge on our evolving system of third-party governance in the United States. Leading scholars have made critical advancements toward understanding some key dimensions of this new type of governance by elevating the concept of network governance as a core unit of analysis in public administration research. Yet at the same time, such work has raised new questions about the performance of federally inspired or utilized implementation networks of the kind that were crucial to the Recovery Act.

For example, Robert Agranoff and Michael McGuire have investigated the role of networks in local public and nonprofit service delivery arrangements.[25] Their work, based largely on a series of detailed case studies, allowed them to distill and convey valuable lessons about the effectiveness of networks and to launch a more sophisticated discussion of the roles that various actors, including public managers, play in local, community-based initiatives. Similarly, Brinton Milward and Keith Provan have written a number of seminal studies on the formative role that networks play in multiple arenas of public administration, from local social service delivery to the "dark networks" involved in many illicit activities.[26] Finally, Stephen Goldsmith and Donald Kettl have explored how networks have evolved to become central collective action vehicles in achieving national objectives, and thus have begun a conversation about the ability of federal policymakers and managers to effectively utilize networks in federal policy implementation.[27]

A related stream of public administration research has focused on network approaches to enhancing collaboration between the public and private sectors in contemporary governance.[28] For example, Rosemary O'Leary, Lisa Blomgren Bingham, and Catherine Gerard have examined the factors that facilitate or inhibit collaboration in networks based on a series of cases drawn from local service delivery in the environment, emergency management, and social service fields.[29] More recently, John Donahue and Richard Zeckhauser have developed an intriguing framework for understanding and evaluating collaborative ventures between the public and private sectors in the pursuit of public goals.[30]

Finally, Lester Salamon and others have approached contemporary governance from the perspective of policy instruments, focusing on the "tools" used by national government leaders and managers to achieve national policy goals through nonfederal third parties. Such tools include grants, contracts, loans, loan guarantees, regulations, vouchers, and other policy instruments. This work constitutes a promising initiative to systematically understand the political, design, and management challenges associated with each tool in achieving effective, efficient, and equitable outcomes.

Despite the important contributions of these studies and related research, their findings fail to address core elements in the implementation of the Recovery Act. For example, such research has tended to focus on the local, ground-level aspects of service delivery while giving little systematic treatment to the different roles played by federal government actors in different policy and implementation networks. Similarly, most network studies have placed a primary research emphasis on horizontal collaboration between local institutions rather than the vertical collaboration between actors at different levels of government that was central to ARRA.

Federal officials are consigned to work within a networked governance world every bit as much as local officials, but there is little research providing guidance for these officials about how to navigate in a world where expectations are centralized while delivery is decentralized. In many cases, federal policymakers have little choice but to work with and through existing networks of state, local, nonprofit, and business actors. For example, as federal expenditures to tame wildfires have grown exponentially, federal officials in the Forest Service have searched for levers to prevent and mitigate the damage caused by these incidents. In the US system, they must seek the support and engagement of networks of local officials, insurance companies, and realtors, among many others, to provide for more fire-safe building and zoning patterns in rural areas throughout the nation. This is only one of many areas where federal managers are dependent on local networks to achieve national policy outcomes. Clean water, homeland security, transportation planning, and public health protection are other areas where federal managers and policymakers are searching for more effective ways to tap the potential of networks for national programs.

Indeed, some of the most important failures of domestic federal policies in recent years appear to have been associated with inadequate understanding of the pros and cons of alternative policy tools and the behavior of complex policy networks. For instance, the failures of government agencies in dealing with Hurricane Katrina reflect disconnects and miscommunications both across and within levels of government, all of which were responsible for significant roles in preparing for and responding to this natural disaster. Similarly, the failings of housing finance entities like Fannie Mae and Freddie Mac, which contributed to the financial crisis of 2008–9, illustrate the limited capacity of government to effectively oversee an extensive third-party network of public, private, and quasi-public actors.

Consequently, a large number of the high-risk areas delineated biennially by the US Government Accountability Office (GAO) stem from failures in policy networks and third-party governance, ranging from contracting failures at the National Aeronautics and Space Administration to fraud and abuse in Medicare payments to systemic weaknesses in managing low-income housing programs.[31] Thus, though the process of engaging various public and private agencies in the implementation of government programs has many benefits, it can also have profound costs. New policy design and management strategies are required so those involved can avoid these vulnerabilities in the future.

Confronting Gaps in Our Knowledge of Implementation and Network Governance

Although public administration's focus has rightly shifted from "government" to "governance" in order to encompass and understand the roles played by new policy tools and administrative networks in achieving public goals, it is important not to lose sight of the critical role that government still plays in policy networks. Indeed, *there is a need today to bring government back into governance*. Just as government increasingly operates through the channels of networks, networks often operate at the behest of and within the shadow of government and public policy. We need to better understand the key role that government policymakers and managers play in a system of shared governance. In some networks, like the partnership involved in managing the Chesapeake Bay watershed, federal environmental officials provide the administrative services of a network hub—a vital function that is critical to network sustainability. In other cases, government agencies act as the lead organizations within a policy or implementation network.[32] Thus, as federal officials undoubtedly have become more dependent on networks, many networks have likewise become more reliant on or influenced by the government.

There is also a critical need to deepen our understanding of *the federal role in networked governance*. In some network studies, government officials are described as one actor among many, consigned to accept the norms and boundaries set by the network itself as the price of admission. Although this no doubt characterizes federal roles in some network settings, in others the federal government has been far more influential. For example, the Head Start federal categorical grant program effectively created an entirely new network of early childhood education providers at the local level. And under the Intermodal Surface Transportation Efficiency Act, federal highway grant requirements empowered metropolitan planning organizations with a new role in approving projects developed by state and local officials. There are also various federal mandates whereby the federal government seeks to re-purpose existing networks. For example, local fire chiefs have been asked to focus on national homeland security goals—a focus that at the very least competes with and may trump local emergency management priorities. In federal school voucher and charter school initiatives, the federal government is seeking to inspire the creation of entirely new networks of public and private educational entities alongside the existing public school networks.

A similar gap applies to the highest realms of policymaking and governmental management. With each new presidential administration, rekindled attention is given to the management of government and the reforms that are needed to improve the performance of federal programs. To date, all new administrations have defined their management agendas in traditional hierarchical terms, assessing how well agencies are managing themselves with respect to human capital, performance, financial management, and information technology. Notwithstanding the fact that most performance goals are now achieved using indirect governance tools to influence networks of private and nonprofit organizations, businesses, and state and local governments, presidential management agendas have largely missed this important dimension. Actors in the federal management community have begun to acknowledge the importance of collaboration as an emergent theme, but there are as yet no systematic agenda items or management approaches that assess or provide guidance for agencies on managing in complex, networked environments.

Implementation Insights from ARRA: A Laboratory for Indirect Governance

A principal inspiration for this book is that the implementation of the American Recovery and Reinvestment Act provided an incomparable laboratory for understanding the dynamics of third-party governance in federal program design, management, and implementation. The economic and fiscal context of the Recovery Act, combined with its own exceptional programmatic features, provided a unique stress test of the contemporary governance system.

As with any large initiative, ARRA's design reflected a combination of deliberate policy choices and necessary legislative compromises. But the final product testified to the prominence of complex tools of indirect governance in contemporary federal policy. In total, the final version of the Recovery Act authorized $787 billion for a combination of new programs and existing ones. This complex composition arose in part from contentious debates in Congress over the relative mix of spending increases and tax cuts in the stimulus package. Republicans sought a package that emphasized tax reductions. But most Democrats believed that spending programs provide a more effective economic stimulus. They preferred a mixed program with relief for hard-pressed state and local governments, safety net assistance for those who had lost jobs or were unable to find work, and investments in both long-term and short-term infrastructure projects. The final Recovery Act package combined all these, with a little more than one-third—or $275 billion—going to states and localities in the form of grants; roughly another third, $288 billion, provided in the form of various types of tax reductions and expenditures; and the remainder a mix of federal spending, often provided through indirect tools such as contracts, grants, and loans, to a wide range of public, nonprofit, and private entities for purposes such as enhanced information technology systems in health care, clean energy production and transmission, and improvements to federal facilities and infrastructure.

The assortment of grants in the Recovery Act was also complex, incorporating a mix of very flexible aid to the states; new money for traditional Democratic priorities in education, social services, and infrastructure; and new programs designed to stimulate innovation at the state and local levels. Much of the Recovery Act's funding was primarily intended to help state and local governments finance their own policy agendas. Experience from prior countercyclical programs suggested that the more such aid is aligned with state and local goals, the faster it would be implemented to stimulate or save jobs and boost economic growth.[33]

In the area of flexible assistance to state and local governments, ARRA's two principal initiatives were a 6.2 percent increase in the federal matching rate for Medicaid and the State Fiscal Stabilization Fund for education and government services. Both were designed in large part to help cushion state budgets from the rapid falloff in state tax revenues and, in the process, minimize layoffs of state and local government employees. Together, they provided by far the largest amount of flexible federal aid to state governments since General Revenue Sharing was eliminated in 1980.

In addition to these forms of flexible assistance, other stimulus funding was provided through increases in existing federal aid programs, such as Title I education grants, federal highway grants, Community Development Block Grants, and social services programs. Overall, the Recovery Act provided funding through more than ninety separate federal grant programs. Using such established programs generally had the advantage of enabling faster state and local spending—one of the goals of stimulus spending—by taking advantage of existing administrative structures, procedures, and implementation networks. Such an approach did little to advance program innovation and reform, however.

Consequently, additional stimulus funds went into new initiatives and infrastructure enhancements, such as expanding broadband access in underserved areas, developing high-speed rail networks, and improving transportation infrastructure. Such infrastructure investments promised greater potential for enhancing long-term economic growth and promoting the Obama administration's specific new policy objectives, but such aid entailed a much longer implementation time frame.

Finally, a little more than one-third of the Recovery Act's funds were delivered in the form of tax cuts of various kinds. The largest was the $116 billion Making Work Pay tax cut, which adjusted payroll withholding rates to provide the average taxpayer with a few dollars more in each paycheck. Other individual tax cuts were provided for alternative minimum tax relief, child care, higher education, and an expanded Earned Income Tax Credit. Finally, a range of business tax cuts were included for such purposes as health information technology, green energy production, and more capital depreciation.

In addition to its heavy reliance on instruments of indirect governance, the Recovery Act was equally noteworthy for its novel administrative provisions. The law mandated unprecedented transparency for tracking the distribution and spending of funds by state and local governments, nonprofit organizations, and private contractors. This was accompanied by strict accountability provisions and processes, including a newly established Recovery Accountability and Transparency Board, intensive GAO tracking and evaluation of program implementation, and enhanced monitoring by departmental inspectors general. The ambivalent message sent by the Obama administration was to spend stimulus funds as quickly as possible, but to do so without making any mistakes and with unprecedented openness.

The innovative approach and ambitious agenda of the Recovery Act thus provide an ideal testing ground for examining policy implementation under conditions of shared and networked governance. Multiple programs under the act relied heavily on state and local governments, nonprofit organizations, private companies, and taxpayers in order to accomplish program goals and provide needed services. Moreover, the act's requirement that all funds be spent or obligated within a brief, two-year window, subject to new federal management and accountability systems, raised the stakes for third-party governance as never before.

Methodology and Research Design

In order to utilize the Recovery Act as a laboratory for exploring the federal role in diffuse policy implementation networks, this book employs a series of programmatic case studies based on field research.[34] In doing so, it builds on second- and third-generation models of implementation research design. Whereas early implementation research typically examined a single program, often in a single locale, later generations of implementation research have sought to enhance the reliability and generalizability of findings by systematically examining multiple programs in multiple locations.[35] Accordingly, this project examines six different Recovery Act programs across multiple states.

Each of the case study programs selected for this volume met several important criteria. First, each program was a policy priority under the Recovery Act, including education, energy, and infrastructure assistance. Second, each program received significant increases in funding as part of the stimulus legislation. Together, these two criteria assured that the programs received sufficient funding and managerial attention to constitute a legitimate test of the third-party governance paradigm. Third, each program represented a mix of indirect policy tools, including project grants, formula grants, and tax expenditures. This variation allowed for comparisons across indirect program types. Finally, the mix of case study subjects included both new and established programs in order to examine the consequences for implementation of existing networks versus newly created implementation networks. The framework for program selection is illustrated in figure 1.1.

Specifically, the six case study programs included in this volume are the following:

- *The State Fiscal Stabilization Fund (SFSF):* This program provided assistance to states and local school districts to avoid teacher and other government employee layoffs, modernize school facilities, and meet other priority educational and fiscal needs. It was a formula grant distributed through a mix of new and established implementation networks in the states. A separate project grant component of SFSF, the Race to the Top (RTTT) program, is also examined briefly.
- *The Federal-Aid Highway Program:* This program represented the largest federal infrastructure assistance program to state governments for the building, repair, and maintenance of highways, roads, and bridges. This is a formula grant program that provided assistance through existing implementation channels.

	TOOL:	FORMULA GRANT	PROJECT GRANT	TAX EXPENDITURE
	ESTABLISHED	Highway grants	Race to the Top	New Markets
NETWORK		SFSF		
	NEW	Weatherization	Broadband	Advanced energy

Figure 1.1. The Analytical Framework for Case Selection
Source: Timothy J. Conlan, Paul L. Posner, and Priscilla M. Regan.

- *Weatherization Assistance:* The Department of Energy provided weatherization assistance grants to states according to a formula, which then passed through federal funds to local governmental and nonprofit agencies on a project basis to help low-income individuals weatherize their homes. The dramatic expansion of the scale of this program required the establishment of new networks at the local level.
- *Broadband Access Grants:* The stimulus plan established a new project grant program to states, localities, and nonprofits to increase broadband internet access to rural, unserved, and underserved areas. This was a new grant program requiring the creation of new administrative networks.
- *The New Markets Tax Credit:* This expansion of an existing tax credit program was intended to encourage private equity investment in low-income communities. It provided a 39 percent credit against federal tax liability for investors that made equity investments in certified community development entities.
- *Advanced Energy Investment Credits:* This was a new 30 percent tax credit for facilities that made investments to produce cleaner energy.

For each case study, multiple interviews were conducted with program officials and participants in the relevant policy community in Washington as well as in a sample of three different states per program.[36] More than two hundred interviews were conducted for the case studies as a whole. Interview subjects at the national level included federal agency administrators and White House staff members, congressional committee staff members, program evaluators in GAO and other relevant federal agencies, interest group representatives, and policy specialists in various Washington think tanks. Information from these interviews was supplemented with government documents, program data, GAO and departmental inspector generals' reports, and independent policy analyses.

In addition to Washington-based research, fieldwork was conducted in three different states for each program studied. Virginia served as a common control state for each case study, and two additional states were selected per program based on factors critical to that particular program. For example, state selection for chapter 3, which examines implementation of the State Fiscal Stabilization Fund for education, was driven by considerations of state educational system organization, political leadership, and participation in Race to the Top. The three case study states were Delaware, Virginia, and Minnesota. Virginia and Minnesota typify two major methods of local school system organization: by county (Virginia) and independent school district (Minnesota). Because partisan conflict over the Recovery Act was clearly visible in Congress and in some early, highly publicized refusals by Republican governors to accept ARRA funds for expanded unemployment benefits and high speed rail, state political control was also taken into account in the selection process. Republicans controlled the statehouse and the general assembly throughout most of the study period in Virginia, Democrats exercised unified control over state government in Delaware, and Minnesota underwent transition from a Republican to a Democratic governor during the study period. Finally, Delaware's selection as one of two first-round recipients of RTTT funds allowed for some preliminary field research on that component of SFSF.[37]

In each state where field research was conducted, a broad range of governmental and often nongovernmental actors was interviewed, reflecting those with key roles in the policy implementation network. These included, as appropriate for each case, gubernatorial staff, state budget office officials, departmental and program administrators, interest group experts, and local policy experts. Additionally, relevant data, policy, and news reports at the state level were consulted. In all, fieldwork for one or more programs was conducted in a regionally and demographically diverse group of nine states: California, Delaware, Florida, Minnesota, New Mexico, New York, Virginia, Washington, and West Virginia. The significant economic, political, and demographic characteristics of the case study states are displayed in table 1.1.

The Outline of This Book

The remainder of this book consists of nine additional chapters. Chapter 2 sketches the economic context of the stimulus plan, outlines its overall structure and principal provisions, and provides an overview of the politics of

Table 1.1. Characteristics of the States Selected for Field Research

State	Region	Party Control of State Executive, 2009–10	Party Control of State Legislature, 2009–10	Total State Population (millions)	Per Capita Income (dollars)	Tax Revenue Change, 2008–10
California	West	Republican	Democratic	37.3	41,893	−8.7
Delaware	East	Democratic	Democratic	0.9	39,425	−5.6
Florida	South	Republican	Republican	18.8	38,325	−15.2
Minnesota	Midwest	Republican	Democratic	5.4	42,528	−6.1
New Mexico	West	Democratic	Democratic	2.1	32,940	−17.6
New York	East	Democratic	Democratic	19.0	49,119	−2.2
Virginia	South	Republican	Split	8.3	44,134	−10.4
Washington	West	Democratic	Democratic	7.1	42,024	−10.3
West Virginia	South	Democratic	Democratic	1.8	31,806	−1.6

Sources: National Conference of State Legislatures, "2010 State and Legislative Partisan Composition," www.ncsl.org/documents/statevote/LegisControl_2010.pdf; for the tax revenue change, US Bureau of the Census, "State Government Tax Collections."

enacting and implementing the legislation. Chapters 3 and 4 examine the implementation of large formula grants to the states under conditions of severe fiscal and managerial stress. Chapter 3, by Timothy Conlan, focuses on the State Fiscal Stabilization Fund, which provided a temporary fiscal lifeline to states struggling to maintain support for education and general state services in the midst of sharply declining tax revenues. Chapter 4, by Sheldon Edner, examines the challenges faced by a stable and well-defined policy implementation network in the face of federal pressure to quickly identify and begin work on "shovel ready" infrastructure projects, focusing on those for the federal highway network.

The next two chapters focus on the trials and tribulations that ensue when the federal government attempts to create new or vastly expanded intergovernmental programs virtually overnight. Chapter 5, by Priscilla Regan, examines the challenges involved in creating and implementing a new federal effort to promote greater access to broadband internet service in underserved areas. Chapter 6 is Alan Abramson's study of the federal government's effort to rapidly scale up a small existing program to provide weatherization assistance to needy homeowners. Relying heavily on implementation assistance from small or inexperienced local governments and nonprofit organizations, the weatherization program is a poster child for the management challenges posed by third-party governance.

The subsequent chapters of the book shift focus to an alternative tool of indirect governance: federal tax credits. In chapter 7 Lehn Benjamin examines the complex intersection of very different policy communities that had to come together in order to make effective use of New Markets Tax Credits in community revitalization efforts. In chapter 8 Stefan Toepler and Matthew Sommerfeld question whether the network concept serves as a helpful construct in certain instances. The unique process of implementation in certain tax credit programs involved very little network structure and underscores the value of the tools concept in understanding policy design and implementation.

The final two chapters depart from the program-specific approach and address crosscutting themes in the implementation process. In chapter 9 Paul Posner suggests that ex ante design and ex post audits were successful in warding off the characteristic fraud and abuse that can plague urgent and highly visible national initiatives. However, such outcomes were achieved at the expense of high administrative costs and significant conflict among competing networks of top political executives, program managers, and audit officials. Finally, in chapter 10 Paul Posner, Timothy Conlan, and Priscilla Regan distill conclusions and examine broader lessons that can be learned from the Recovery Act's implementation.

Notes

1. See, e.g., Congressional Budget Office, *Estimated Impact of the American Recovery and Reinvestment Act on Employment and Economic Output from January 2011 through March 2011* (Washington, DC: Congressional Budget Office, 2011); and Alan S. Blinder and Mark Zandi, "How the Great Recession Was Brought to an End," July 27, 2010, www.economy.com/mark-zandi/documents/End-of-Great-Recession .pdf. For a brief overview of these and other studies, most of which found significant positive effects, see Dylan Matthews, "Did the Stimulus Work? A Review of the Nine Best Studies on the Subject," *Washington Post*, August 11, 2011, www.washingtonpost .com/blogs/wonkblog/post/did-the-stimulus-work-a-review-of-the-nine-best-studies -on-the subject/2011/08/16/gIQAThbibJ_blog.html.

2. See, e.g., Gary Burtless and Tracy Gordon, "The Federal Stimulus Programs and Their Effects," in *The Great Recession*, ed. David B. Grusky, Bruce Western, and Christopher Wimer (New York: Russell Sage Foundation, 2011), 249–93; George Mason University Centers on the Public Service, *The Implementation of the Recovery Act: Networks Under Stress* (Fairfax, VA: George Mason University, 2013), http://psc .gmu.edu/wp-content/uploads/ARRA_Overview_Mar_13.pdf; and Richard F. Callahan, Sandra O. Archibald, Kay A. Sterner, and H. Brinton Milward, *Key Actions That Contribute to Successful Program Implementation: Lessons from the Recovery Act* (Washington, DC: IBM Center for the Business of Government, 2012).

3. Pew Research Center for the People and the Press, "Republicans Draw Even with Democrats on Most Issues: Pessimistic Public Doubts Effectiveness of Stimulus, TARP," April 28, 2010, 1.

4. The remaining 27 percent were uncertain whether the benefits outweighed costs. See Justin Wolfers, "What Debate? Economists Agree the Stimulus Lifted the Economy," *New York Times*, July 29, 2014, www.nytimes.com/2014/07/30/upshot/what -debate-economists-agree-the-stimulus-lifted-the-economy.html?_r=0&abt=0002 &abg=1.

5. Pew Center for the People and the Press, "Stimulus News Seen as More Negative than Positive," press release, February 11, 2009, www.people-press.org/2009/02 /11/stimulus-news-seen-as-more-negative-than-positive.

6. See, e.g., Scott Mayerowitz and Nathalie Tadena, "Stimulus Waste? The $3.4 Million Turtle Crossing," abcnews.com, July 10, 2009, abcnews.go.com/Business /Economy/story?id=8045022; and Geoff Earle, "$timulus Stinkers Come under Fire," *New York Post*, June 17, 2009, nypost.com/2009/06/17/timulus-stinkers-come -under-fire. This story was also inaccurately headlined in one conservative website as a $6 billion project. See "Government Waste: The Six Billion Dollar Turtle Tunnel," *Examiner.com*, www.examiner.com/article/government-waste-the-six-billion -dollar-turtle-tunnel.

7. Jonathan Karl, "GMA Investigation: Stimulus Waste or Future Investment?" *Good Morning America*, May 15, 2009, http://abcnews.go.com/Politics/story?id=7594607 &page=1.

8. See, e.g., CNN, "Stimulus Project," www.cnn.com/SPECIALS/2010/stimulus .project; and ProPublica, "Eye on the Stimulus," www.propublica.org/ion/stimulus.

9. ProPublica and WNYC formed a partnership called Shovel Watch (www .shovelwatch.org), which was intended to "provide documents, data, and original reporting to help citizens monitor the progress and effectiveness of the largest domestic spending bill in US history.

10. For the details, see chapter 9 in this book.

11. Gregory Korte, "Five Years since Stimulus: Many Fraud Cases, Few Losses," *USA Today*, February 16, 2014, www.usatoday.com/story/news/politics/2014/02/16 /recovery-act-stimulus-fraud-convictions/5400705/.

12. US Congress, House, "Preventing Stimulus Waste and Fraud: Who Are the Watchdogs? Hearing before the Committee on Oversight and Government Reform," 111th Cong., 1st sess. March 19, 2009, 31.

13. Korte, "Five Years Since Stimulus."

14. Paul C. Light, "A Cascade of Failures: Why Government Fails, and How to Stop It," Brookings Institution, July 2014.

15. See, e.g., White House, "A Second Look at the Second Opinion: Coburn Report Riddled with Falsehoods, Outdated Information, and Misleading Assertions," n.d., cited by Kate Phillips, "Scuffles Over Stimulus Projects," *New York Times*, June 16, 2009, http://thecaucus.blogs.nytimes.com/2009/06/16/scuffles-over-stimulus -projects/?_r=0.

16. Jerry Brito and Veronique de Rugy, "Stimulus Facts," Working Paper 09-46 (Fairfax, VA: Mercatus Center at George Mason University, 2009).

17. Nate Silver, "Study Claiming Link between Stimulus Funding and Partisanship Is Manifestly Flawed," *FiveThirtyEight*, April 1, 2010, http://fivethirtyeight.com /features/study-claiming-link-between-stimulus.

18. Jason Reifler and Jeffrey Lazarus, "Partisanship and Policy Priorities in the Distribution of Economic Stimulus Funds," Working Paper (Rochester: Social Science Research Network, 2010), 13, http://papers.ssrn.com/sol3/papers.cfm?abstract_id=1670161.

19. Martha Derthick, *New Towns In-Town* (Washington, DC: Brookings Institution Press, 1972); and Jeffrey L. Pressman and Aaron B. Wildavsky, *Implementation: How Great Expectations in Washington Are "Dashed" in Oakland: Or, Why It's Amazing That Federal Programs Work at All, This Being a Saga of the Economic Development Administration as Told by Two Sympathetic Observers Who Seek to Build Morals on a Foundation of Ruined Hopes* (Berkeley: University of California Press, 1984).

20. Daniel A. Mazmanian and Paul A. Sabatier, *Implementation and Public Policy* (Lanham, MD: University Press of America, 1999), 266; see also Malcolm L. Goggin, Ann Bowman, James Lester, and Laurence O'Toole, *Implementation Theory and Practice: Toward a Third Generation* (Glenview, IL: Scott Foresman, 1990).

21. Paul Manna, *Collision Course: Federal Education Policy Meets State and Local Realities* (Washington, DC: CQ Press, 2011).

22. Michael Kirst and Richard Jung, "The Utility of a Longitudinal Approach in Assessing Implementation: A 13-year View of Title I, ESEA," *Educational Evaluation and Policy Analysis* 2, no. 5 (Sept.-Oct. 1980): 17–34.

23. Paul Peterson, Barry Rabe, and Kenneth Wong, *When Federalism Works* (Washington, DC: Brookings Institution Press, 1986).

24. Paul L. Posner, "The Political Reality of the Stimulus," *Governing*, February 20, 2013, www.governing.com/columns/mgmt-insights/col-political-reality-economic-stimulus-obama-roosevelt-decentralized-government.html.

25. See Robert Agranoff, *Managing within Networks* (Washington, DC: Georgetown University Press, 2007); and Robert Agranoff and Michael McGuire, *Collaborative Public Management: New Strategies for Local Government* (Washington, DC: Georgetown University Press, 2003).

26. See, among others, H. Brinton Milward and Keith Provan, "A Preliminary Theory of Network Effectiveness: A Comparative Study of Four Mental Health Systems," *Administrative Science Quarterly* 40, no. 1 (1995): 1–33; Jörg Raab and H. Brinton Milward, "Dark Networks as Problems," *Journal of Public Administration Research and Theory* 13, no. 4 (2003): 413–39; and H. Brinton Milward and Keith G. Provan, *A Manager's Guide to Choosing and Using Collaborative Networks* (Washington, DC: IBM Center for the Business of Government, 2006).

27. Stephen Goldsmith and Donald Kettl, eds., *Unlocking the Power of Networks* (Washington, DC: Brookings Institution Press, 2009).

28. Stephen Goldsmith and William Eggers, *Governing by Network: The New Shape of the Public Sector* (Washington, DC: Brookings Institution Press, 2004).

29. Rosemary O'Leary, Lisa Blomgren Bingham, and Catherine Gerard, eds., "Special Issue on Collaborative Public Management," *Public Administration Review* 66, supplement (December 2006).

30. John Donahue and Richard Zeckhauser, *Collaborative Governance* (Princeton, NJ: Princeton University Press, 2011).

31. GAO, *High-Risk Series: An Update*, GAO-15-290 (Washington, DC: Government Accountability Office, 2015).

32. Milward and Provan, *Manager's Guide.*

33. See GAO, *Federal Assistance: Temporary State Fiscal Relief*, GAO-04-736 (Washington, DC: GAO, 2004); and GAO, *Medicaid: Strategies to Help States Address Increased Expenditures during Economic Downturns*, GAO-07-97 (Washington, DC: GAO, 2006).

34. For a classic treatment of the field network approach as a methodology for studying implementation, see Richard P. Nathan, "The Methodology for Field

Network Evaluation Studies," in *Studying Implementation: Methodological and Administrative Issues*, ed. Walter Williams (Chatham, NJ: Chatham House, 1982).

35. Peterson, Rabe, and Wong, *When Federalism Works*; Mazmanian and Sabatier, *Implementation*; Goggin et al., *Implementation*.

36. Interviews were conducted both to document how federal managers were working with partners in state and local governments, nonprofit organizations, and other institutions to advance federal priorities associated with ARRA and also to identify management strategies and practices that seemed particularly effective for achieving public objectives in the shared governance environment. Interviewees were asked a set of open-ended questions, including how their program was changing in response to ARRA; what were their greatest challenges; how their program had worked with third parties in the past and how that has changed as a result of ARRA; how they conceptualize the networks with which they deal and how do they make strategic choices in working with and through them to deliver public goods; what were the accountability tools traditionally used and how these have changed in response to ARRA; and whether ARRA implementation has demanded new management skills and competencies. Other questions would be raised as new information and leads were developed.

37. The specific rationale for state selection for other programs in this volume is discussed in each case study chapter.

2

Economic Crisis and Policy Response

THE CONTEXT, DESIGN, AND POLITICS OF THE RECOVERY ACT

Timothy J. Conlan and Paul L. Posner

THE AMERICAN RECOVERY and Reinvestment Act (the Recovery Act, or ARRA) was developed in response to the worst economic crisis since the 1930s. According to the President's Council of Economic Advisers, by late 2008, "the possibility of a second Great Depression was frighteningly real."[1] Credit markets had frozen, the gross domestic product (GDP) was in freefall, unemployment was accelerating, and recessionary conditions were spreading quickly around the globe. As a result, unprecedented economic policy initiatives were undertaken by the Federal Reserve Board, the Bush administration, and the Obama administration in 2008 and 2009, including but not limited to the Recovery Act.

This chapter begins with a brief examination of the causes, scope, and consequences of the Great Recession and global financial crisis. It then summarizes the principal policy responses of the federal government, both monetary and fiscal, before turning in greater detail to the design, enactment, and composition of ARRA. The politics of the Recovery Act are examined, including how partisanship shaped the congressional design and enactment of the legislation and created the political context for implementation of the act at the state and local levels. Finally, historical parallels to and differences from the policies of the New Deal are briefly discussed.

Global Financial Crisis: The Economic Context
of the Recovery Act

The Great Recession, as it was known in the United States, officially began in December 2007 and extended through 2009. All told, 7 million jobs were lost and unemployment ultimately reached 10 percent.[2] Housing prices collapsed from their bubble-induced peak in 2006, putting millions of homeowners under water on their mortgages and inducing a wave of home foreclosures. The Dow Jones Industrial Average lost more than 50 percent of its value between 2007 and 2009, and GDP declines spread globally to the United Kingdom, Germany, Japan, and elsewhere.

The roots of the crisis lay in broad changes in economic behavior and finance. Consumption grew to record levels even as the incomes of most Americans remained stable or declined and domestic savings—personal, corporate, and governmental—continued their long-term decline. Debt and inflows of overseas capital helped make up the difference. The flow of capital from abroad allowed interest rates to remain lower than they otherwise would have been, thus enabling continued high levels of consumption.

Nowhere were these trends more evident than housing. Sophisticated financing strategies—such as the securitization of mortgages and the proliferation of riskier, subprime mortgages—attracted record levels of money into housing and encouraged a bubble in housing prices.[3] Securitized housing loans were sold to investors throughout the world, appearing on the balance sheets of many financial institutions. This speculative housing finance market worked as long as housing prices kept rising. But once the bubble burst, home prices fell dramatically in many markets. As the underlying value of the loans themselves became more suspect, the securitized instruments contaminated balance sheets and eroded investor confidence across the financial sector. The widespread use of credit default swaps to insure debt and investments further spread the risk of these bad loans worldwide.

By the fall of 2008, these conditions generated a financial crisis that accelerated even as the presidential campaign got fully under way. With asset values and balance sheets declining or uncertain, trading across financial institutions ground to a halt. Unable to accurately assess risks, banks and other financial institutions became unwilling to make new loans, even to each other. Unable to raise funds due to concerns about the presence of "toxic" debts on their balance sheets, major financial institutions such as Lehman Brothers and the giant insurance firm American International Group (AIG) began to fail.

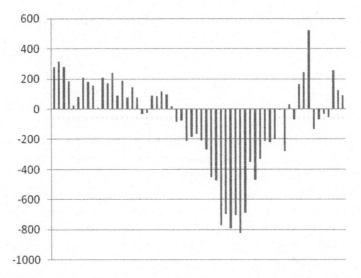

Figure 2.1. Monthly Change in Nonfarm Employment, 2006–10
Note: In thousands, seasonally adjusted.
Source: US Bureau of Labor Statistics.

As the flow of credit slowed, the housing crisis spread to the broader economy. Job losses in late 2008 reached their highest levels since the 1930s, and the stock market tumbled. Stocks lost one-quarter of their value in just September and October 2008. GDP declined 5.4 percent in the fourth quarter of 2008 and 6.4 percent in the first quarter of 2009. The economy was hemorrhaging more than 600,000 jobs per month (see figure 2.1).

Government finances and services were also deeply affected. Federal revenues declined 18 percent—or by $463 billion—from fiscal year (FY) 2007 to FY 2009 and did not return to FY 2007 levels for four years. State income tax revenues fell an average of 10.3 percent from FY 2007 to FY 2010, and income tax revenues in a dozen states plummeted by more than 20 percent.[4] State corporate income tax receipts fell by almost 30 percent during this same period.

Revenue effects at the local level were more variable, as local governments' reliance on real property taxes and the lag time involved in assessing changes in property values delayed the impact of business cycle changes on property tax revenues. Thus, though state tax revenue declined significantly in 2008 and 2009, local tax revenues nationwide did not decline until 2010, when they fell by nearly 2 percent.[5] Localities where the housing bubble was most severe—Florida, Nevada, and California, for example—experienced even more significant revenue declines. And those communities with the weakest economies and finances—such as Detroit; San Bernardino, California; and Central Falls, Rhode Island—were among a group of cities that declared bankruptcy in order to reconcile burgeoning costs with declining revenues.[6]

On the expenditure side, the recession caused spending for safety net programs like Medicaid and unemployment benefits to rise, further contributing to rising federal deficits and serious budgetary shortfalls in many states.[7] The National Conference of State Legislatures estimated that states were facing budget shortfalls of $117 billion in FY 2009 and $174 billion in FY 2010 due to falling revenues and expenditure demands.[8] Although the federal government can and does run deficits during downturns, states and localities do not enjoy this luxury, thanks to pressure from bond markets and balanced budget requirements. The large fiscal gaps facing states were filled to a great extent by spending reductions, prompting unprecedented declines in state and local government employment when compared with earlier recessions.[9]

Federal Policy Response: A Three-Pronged Strategy

Ideally, monetary and fiscal policy are used in coordination to blunt the economic impact of spikes in the business cycle—an ideal that often does not materialize in the real world. However, the Great Recession was one occasion when there was close collaboration between monetary policy stimulus and fiscal policy. Indeed, it was fitting that the largest downturn since the Great Depression would be greeted with the deployment of aggressive monetary policy, unprecedented financial bailouts, and a stimulus program that set postwar records for magnitude and timing. Estimates by Alan Blinder and Marc Zandi show that, all together, the federal programs averted a broader depression. Real GDP remained 15 percent higher, and the unemployment rate was about 6 percent age points lower than if none of these policies had been put in place.[10] Specifically, the federal response had three major elements:

- Traditional and nontraditional monetary policy responses, including nearly zero short-term interest rates and novel Federal Reserve Board credit-easing strategies;
- Treasury acquisition of and assistance to financial institutions and selected major industries to help avert a financial and economic collapse, through the Troubled Asset Relief Program; and

- The federal fiscal stimulus provided by automatic stabilizers and, most important, the approximately $800 billion American Recovery and Reinvestment Act (ARRA).

Although the remainder of this book focuses exclusively on ARRA, the other responses warrant brief attention for their complementary roles in shaping the economic and political context for ARRA's implementation.

Monetary and Financial Assistance Policies

The monetary and financial assistance policies of the Federal Reserve and the Treasury Department were designed to prevent the meltdown of US and global financial credit markets. As markets became unable or unwilling to provide the financing and credit that business firms require for their operations, the Federal Reserve and Treasury became lenders and financiers of last resort. Breaking with long-standing traditions of limited government, the federal government took bold action to keep firms alive that were perceived to be "too big to fail," such as the insurance giant AIG.[11]

Monetary policy was an essential part of this response, as interest rates were lowered to near zero by the Federal Reserve. When this proved inadequate, however, monetary officials created new "quantitative easing" tools to restore the credit markets. The Federal Reserve purchased long-term financial assets in the form of debt issued by the Treasury and by government-sponsored enterprises such as Fannie Mae and Freddie Mac. The ultimate goal of these actions was to support credit markets, put continued downward pressure on interest rates, and bolster the stock market. The Federal Reserve dramatically ramped up credit easing instruments beginning in October 2008 to jump-start lending in the critical weeks and months following the collapse of the financial system.

The Troubled Asset Relief Program

Reinforcing the Fed's aggressive liquidity infusions and asset purchases was the US Treasury Department's Troubled Asset Relief Program (TARP). TARP arose as a proposed Treasury Department response to the financial shock caused by the failure of Lehman Brothers, a large investment firm, and the imminent bankruptcy of a large insurer, AIG, in September 2008. Both failures underscored the extent to which financial-sector balance sheets had become infected by questionable assets stemming from the housing bubble. Their failures sparked panic and a liquidity crisis on Wall Street that froze lending and spread the contagion to other large banks and investment firms. These unprecedented events convinced Federal Reserve chairman Ben Bernanke and Treasury secretary Henry Paulson that dramatic new actions would be needed to unfreeze the drastically reduced flow of credit caused by illiquid mortgage-related assets.

Their solution was a program to quickly remove troubled assets from the system on a scale significant enough to restore market confidence. The Bush administration's first proposal, on September 20, 2008, was an astonishingly short three-page legislative proposal requesting authority to purchase the troubled assets of financial institutions, particularly residential and commercial mortgage-related assets. Despite the emergency, this proposal was a nonstarter in Congress. To begin with, the public was deeply opposed to "bailing out Wall Street," which had enjoyed unparalleled prosperity during the bubble and was widely blamed for having caused the crisis. Moreover, this plan would make the federal government a major owner of private-sector assets and create unknown, but potentially huge, financial risks for taxpayers without the benefit of oversight or review. Finally, the size of the budget request was enormous. As the *New York Times* reported, "A $700 billion expenditure on distressed mortgage-related assets would roughly be what the country has spent so far in direct costs on the Iraq war and more than the Pentagon's total yearly budget appropriation. Divided across the population, it would amount to more than $2,000 for every man, woman and child in the United States."[12]

Consequently, Congress revised and expanded the legislation to include greater oversight and taxpayer protections and sought to sell it more as help to struggling homeowners and auto workers. It was rushed through the process and signed into law on October 3, 2008, with bipartisan support.[13] In its final form, TARP authorized up to $700 billion to provide capital and other support to financial institutions, funds and guaranteed assets for certain credit markets, financial assistance for the automotive industry, and compensation to some mortgage servicers for homeowner loan modifications (see figure 2.2).

Although appealing in theory, it proved to be very difficult for the Treasury to set a purchase price for toxic assets with unknown risks and prospects. Given the emergency facing worldwide credit markets, the Treasury adapted quickly by providing capital injections to major financial institutions to restore their balance sheets and restore the confidence of markets in the financial solvency of these institutions. Tens of billions of dollars were later committed to save General Motors and Chrysler from bankruptcy as car sales plummeted with the deepening recession. Despite reassurances from the Bush and Obama administrations that these actions were not intended to bail out Wall Street or pick winners among industries but rather to maintain a credit

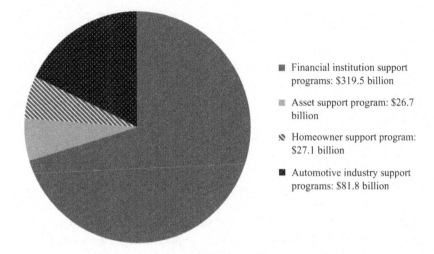

■ Financial institution support
  programs: $319.5 billion

▨ Asset support program: $26.7
  billion

❧ Homeowner support program:
  $27.1 billion

■ Automotive industry support
  programs: $81.8 billion

Figure 2.2. TARP Expenditures, 2008–9
Note: This graph shows gross disbursements, not net present value, as of September 2009.
Source: US Department of the Treasury, "Transactions Report," October 2, 2009.

lifeline to Main Street and limit industrial layoffs, this approach was deeply unpopular with the public, and it also colored subsequent public evaluations of the Recovery Act.

To counter negative perceptions, the Treasury Department, under both presidents Bush and Obama, created several programs under TARP to help homeowners facing foreclosure. However, these programs were all modest in size and slow to gear up.[14] Many regarded them as mere window dressing. The Congressional Oversight Panel, one of several entities charged with monitoring TARP's implementation, asserted that "the program's potential was oversold as a means to 'protect home values, college funds, retirement accounts, and life savings' and 'preserve homeownership and promote jobs and economic growth' when TARP was always intended by Congress and Treasury to primarily recapitalize banks rather than buy assets."[15]

Indeed, most TARP expenditures were utilized to recapitalize financial institutions, followed by support for the automotive industry. The purchasing of assets and assistance to prevent foreclosures made up the remaining support programs. Rather quickly, the Treasury determined that it would not need the full amount authorized, and in March 2009 the Congressional Budget Office (CBO) estimated that TARP would ultimately cost about $350 billion and not $700 billion. Since then, the costs were reestimated several times, and the budgetary effects changed significantly so that the net cost to taxpayers will be $28 billion, according to the CBO's most recent ten-year projection.[16]

The CBO concludes that the federal government's net costs stem from the assistance to AIG, aid to the automobile industry, and the continuing grants to forestall home mortgage foreclosures. Both AIG and the US automobile companies avoided bankruptcies with the infusion of TARP funds (in exchange for stock in the companies). When these institutions returned to profitability, the federal government sold its shares at a modest loss in order to quickly return them to full private ownership. The bulk of TARP purchases of assets of financial institutions, however, realized net gains for the federal budget, as federal receipts from sales outweighed the initial purchase costs.

Thus, TARP accomplished its primary purpose of increasing liquidity and stabilizing the financial markets at a much lower cost than anticipated. Yet when asked in a Bloomberg poll in December 2014 how TARP had affected the economy, only 24 percent of the public said it had helped. Forty-three percent said that it had weakened the economy, and another 21 percent that it had made no difference.[17] When asked whether the money extended to banks would be repaid, 60 percent thought that the funds would be lost and only 33 percent believed that most would be recovered.[18] Given the amount of attention paid to the initial $700 billion estimate for TARP, the public would most likely be amazed to learn that the current estimate has dwindled to $28 billion.

The Recovery Act: Fiscal Stimulus on Steroids

Direct fiscal stimulus was the third leg of the recovery triad—attempting to reduce the severity and length of the recession by using federal spending and tax cuts to boost consumption. A modest stimulus bill passed in early 2008 with the support of the Bush administration. The centerpiece of the legislation was an advanced, refundable tax credit that sent $106 billion in "rebate" checks to most American taxpayers.[19] Although Democrats in Congress sought to add some spending items to the legislation, such as increased food stamp funding and an extension of unemployment insurance benefits, the Bush administration and congressional Republicans insisted on limiting the bill to tax cuts, which could be promptly administered.[20] Democrats accepted this approach when the tax cuts were made refundable, meaning that even low-income workers who paid too little in income taxes to take full advantage of a standard tax credit were allowed to receive a benefit reflecting the value of their payroll taxes as well.

This early stimulus attempt, which passed in early February 2008 just as the recession was beginning to take hold, proved to be too small and poorly designed to head off the emerging economic crisis. Most recipients of the

$300–$600 rebate checks indicated that they intended to pay off existing debt or save the money as a hedge against growing economic uncertainty. Only 22 percent said they planned to spend the money, which was the goal of the stimulus plan.[21] As the economy worsened dramatically in late 2008, a growing consensus emerged in Washington that more fiscal stimulus would be needed. The focus on developing significant new stimulus legislation accelerated with Barack Obama's election.

Work on the stimulus plan was well under way even before Obama took office on January 20, 2009. His campaign team touched base with key congressional figures, such as Appropriations Committee chair David Obey, even before the election, and Obama's incoming economic team began discussing the contours of a stimulus plan immediately after the election. The guiding principles of the policy response were that funding should be "timely, targeted, and temporary." That is, stimulus programs should be structured to spend out quickly and passed as soon as possible; they should be targeted to those most in need and most likely to spend the funds immediately; and the added funding should be phased out as the economy recovered. This was a formulation first developed by Lawrence Summers in congressional testimony on the Bush stimulus bill in January 2008.[22] Summers would go on to become a key economic adviser to President Obama and head of the President's National Economic Council, and these principles were utilized in shaping Obama's recovery plan.[23]

By mid-December, the Obama economic team had agreed that a stimulus of about $800 billion would be needed.[24] Some advisers believed more was needed, with estimates running as high as $1.2 trillion given the scale of the deepening recession, but this was deemed to be politically unachievable. In terms of structure, administrative officials agreed on several core elements, such as providing the stimulus through a mix of new spending and tax cuts; providing significant amounts of aid to the states, which were on the verge of hemorrhaging jobs; and addressing pent-up demands for new and revitalized infrastructure. In terms of policy, the president wanted to focus on energy, education, health care, and protecting the vulnerable.[25]

Finally, the president sought to use the stimulus as an opportunity to address his "change" agenda, creating "iconic programs" that would constitute an "updated version of the New Deal."[26] This led to the inclusion of new, but not always fully vetted, initiatives such as $9 billion in grants for high-speed rail, $7.2 billion for the extension of broadband internet access into rural and underserved areas, and a $17 billion initiative for converting health care records into electronic form. Major initiatives to promote clean energy were another expression of this. As Rebecca Nelson and Ben Geman reported in *National Journal*, "Just a month after his election, on December 16, 2008, the soon-to-be president met with his transition team in Chicago to talk about how to handle the fiscal crisis. Discussing what would be included in the massive economic stimulus, he told his advisers, including [Carole] Browner, 'I want a big commitment to green energy. A big investment.' . . . The stimulus Obama ultimately signed in 2009 would steer some $90 billion into low-carbon energy initiatives and technologies."[27]

Incoming administration officials began working with Congress during the presidential transition period as well. Meetings were held with top Democratic congressional leaders, most notably House Appropriations chair David Obey, who was designated lead negotiator on the bill by House speaker Nancy Pelosi. For a time, the president's soon-to-be chief of staff and former congressman, Rahm Emanuel, hoped to have a bill ready for the president's signature on or soon after inauguration day: January 20, 2009.

Although this inaugural deadline proved to be unrealistic, Congress acted with unprecedented speed to write, revise, and pass a gigantic piece of economic recovery legislation early in the 111th Congress. The incoming president met personally with both Democratic and Republican leadership teams in Congress on January 5, just two days after the new Congress convened.[28] In the House, Speaker Pelosi unveiled an $825 billion stimulus package on January 15, and the House Appropriations Committee marked up and passed a bill containing many of the spending elements of the stimulus legislation on January 21, 2009. Other committees acted the following day to adopt the tax and entitlement provisions of the package. The full House debated and passed the bill on January 28, the Senate followed suit on February 10, and the president signed the final version that compromised House/Senate differences on February 17, 2009—less than one month after his inauguration.[29]

Although congressional Democrats shared the president's interest in quick passage of a bill to address the deepening recession, they also wanted their own imprint on the legislation. For example, many were leery of the new administration's wish to send considerable aid to state and local governments, many of which were controlled by Republicans. As Michael Grunwald recounted,

> Democrats on the Hill didn't love everything in Obama's plan. For starters, $200 billion worth of aid to states sounded like a truck load of political spinach . . . . Why . . . write checks that would make them look like bigger spenders and their governors look like better stewards? State aid was especially unappealing to Democrats from states with conservative Republican governors . . . . They had slashed taxes irresponsibly when times were flush; why help them avoid the consequences now.[30]

They ultimately went along with the idea of providing substantial fiscal relief to states, in part because of convincing evidence that this was an effective form of short-term economic stimulus that would help mitigate pending layoffs of state and government employees. As the Congressional Research Service put it, "Congressional interest in state budgetary finances has increased in recent years, primarily because state action to address budget shortfalls, such as increasing taxes, laying off or furloughing state employees, and postponing or eliminating state infrastructure projects, could have an adverse effect on the national economic recovery."[31] This was reinforced by the recognition that many of the federal policies that Democrats cared most deeply about—providing health care to the poor, support for education, community development, and mass transit, to name just a few—were implemented by state and local governments with assistance from federal grants.

Nevertheless, Congress did insist on other changes in the administration's stimulus agenda. In particular, the president-elect and his incoming education secretary, Arne Duncan, wanted to make stimulus aid to education conditional on governors accepting fundamental education reform. Congressional Democrats refused. Appropriations chair Obey is quoted as saying, "If you guys want to reform the hell out of the education system, do it when people aren't drowning."[32] The compromise was to put most of the education money—more than $70 billion in all—into existing programs and a highly flexible "education stabilization fund." Only $4.5 billion was reserved for a competitive education reform program, Race to the Top.

Democrats were also highly skeptical of including substantial tax cuts in the stimulus bill, believing that they would be relatively ineffective. However, they went along with the administration's insistence that a variety of tax cuts be included as a way of appealing for Republican support. Finally, although the new president insisted that the stimulus bill not include any legislative earmarks, members of Congress wanted to be sure that their own priorities were reflected in the package, and a large number of programmatic cats and dogs were included in the bill, ranging from federal facilities improvements to agricultural spending to nuclear waste cleanup.

The House's passage of an $825 billion stimulus bill went smoothly, reflecting the Democrats' 257–178 majority in the chamber and their resulting control over proceedings under House rules. The situation was more challenging in the Senate, where the Democrats needed Republican help to stop filibusters and bring the legislation to a vote.[33] Senate Democratic leaders also needed to retain the votes of all party members, including moderates representing Republican-leaning states, such as senators Ben Nelson of Nebraska and Evan Bayh of Indiana. This necessitated concessions to senators who were concerned about the size of the stimulus package and its impact on federal deficits and who tended to prefer that a greater share of the package go to tax cuts rather than direct federal spending.

As it moved through the Senate Appropriations and Finance committees, the Senate version of the stimulus bill actually grew larger than the House bill—up to $940 billion—as costly new provisions were added and others were expanded. One of these was a $72 billion "patch" to the alternative minimum tax in order to keep upper-middle-income taxpayers from becoming subject to what was once known as the "millionaires' tax."[34] At the same time, however, a group of Senate moderates, led by Susan Collins (R-ME) and Ben Nelson (D-NE), worked to fashion a compromise that could bring the overall cost of the package down to below $800 billion and attract the necessary sixty votes. Their compromise, which cut $83 billion in spending from the Senate bill and had $25 billion less in tax cuts, was accepted by the White House and by the Democratic Senate majority leader, Harry Reid, and was substituted for the committee bill on the floor.[35] This allowed three Republicans—Collins, Olympia Snowe (R-ME), and Arlen Specter (R-PA)—to vote for the bill.

To facilitate rapid agreement between the chambers, the conference committee of House and Senate negotiators was kept small and included key legislators such as Senate majority leader Reid and House Appropriations chair Obey. At the same time, *CQ Almanac* reported that "the final deal was driven largely by the three centrist Republicans who supported the Senate bill."[36] To keep the Senate moderates on board, the compromise stimulus bill was kept to $787 billion, and tax cuts made up 35 percent of the total value.[37] Many other provisions—such as education spending, Medicaid allocations, and health insurance subsidies—essentially split the difference between the two bills. The conference report was passed by the House and Senate on February 13, 2009. It was signed by President Obama on February 17, 2009, who called it "the most sweeping economic recovery package in our history."[38]

Party Polarization and the Crafting of ARRA

Although the size and scope of the Recovery Act may have represented a "sweeping" accomplishment for the president in substantive terms, it was a disappointment in political terms. As the Senate's negotiations over ARRA suggest, the partisan politics of crafting and passing the legislation were difficult and complex. President Obama and his team clearly wanted and, given the scale of the economic emergency, expected to enact the legislation with bipartisan support. As David Axelrod, the president's top communications adviser put it, "There was an assumption that in a time of national emergency you could get bipartisan support."[39] This would signify an important change of tone in Washington politics, which was something the president had run on. It would also strengthen public acceptance of the legislation when the inevitable bumps occurred during implementation. Consequently, the president tried hard to attract Republican support, meeting with congressional Republicans on more than one occasion and insisting that his own advisers and congressional Democrats be open to Republican ideas in putting the package together.[40] In the end, however, President Obama attracted very little Republican support for the legislation. Apart from the three Republican moderates who voted for the legislation—one of whom (Arlen Specter) subsequently changed parties and ran for reelection as a Democrat—the bill failed to attract even a single Republican vote in the House of Representatives, at any stage in the process.

This failure reflected both policy and political differences between the parties. Republicans as a group wanted to spend less on a stimulus and, within those constraints, focus more on tax cuts. Many expressed sticker shock at an $800 billion stimulus plan. "Oh, my God," was the reaction of House Republican leader John Boehner (R-Ohio) when House Democrats unveiled their $825 billion proposal in January 2009: "My notes here say that I'm disappointed. I just can't tell you how shocked I am at what I'm seeing."[41] Boehner and his colleagues were particularly concerned about the impact of so much additional spending on an already-exploding federal deficit, which had reached $1.2 trillion in George W. Bush's final budget proposal.

Yet, apart from such substantive concerns, congressional Republicans also had strategic political reasons for opposing the Recovery Act. They were leery of giving President Obama any sort of political victory, which might build political capital and snowball into additional wins.

Nevertheless, the near-unanimity of Republican opposition to the Recovery Act surprised the Obama White House. They had assumed that a number of more moderate Republicans, especially those representing states and districts carried by the president in a landslide election victory, would be inclined to support the new president's top priority during a honeymoon period. But at a dinner held the very evening of Barack Obama's inauguration, a number of influential Republican policymakers—including House Republican whip Eric Cantor (R-VA), Republican Conference chair Kevin McCarthy (R-CA), and Budget Committee ranking Republican Paul Ryan (R-WI)—agreed on a strategy of "united and unyielding opposition to the president's economic policies."[42] At a meeting of the House GOP Conference on January 27, 2009—the day before the stimulus bill came up for a vote on the House floor, both Cantor and minority leader John Boehner urged all members to vote "no" on the stimulus bill—just shortly before the president was scheduled to appear before the group to answer questions and urge support.[43] And not a single House Republican did vote for the legislation. As Representative Mike Castle (R-DE), a moderate Mid-Atlantic Republican, put it, "The caucus had decided we weren't going to give Obama a bipartisan victory on this."[44]

Surprisingly, even Republican members of the Appropriations Committee, who tended to be more pragmatic than ideological and were often supportive of the types of infrastructure spending in the stimulus bill, refused to break ranks. Michael Grunwald recounts a meeting between Appropriations chair David Obey and Ranking Republican Jerry Lewis (R-CA) as follows: "Obey asked whether Republicans had anything they wanted in the stimulus. Jerry's response was: 'I'm sorry, but leadership tells us we can't play,'" Obey recalls. "Exact quote: 'We can't play.' What they said right from the get-go was: It doesn't matter what the hell you do, we ain't gonna help you."[45]

Significantly, the hyperpartisanship that developed during the legislative crafting of the Recovery Act presaged many of the partisan conflicts that emerged during its implementation. Although governors of all political stripes gladly accepted the federal government's $144 billion fiscal lifeline of Medicaid and education funding, few Republicans were willing to credit President Obama or congressional Democrats for help in patching the massive holes developing in state budgets.[46] Moreover, a number of Republican governors went to considerable lengths to publicly reject certain elements of the Recovery Act, such as grants to states for high-speed rail and expanded unemployment benefits for the long-term unemployed. Partisan polarization *between* the federal government and the states became part of the context of implementing the Recovery Act.[47]

The Politics of Design and Implementation

It has become axiomatic that the implementation of many policies is a direct reflection of the trade-offs made during the frenzied politics of policy formation. This certainly held true for the Recovery Act. Given the substantial political and economic pressures to spend money rapidly and gain quick congressional adoption, a premium was placed on utilizing existing programs as conduits or carriers of stimulus funding. This category included major intergovernmental provisions in ARRA, such as increasing the federal matching rate for Medicaid, as well as added funds for Title I education grants and federal highways. Expedited passage was also promoted by distributing ARRA funds broadly, benefiting many different committees and members whose support was essential.

Yet, the opportunity to pass a large bill very quickly encouraged hitching up new untested proposals to the fast-moving legislative train as well. Signature new policy initiatives like high-speed rail, expanded broadband access, health information technology, and green energy initiatives were thus incorporated into the Recovery Act, even though some might have benefited from a more deliberate legislative process. In both instances, the process closely resembled the garbage can approach described by John Kingdon, when "policy windows" open suddenly and political entrepreneurs rush in with ready-made proposals.[48]

Overview of the Recovery Act's Structure and Design

As passed, ARRA constituted an enormous and diverse amalgam of business and individual tax cuts; aid to state and local governments and needy individuals; and funding for infrastructure, innovation, and facilities modernization. Table 2.1 lists the major programs receiving stimulus funds. They range in size from the very large, such as the Making Work Pay Tax Credit ($116.2 billion) and increased federal Medicaid payments to states ($86.6 billion), to the relatively modest, such as increases in the carryover of net operating losses for businesses ($947 million) and increased funding for various programs of the National Aeronautics and Space Administration ($1 billion).

Because of the large number and complexity of programs in the Recovery Act, it can be helpful to group them in ways that shed light on the law's areas of programmatic emphasis, varying implementation approaches, economic effectiveness, and political consequences. For example, figure 2.3 displays ARRA expenditures by function and purpose. It graphically displays areas of primary emphasis, such as tax relief, state and local government fiscal relief, infrastructure, health care, and education.

Conversely, this functional grouping fails to adequately convey the varying implementation approaches and administrative mechanisms utilized to deliver Recovery Act funding and services. For example, state and local governments received much more than the $144 billion in fiscal relief indicated in figure 2.3. This category was made up solely of the highly flexible funding provided to states by the increased federal matching rate for Medicaid and by the State Fiscal Stabilization Fund (see chapter 3). Much of the funding for education and training, protecting the vulnerable, infrastructure, and energy was also provided in the form of federal grants to state and local governments. Thus, the total amount of grant-in-aid funding under the Recovery Act was nearly double ($275 billion) the amount suggested in figure 2.3.

Table 2.1. Major Programs Funded by the Recovery Act

Education and Employment
- State Fiscal Stabilization Fund: $53.6 billion
- Extended unemployment benefits: $39.2 billion
- Increase in Pell grants: $15.6 billion
- Increased Title I grants for disadvantaged students: $13.0 billion
- Special education programs: $12.2 billion
- Expanded job-training programs: $4.0 billion
- Assistance to Dislocated Workers: $1.6 billion

Transportation
- Highway construction projects: $27.5 billion
- Rail transportation, including high-speed rail: $9.3 billion
- Mass transit: $8.4 billion

Housing and low-income assistance
- Additional SNAP (food stamps) spending: $20.0 billion
- Public housing capital fund: $4.0 billion
- Section 8 rental assistance: $2.0 billion
- Redevelopment of abandoned and foreclosed houses: $2.0 billion
- Child care services: $2.0 billion
- Head Start and Early Head Start expansion: $2.1 billion

Health
- Medicaid matching rate increase: $86.6 billion
- Increased COBRA subsidies: $25.1 billion
- Biomedical research: $10.0 billion

Energy, the environment, and science
- Electric utility grid modernization: $11.0 billion
- Energy efficiency and conservation grants: $6.3 billion
- Loan guarantees for renewable-energy projects: $6.0 billion
- Environmental cleanup of weapons-production sites: $6.0 billion
- Clean- and drinking-water infrastructure improvements: $6.0 billion
- Weatherization Assistance Program: $5.0 billion
- Improved energy efficiency of federal buildings: $4.5 billion
- Fossil energy research and development: $3.4 billion
- National Science Foundation: $3.0 billion
- Grants for manufacturing advanced battery systems: $2.0 billion
- Hazardous-waste cleanup programs: $1.2 billion
- NASA climate science, aviation safety and exploration programs: $1.0 billion

Other
- Expand broadband internet access in underserved areas: $7.2 billion
- Improve Defense Department housing, hospitals, and child care: $6.5 billion
- Law enforcement: $4.0 billion

Table 2.1. (*cont.*)

➤ Repair, restoration, and improvement of facilities on public and tribal lands: $3.1 billion

➤ Homeland Security projects: $2.8 billion

Individual tax cuts
• "Making Work Pay" credit: $116.2 billion
• Alternative minimum tax relief: $69.8 billion
• Child tax credit: $14.8 billion
• Retiree assistance payments: $14.2 billion
• HOPE scholarship tax credit expansion: $13.9 billion
• Homebuyer credit: $6.6 billion
• Earned income tax credit: $4.7 billion

Business tax cuts
• Health information technology: $20.8 billion
• Energy production credit: $13.1 billion
• Bonus depreciation: $5.1 billion
• Net operating losses: $947 million

Source: CQ Press, *CQ Almanac* (Washington, DC: CQ Press, 2009).

More than fifty new tax provisions were enacted as part of ARRA. As with the other tools of government, the tax provisions included both new programs, such as the Making Work Pay Tax Credit for working families and the American Opportunity Tax Credit for higher education, and enhancements to existing programs, such as increasing the earned income tax credit and the refundable portion of the child tax credit.[49]

Consequently, the administration's Recovery Act website—Recovery .gov—also grouped programs by their principal administrative approaches. As shown in figure 2.4, the White House classified the varied elements of the Recovery Act into three roughly equal approaches: tax cuts, direct assistance to states and needy individuals, and various infrastructure "projects." Many of the tax cuts and direct assistance programs were well constructed to meet the administration's original goals of a "timely, targeted, and temporary" stimulus. Their funds could be obligated, delivered, and spent quickly, mostly within the law's goal of two years after passage. As table 2.2 illustrates, virtually all the tax relief (refundable tax credits and revenues) and 80 percent of the direct assistance (Medicaid, unemployment compensation, SNAP, and State Stabilization Fund) outlays were spent between 2009 and 2011. In contrast, infrastructure, research, and innovation projects funded by the Department of Transportation, Department of Energy, and other agencies (e.g., broadband access grants in the Departments of Agriculture and Commerce)

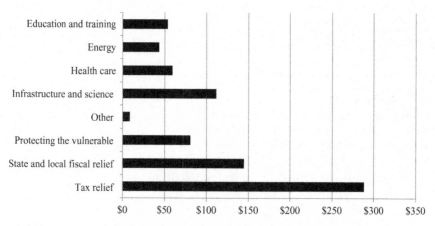

Figure 2.3. ARRA Expenditures by Function (billions of dollars)
Source: Recovery Accountability and Transparency Board (www.recovery.gov).

had longer spending tails extending out to 2015 and beyond due to slower startup and project completion timetables.

Programmatic Structure and the Implications for Implementation and Evaluation

These issues of program design have important implications for ARRA's implementation. Scholars have long recognized that many issues of policy implementation can be traced back to the policy approach selected. One of the core lessons that Pressman and Wildavsky drew from their study of federal programs in Oakland was "to make the difficulties of implementation a part of the initial formulation of policy. Implementation must not be conceived as a process that takes place after, and independent of, the design of policy."[50] Paul Manna has likewise traced many of the difficulties in implementing the No Child Left Behind education program to the legislation's fundamental design—"the disconnect that existed between [this legislation's] theories of action and the policy world that implemented the law."[51]

It follows, then, that ARRA's implementation experience, which is explored in detail in the following chapters, begins with the diverse set of policy instruments employed by the different programs contained within it. The design of the Recovery Act established parameters for the subsequent implementation and political evaluations of Obama's stimulus initiative. In particular, the heavy reliance on tools of third-party governance—tax incen-

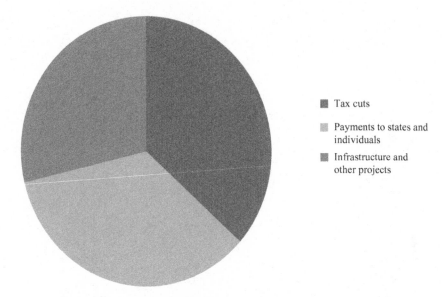

■ Tax cuts

▦ Payments to states and
   individuals

▓ Infrastructure and
   other projects

Figure 2.4. Alternative Funding Approaches under ARRA
Source: Recovery Accountability and Transparency Board (www.recovery.gov).

tives, formula grants, project grants, Section 8 vouchers, loan guarantees, and contracts to both for profit and nonprofit service providers—raised inherent administrative challenges associated with each individual tool. More than two-thirds of the stimulus package depended on the actions of other levels of government and private and nonprofit entities to carry out federal purposes.[52] For example, the nearly one hundred separate grants-in-aid receiving funds through the Recovery Act inevitably raised classic dilemmas that arise whenever grants are used as a tool of governance. These included tensions between federal accountability and state adaptation to local conditions, between recipient need and management capacity, and between program specialists' expertise and cross-program coordination. All emerged in the implementation of the Recovery Act's grant programs, just as they have in other grant programs of the past.[53] Consequently, the Recovery Act provided an ideal testing ground for exploring the federal role in diffuse policy implementation networks as well as the skill sets required by successful managers within those networks.

The third-party governance approach also had implications for public assessments of the Recovery Act. Despite its high political profile during the enactment debates and subsequent media reports of wasteful spending, ARRA

Table 2.2. Estimated Budgetary Effects of ARRA (billions of dollars, by fiscal year)

Outlays	2009	2010	2011	2012	2013	2014	2015	2016–19	2009–19
Medicaid	32	40	12	4	3	2	2	4	99
Other Health and Human Services	2	12	11	7	8	7	2	3	53
Refundable tax credits	3	45	38	6	5	0	0	0	97
Unemployment compensation	28	33	3	0	0	0	0	0	64
SNAP	5	11	12	8	6	6	0	0	48
State Stabilization Fund	12	23	12	2	1	1	1	0	54
Other education (incl. Pell Grants)	9	19	11	3	1	1	0	0	44
Department of Transportation	4	17	11	5	3	1	2	3	46
Department of Energy	1	8	11	8	3	1	1	1	34
Build America Bonds	0	1	4	4	4	4	4	16	36
Social Security Administration	13	0	0	0	0	0	0	0	14
Other	7	25	21	12	6	2	1	0	74
Total outlays	114	235	147	59	41	26	14	28	663
Revenues	–65	–167	2	13	4	7	9	24	–173
Total effect on the deficit	–179	–401	–145	–47	–37	–19	–5	–4	–836

Note: The original estimate of $787 billion for ARRA was revised to $836 billion as of February 2015, reflecting the increased funding for refundable tax credits and unemployment compensation added as part of PL 111–312.
Source: Congressional Budget Office.

was a classic expression of what Suzanne Mettler has called "the submerged state."[54] Most of the programs explored in this volume were virtually invisible to the vast majority of American citizens despite the attention showered on the overall umbrella of "the stimulus." Although this may be understandable for specialized components of ARRA, such as expanded broadband internet access grants (see chapter 5) or advanced energy tax credits (explored in chapter 8), the $53 billion State Fiscal Stabilization Fund (chapter 3) was equally opaque to the broader public. These programs were all classic examples of indirect governance, whose accomplishments and problems seemed equally invisible to the citizenry. Even the hundreds of thousands of public school teachers who avoided layoffs because of the stabilization fund were mostly unaware of their narrow encounter with fate.

Indeed, even the stimulus programs that most directly affected the largest number of American taxpayers were barely noticed by the citizenry. The largest single expenditure in the Recovery Act—the Making Work Pay Tax Credit—provided $116 billion in tax relief to tens of millions of Americans. And yet this credit was deliberately designed in such a way as to go almost unnoticed. Rather than send each taxpayer a sizeable rebate check, as the Bush administration had done with its 2008 stimulus, this credit adjusted tax withholding schedules so as to provide a few extra dollars per paycheck. The administration's economists feared that if tax payers noticed the extra money, they might not spend it—as happened with most of the earlier stimulus program. Obama's policy advisers turned instead to behavioral economics to "nudge" taxpayers in the desired direction. Unfortunately for congressional Democrats, who reluctantly went along with this approach, the nudge was so gentle that no political credit accrued to the party in the next election.[55] The Democrats lost their sizeable majority to the Republicans in 2010, a result attributed in part to an angry electorate which felt that it had received little help from an unresponsive government at a time of desperate economic need. As Rahm Emanuel later bemoaned, "the geniuses on our economic team wanted the money dripped out so nobody fricking saw it."[56]

We return to examine this theme of indirect governance and political credit claiming in chapter 10. It is worth noting, however, that this experience highlights a final factor that is helpful for understanding the Recovery Act writ large: historical context. In design and execution, ARRA was very different from the original New Deal. These two signature responses to economic crisis differed dramatically in substance, administration, and politics.

The programs of the New Deal are often characterized as relief, recovery, and reform. They not only helped to grow the economy (although they did not end the Great Depression), they also created a series of new federal institutions that greatly, and permanently, expanded the role of the federal government in American life. In their wake, the federal government was committed to providing at least minimal assistance to the poor, the unemployed, and the elderly; to protecting the rights of workers and unions; to stabilizing the banking system; to regulating the financial markets; to subsidizing agricultural production; and to undertaking countercyclical monetary and fiscal policy during future economic downturns. Moreover, the public works projects undertaken during the New Deal transformed the face of the nation and led to sustainable longer-term economic growth in underdeveloped regions of the nation.[57]

To accomplish these things, the New Deal was often experimental and eclectic, employing multiple strategies to promote jobs and regulate the economy. These included

- Relief and welfare provided to needy individuals and families, starting with the Federal Relief Administration, which featured grants to states for welfare payments, through to the new Social Security welfare and unemployment insurance programs;
- Traditional public works projects deployed through the Public Works Administration, which featured major building projects using private contractors;
- Work provided to employable adults through projects funded under the Works Progress Administration, the Civil Works Administration, and the Civilian Conservation Corps;
- Confidence in the nation's banking and financial institutions through new regulatory and insurance programs;
- Economic regulation of wages, subsidies provided to agriculture, and recognition of unions, among other programs; and finally
- Targeting to specific economic and geographic sectors of the nation through such programs as housing assistance, energy supply and regulation, and the Tennessee Valley Authority.

Like the Recovery Act, this list of approaches includes many examples of indirect governance, such as relief grants provided to state and local governments. But there was also much more reliance on direct provision of services by the federal government, as in Social Security's old age pensions, and signature, high-profile programs intimately connected with the national government, such as the Tennessee Valley Authority, rural electrification, and bank deposit insurance. Tax cuts were not in the tool kit for the New Deal. Indeed, tax increases were enacted at the federal and state levels to help contain deficits and fund programs. During the 1930s, federal revenues grew from 4.8 to 6.8 percent of GDP.

Thus, there were marked differences between the New Deal and ARRA—in their magnitude, strategies, and political support. It is worth bearing these differences in mind as we turn next to analyze the implementation of the Recovery Act's specific programs in the following chapters. We will return to explore these themes in the concluding chapter of the book.

Notes

1. Council of Economic Advisers, *Economic Report of the President: Transmitted to the Congress February 2010* (Washington, DC: White House, 2010), 25, www.whitehouse .gov/sites/default/files/microsites/economic-report-president.pdf.

2. Ibid.

3. For an illustration of the historic bubble in prices, see ibid., 27. Home mortgages were securitized by pooling many different loans together and selling them as shares backed up by the asset value of the mortgages. This allowed mortgage lenders to convert their long-term mortgage holdings into capital for new lending. By including pieces of many loans in each security, the process also offered investors the promise of lower risk. Loans could also be grouped by level of risk, with riskier securities offering higher returns. In theory, this would allow investors to choose their desired level of risk and return. However, the instruments became so complex, and the process encouraged the origination of so many more vulnerable subprime mortgages, that even sophisticated investors and rating agencies were unaware of the number of bad loans in their portfolios and unprepared for consequences when housing prices began to decline.

4. National Governors' Association and National Association of State Budget Officers, "Fiscal Survey of States," June 2010, 1, 53.

5. Harold Wolman, *National Fiscal Policy and Local Government during the Economic Crisis* (Washington, DC: German Marshall Fund, 2014), 20.

6. George Mason University Centers on the Public Service, "The GMU Municipal Sustainablity Project: Resources for a Robust Recovery," http://fiscalbankruptcy .wordpress.com/the-reports/.

7. Council of Economic Advisers, *Economic Report of the President: Transmitted to the Congress March 2014* (Washington, DC: White House, 2014), table B-24, www .whitehouse.gov/sites/default/files/docs/full_2014_economic_report_of_the _president.pdf.

8. National Conference of State Legislatures, *State Budget Update: March 2011* (Washington, DC: National Conference of State Legislatures, 2011), 8.

9. Lucy Dadayan and Donald J. Boyd, *The Depth and Length of Cuts in State-Local Government Employment Is Unprecedented*, Issue Brief (Albany: Nelson A. Rockefeller Institute of Government at the State University of New York, 2013), www.rockinst.org /pdf/government_finance/2013-01-09-State-Local_Government_Employment.pdf.

10. Alan S. Blinder and Mark Zandi, "How the Great Recession Was Brought to an End," July 27, 2010, www.economy.com/mark-zandi/documents/End-of-Great -Recession.pdf.

11. A useful perspective on the atmosphere of crisis response and the development of these policies is provided by then Federal Reserve chairman Ben Bernanke

in his memoir, *The Courage to Act: A Memoir of a Crisis and Its Aftermath* (New York: W. W. Norton, 2015).

12. D. M. Herszenhorn, "Administration Is Seeking $700 Billion for Wall Street," *New York Times*, September 20, 2008, www.nytimes.com/2008/09/21/business/21cong .html.

13. For more details on TARP's enactment, see Timothy J. Conlan, Paul L. Posner, and David R. Beam, *Pathways of Power: The Dynamics of National Policy Making* (Washington, DC: Georgetown University Press, 2013).

14. US Department of the Treasury, "Transactions Report," October 2, 2009.

15. Congressional Oversight Panel, "March Oversight Report: The Final Report of the Congressional Oversight Panel 155–156," US House of Representatives, 2011.

16. Congressional Budget Office, "Report on the Troubled Asset Relief Program, March 2015."

17. Robert J. Samuelson, "TARP's Success Story," *Washington Post*, March 28, 2011.

18. Congressional Oversight Panel, "March Oversight Report."

19. "Stimulus Bill Provides Tax Rebates," in *CQ Almanac 2008*, 64th edition, ed. Jan Austin (Washington, DC: Congressional Quarterly, 2009). 7-17–7-19, http:// library.cqpress.com/cqalmanac/cqal08-1090-52026-2174946.

20. Barbara Sinclair, *Unorthodox Lawmaking: New Legislative Processes in the US Congress*, 4th ed. (Washington, DC: CQ Press, 2012), 166–68.

21. Matthew Shapiro and Joel Slemrod, "Did the 2008 Tax Rebates Stimulate Spending?" NBER Working Paper 14753 (Cambridge, MA: National Bureau of Economic Research, 2009), www.nber.org/papers/w14753.

22. Lawrence Summers, "Fiscal Stimulus Issues: Testimony before the Joint Economic Committee, January 16, 2008," www.hks.harvard.edu/news-events/news/testi monies/lawrence-summers-testifies-before-joint-economic-committee.

23. Michael Grunwald, *The New New Deal*, ebook edition (New York: Simon & Schuster).

24. Ibid.

25. Ibid.

26. Ibid.

27. Rebecca R. Nelson and Ben Geman, "Obama Reaches for Green Legacy, but Will History Books Agree?" *National Journal*, August 3, 2015, www.nationaljournal .com/s/70708/obama-reaches-green-legacy-will-history-books-agree.

28. Sinclair, *Unorthodox Lawmaking*, 172–73.

29. US Congress, *HR1: American Recovery and Reinvestment Act of 2009*, www .congress.gov/bill/111th-congress/house-bill/1.

30. Grunwald, *New New Deal*.

31. Robert Jay Dilger, *State Government Fiscal Stress and Federal Assistance* (Washington, DC: Congressional Research Service, 2014), 3.

32. Grunwald, *New New Deal*.

33. Democrats began the 111th Congress with fifty-eight votes in the Senate, including two independents (Senator Bernie Sanders and Senator Joseph Lieberman) who caucused with them. They briefly achieved a sixty-vote majority in July 2009 after Senator Arlen Specter changed parties and Senator Al Franken was declared the winner of a close and highly contested election in Minnesota. Democrats

lost their sixty-vote majority in the second session when Senator Ted Kennedy of Massachusetts died in office and was replaced by the Republican Senator Scott Brown.

34. "Stimulus Bill," 7–18.

35. Sinclair, *Unorthodox Lawmaking*, 179.

36. "Stimulus Bill," 7–19.

37. The ultimate costs of the Recovery Act later rose to an estimated $836 billion due to a thirteen-month extension of ARRA's expanded unemployment insurance benefits and a two-year extension of its Earned Income Tax Credit provisions under the Tax Relief, Unemployment Insurance Reauthorization, and Job Creation Act of 2010, which also extended the middle-class tax cuts advanced by the George W. Bush administration in 2001 and 2003. See Public Law 111-312.

38. President Barack Obama, "Remarks by the President and Vice President at Signing of the American Recovery and Reinvestment Act," White House press release, February 17, 2009, www.whitehouse.gov/the-press-office/remarks-president-and-vice-president-signing-american-recovery-and-reinvestment-act.

39. Quoted by Grunwald, *New New Deal*.

40. Sinclair, *Unorthodox Lawmaking*, 174–75.

41. Shailagh Murray and Paul Kane, "House Offers $825 Billion Stimulus," *Washington Post*, January 16, 2009, www.washingtonpost.com/wp-dyn/content/article/2009/01/15/AR2009011502054.html.

42. Sam Stein, "Robert Draper Book: GOP's Anti-Obama Campaign Started Night of Inauguration," *Huffington Post*, April 25, 2012, www.huffingtonpost.com/2012/04/25/robert-draper-anti-obama-campaign_n_1452899.html.

43. David Espo, "House Republicans Urged to Oppose Stimulus Bill," Associated Press, January 27, 2009.

44. Grunwald, *New New Deal*.

45. Ibid.

46. One notable exception was Florida governor Charlie Crist; his public appreciation for President Obama's help via the Recovery Act is widely credited with costing him the Republican nomination for the Senate in 2010.

47. For more on this, see Timothy J. Conlan and Paul L. Posner, "Inflection Point? Federalism and the Obama Administration," *Publius: The Journal of Federalism* 41 (Summer 2011): 421–46.

48. John Kingdon, *Agendas, Alternatives and Public Policy*, 2nd ed. (New York: Longman, 1995).

49. Treasury Inspector General for Tax Administration, "Semiannual Report to Congress, April 1, 2013 to September 30, 2013," 57.

50. Jeffrey L. Pressman and Aaron B. Wildavsky, *Implementation: How Great Expectations in Washington Are "Dashed" in Oakland: Or, Why It's Amazing That Federal Programs Work at All, This Being a Saga of the Economic Development Administration as Told by Two Sympathetic Observers Who Seek to Build Morals on a Foundation of Ruined Hopes* (Berkeley: University of California Press, 1984), 141.

51. Paul Manna, *Collision Course: Federal Education Policy Meets State and Local Realities* (Washington, DC: CQ Press, 2010), 159.

52. George Mason University Centers on the Public Service, *The Implementation of the Recovery Act: Networks Under Stress*, (Fairfax, VA: George Mason University, 2013).

53. For a detailed examination of these issues, see Timothy J. Conlan, *Grants and the Recovery Act: Classic Challenges, New Dilemmas, and Best Practices* (Fairfax, VA: CGI Initiative for Collaborative Governance, 2009).

54. Suzanne Mettler, *The Submerged State: How Invisible Government Policies Undermine American Democracy* (Chicago: University of Chicago Press, 2011).

55. Michael Cooper, "From Obama, the Tax Cut Nobody Heard of," *New York Times*, October 18, 2010.

56. Quoted by Grunwald, *New New Deal*.

57. Jason Scott Smith, *Building New Deal Liberalism: The Political Economy of Public Works* (New York: Cambridge University Press, 2006).

3

A Lifeline to Struggling States

THE STATE FISCAL STABILIZATION FUND

Timothy J. Conlan

THE STATE FISCAL STABILIZATION FUND (SFSF) was the largest temporary program of broad-based federal assistance for education in American history. It was designed primarily to help states maintain funding for K-12 and public higher education and to avoid large-scale personnel cuts during the depths of the Great Recession. At the same time, it provided an important role for state governors in allocating funds and in certifying their commitment to educational reform.

This chapter explores the design, implementation, and impacts of this unique program. Because the SFSF was intended to be both a fiscal lifeline to struggling states and a major program of support for education, its successful implementation depended on collaboration between different levels of government and between distinctive policy networks. These complex interactions, under conditions of great stress, are an important point of focus in this chapter. In addition, the inclusion within SFSF of a separately administered program to promote educational reform—the so-called Race to the Top (RTTT)—provides an opportunity to explore the challenges of integrating short-term economic goals with a long-term reform agenda.

In order to investigate these issues, twenty-seven interviews were conducted with federal, state, and local officials and other policy experts and participants. Interview subjects included federal legislative and executive branch officials and staff, senior state budget officials and staff, senior leadership and managers in state departments of education, representatives of local education authorities, representatives from a variety of interest groups in the education community, and education experts at policy think tanks and the Government Accountability Office. In addition, a wide variety of published and unpublished sources were examined, including Education Department memoranda and guidance, Recovery Act websites, state reports, formal evaluation studies, and scholarly articles.

Three states—Virginia, Minnesota, and Delaware—were chosen for in-depth analyses and interviews on the basis of several factors. Virginia was selected as the common point of reference for all the programs studied in this volume. Moreover, Virginia is illustrative of those states (along with Maryland, North Carolina, and Tennessee) in which county governments are the primary providers of K-12 education services. Politically, Virginia is also noteworthy for having transitioned from a Democratic to a Republican governor during the implementation of ARRA. Given the important role conferred on governors in the SFSF program, this promised insights into any political dimensions of program administration.

Minnesota differed from Virginia on both the structural and political dimensions. It is representative of those states that utilize independent school districts to deliver educational services. It also had a Republican governor for most of the period of study. Finally, Delaware was chosen in large part to provide some early insights into the RTTT program, the independent competitive grant program created under the umbrella of SFSF. Delaware was one of only two states selected in the first round of RTTT. In addition, Democrats enjoyed unified control of Delaware state government during the period of study.

The Design and Structure of the SFSF Program

With total funding of $53.6 billion, the SFSF was actually a composite of three distinct programs: an *education stabilization fund* of approximately $39 billion; a *government services fund* of almost $9 billion, which could be used for public safety and other governmental functions as well as basic and higher education; and a $5 billion *education innovation fund* called Race to the Top.[1] The first two stabilization funds were distributed by automatic formula to states, with 61 percent based on each state's school-age population and 39 percent based on the state's overall population. The RTTT funds were distributed as competitive state grants awarded at the discretion of the secretary of education.

Unlike most federal aid-to-education programs, which flow from the federal government to state and/or local education agencies, state governors were designated as the statutory recipients of SFSF formula funds. This arrangement enabled better integration of the SFSF funds into state budgetary decision making at a difficult fiscal juncture, and it elevated gubernatorial awareness of the directed purposes of the legislation. However, it also brought new and sometimes unfamiliar actors into the federal aid to education network, which had largely been dominated by education specialists within government and by professional and advocacy groups on the outside.

Although the SFSF program was consciously designed to give states considerable flexibility in allocating and spending funds in areas of greatest need, it also required governors to certify, and be held responsible for, five legislative assurances, some of which already existed under the No Child Left Behind (NCLB) law: (1) to address inequities in teacher preparation and distribution, (2) to establish statewide prekindergarten-to-postsecondary education longitudinal data systems, (3) to improve the quality of NCLB academic assessments, (4) to improve state academic content and student achievement standards, and (5) to comply with the corrective action and school restructuring provisions of NCLB. In addition, governors were required to certify compliance with the statute's maintenance-of-effort (MOE) requirement. Barring a "precipitous decline in financial resources," which could qualify the state for a possible waiver, states were required to continue devoting at least as many state funds to K-12 and higher education as were expended in fiscal year (FY) 2006. Thus, the education stabilization funds allowed states to fill the fiscal gap between what they had spent on K-12 and postsecondary education in FY 2006 and their funding levels in FY 2008 or 2009, whichever was greater. Amounts left over, if any, were to be distributed according to the Title 1 formula for educationally disadvantaged children.

Governors were also required to certify their intent to apply for SFSF funds by April 3, 2009. Because Congress was concerned that some governors might fail to request funding, ARRA also allowed state legislatures to request funding if the governor failed to do so. Early guidance from the Department of Education (ED) also encouraged states to quickly allocate funds to save and create jobs while also ensuring transparency and accountability in the use of funds. Finally, local authorities could use funds for any purposes allowed under major existing aid to education programs; they were, however, prohibited from spending on sports facilities. These latter goals were elaborated in subsequent rules and guidance governing the reporting of jobs created or saved, use of funds, and compliance with statutory requirements such as MOE.

Program Implementation

Despite complications, the implementation of the SFSF program proceeded expeditiously. The first round of grants was distributed quickly. Two-thirds of the funds were made available within two weeks after states applied in April 2009, with the remaining one-third of SFSF funds becoming available later that year in phase two. The initial allotment could be increased to as much as 90 percent of the state's formula share if need was demonstrated. In its sample of 17 states, the Government Accountability Office estimated that, on average, 36 percent of round one SFSF funds were drawn down by August 28, 2009. Proportions ranged from a high of 92 percent of initial funds drawn down by California and Illinois to zero in four other states (Texas, Mississippi, New Jersey, and the District of Columbia).[2] Per legislative intent, SFSF funds were used primarily to fill gaps in states' existing aid formulas to local school districts, known as local educational agencies (LEAs), and to support the maintenance of education payrolls.

This speedy pace of implementation proved challenging to federal, state, and local officials alike. Although the general intent of the program was clear, there were many tasks and issues to be resolved at the national level and many questions from states requesting clarification of the law's application to their particular circumstances. Nationally, the task of implementation was made more complex by the absence of key political appointees—nominated, confirmed, and in place—in the early months of the Obama administration. A special task force with veteran career leadership was established in ED to expedite crucial tasks and respond to state and local requests. This team put together the initial grant application and first set of guidance for recipients in April 2009, just two months after initial passage of the program. These guidelines emphasized four overarching principles intended to guide recipients' use of the funds:

- Spend funds quickly to save and create jobs;
- Improve student achievement through reform;
- Ensure transparency and accountability in spending and reporting; and
- Invest the one-time ARRA funds in a way that avoids the "funding cliff" at the end of two years.[3]

ED staff also dealt with many state and local questions, especially queries concerning MOE requirements. Although the concept of maintaining 2006 levels of spending was clear enough, technical issues concerning differences in state appropriations processes, the timing of state grants to LEAs, and differing state higher education aid formulas created situations that needed federal approval or clarification. At the same time, ED staff staged webinars, communicated with governors' and state budget offices, and used education associations, such as the National Education Association and the National School Boards Association, to get messages out to the education community.

Implementation Partners

Unlike most federal aid-to-education programs, which rely on long-established implementation partnerships with state education agencies and LEAs, state governors were designated as the formal recipients of SFSF funds. Governors, or an authorized representative like the state budget director, were required to sign the state's application for funds, as well as the statutory assurances of compliance with federal education reform goals and MOE requirements.[4] A "statement of support" signature from the chief state school officer was included as an optional and recommended component of the state's application. The chief state school officer of every state except Georgia did sign, but governors in most states retained a central role in program implementation. Secretaries, commissioners, or chief financial officers of state departments of education acted as the principal state contacts for the Education Stabilization Fund in only eight states (seven for the Government Stabilization Fund). By comparison, the state budget director, or a comparable official, served as principal contact in twenty-five states (twenty-six in the Government Stabilization Fund program), as did a member of the governor's staff in sixteen states. Often this was the state's economic recovery officer or a gubernatorial adviser on education policy. In one state, Delaware, the lieutenant governor was appointed to act as the Recovery Act's program coordinator.[5]

The prominent role played by governors and state budget offices in the implementation of SFSF made eminent sense from an overall state budgetary standpoint, given most states' dire fiscal circumstances and the program's goal of fiscal stabilization.[6] From a federal implementation perspective, however, it added a new layer of complexity. A total of 82 percent of the SFSF funds were required to be spent on education, and ED officials sometimes found themselves dealing with state officials who lacked full knowledge of federal and state aid-to-education programs and requirements. As one ED staff member put it, "Rather than dealing with the SEA [state education agency], the money went to the governors, and many offices had never dealt with ED before. You would call and the person on the other end would say, 'that's not my area.' The person picking up the phone wouldn't own it."[7] This was especially vexing given the need for speedy implementation.

Conversely, most states coordinated the effort closely with their state departments of education. One case study state used staff transfers to aid with the coordination and implementation processes. In Minnesota, the state education department's stimulus coordinator transferred to the Department of Management and Budget to help oversee SFSF's implementation, while a budget department staff member joined the finance team at the Minnesota Department of Education. A team composed of staff from both units met regularly to coordinate complex issues like MOE. Delaware, another case study state, also utilized collaboration between the state education department and the governor's office. As one manager noted: "Administration was a joint effort between Education and Budget. Grants were made directly to the governor's office, which caused some issues at the beginning, getting the governor involved. It made sense from a fiscal perspective, but we worked with the governor's staff on the assurances, which were pretty prescriptive. We had already done most of the work on that." These and most other states surveyed by the Center on Education Policy also reported considerable effort on the part of state education officials working with LEAs receiving ARRA funding and overseeing implementation.[8]

Dispatches from the Field: State Experiences with SFSF

State implementation experiences with SFSF can be grouped into four broad sets of issues:

1. Initial start-up and administration,
2. Monitoring, reporting, and compliance,
3. Administrative and political network management, and
4. Programmatic accomplishments.

Each of these sets of issues is examined in turn in the following subsections.

Initial Program Start-Up and Administration

Timing issues proved to be a major concern for officials in all the case study states. Inherent challenges arising from the federal government's insistence on speedy program implementation, in order to maximize the stimulative economic effects of the Recovery Act, were exacerbated by the institutional constraints imposed by state budget processes and legislative sessions. As one state budget official observed, "Everything was rush, rush at the beginning." Another observed that "timing . . . was the key issue. It all came down at the tail end of the legislative session." A third state's official echoed the concern: "It happened in late spring, and we had already laid out our budget before we knew how much we were getting."

Part of the timing difficulties involved dealing with state legislatures during short biennial sessions. In most states, federal grant funds require legislative appropriations, just as state funds do, and most legislative sessions last only 60 to 120 days. When the first phase of SFSF funds were awarded in April 2009, state legislatures were typically in their final days or weeks. This left little time for agreeing on funding allocations with the legislature or for passing appropriations bills. "Senior legislators thought this was new money for hiring new teachers," said one Minnesota official. They had to be educated about the program's limitations and requirements as well as the fiscal necessity of using most SFSF funds to substitute for declines in state revenues. With the session running out in Minnesota, they "gave us discretion," said a budget official.

In Virginia, the legislature provided an administrative appropriation granting discretion for allocating funds to executive branch officials. Without this, said one senior official, "it could have caused real problems." In Delaware, a lack of timely information caused "a real issue with the legislature; . . . we had to go back and amend our application."

Timely information on federal rules and requirements was also a source of early frustration. "Getting timely guidance from the feds, especially early on, was frustrating," said one state official. "There was sometimes no response to our emails. We had to train LEAs without adequate guidance. Ideally, we would have set up a dedicated team with necessary training." Another state education aide observed that "the feds got the money out before the rules were out." To compensate, state budget and education officials relied on their personal and professional networks and their national associations for assistance. "The NGA [National Governors' Association] and chief state school officers' phone calls helped," said one. "As did NASBO [the National Association of State Budget Officers]. I also made use of my informal networks in the Education Department."

Another source of frustration was the lack of administrative funding in the ARRA programs. "This was the worst part of the program," said one state budget official. "It was very foolish." "There were no dedicated administrative dollars for management or training," said another. "Ideally, we would have had a dedicated team for this, but we lacked sufficient staff for thorough review and analysis of recipient reporting."

All the case study states, and a majority of states nationwide, reported difficulties in ramping up the implementation of the SFSF program after they had already experienced—or barely avoided—significant layoffs and furloughs of state personnel. According to one study by the Center for Education Policy, "The capacity of many states to implement ARRA reforms could be constrained by cuts in state education agencies' operating budgets and limited staffing levels. Twenty-three states reported a projected decrease of 5 percent or more in their state education agency (SEA) operating budget for

2011. Another six states projected flat operating budgets for state education agencies for 2011. In many cases, these cuts or freezes for 2011 have come on top of prior years of shrinking state agency budgets."[9]

Ultimately, federal rules were changed to allow for the use of some stabilization funds for state administration, but all the case study states said that this came too late to be helpful in phase one. As one manager reported, "We had already allocated the GSF [Government Stabilization Fund] funds prior to the allowance, so there were no additional funds for management." When some administrative requirements changed in phase two, biennial budgeting made state adaptations difficult: "We could have requested state funding in the biennial budget if we had known," said a Minnesota budget aide.

Monitoring, Reporting, and Compliance

In the earliest stages of writing the Recovery Act, state officials expected the SFSF program to be an extremely flexible block grant. Even as passed, federal education department officials considered it to be, as one put it, "the mother of all block grants." This is because SFSF funds could be spent on virtually any allowable activity authorized by the existing plethora of federal education programs as well as teacher retention and, in the case of the Government Stabilization Fund, many noneducational responsibilities. But the addition of legislative language requiring MOE and state assurances of progress on key elements of educational reform and innovation reduced the anticipated level of flexibility. Although the Government Stabilization Fund remained very flexible and could be applied to a broad range of state services, the larger Educational Fund was more restrictive. The assurances were "pretty prescriptive," said one state official. They "hampered its use as stimulus," agreed a budget aide in another state. "Very complex" was the conclusion of managers in a third.

The biggest constraint, and the one that involved the greatest level of complexity and controversy, was the program's MOE requirement. The statute required that states maintain their level of education spending at no less than their 2006 levels. This was not as restrictive as some initial legislative language, which required maintenance of spending at the 2008 level; such a provision would have likely precluded the use of SFSF funds in many fiscally hard-pressed states, including House speaker Nancy Pelosi's home state of California, due to deep recession-induced declines in state revenues. Nor did the legislation include the common requirement in education programs that federal funds "supplement and not supplant" state funds. Given the recession, states needed the federal funds to "backfill" their lost state revenues if they were to avoid major cuts in education spending and employment.[10] Nevertheless, most states, and two of the three case study states, found that the MOE provision was challenging to meet.

This was especially true in Minnesota. A top budget official noted that the MOE provisions of the SFSF and Medicaid FMAP programs "took the three biggest budget items off the table" for cuts because Medicaid, K-12, and higher education combined to total almost 75 percent of the state's general fund budget. For a time, "there was a question whether we could even use the SFSF funds because of MOE," recalled a state economic analyst. The problem was due in part to a feature of Minnesota's funding formula for elementary and secondary education that made the 2006 amounts look artificially large. The state routinely holds back a portion of education formula funds to LEAs as a reserve and "shifts" them into the next fiscal year. An unusually large shift in 2005 exaggerated the appearance of state funding in 2006. Federal officials at ED eventually ruled that legislative appropriations were an appropriate measure for MOE, as opposed to actual outlays, but "it was hard to get ED to go on the record and say OK," recalled an official. "We didn't want to call a special session of the legislature because of a bad phone call."

Other case study states had less difficulty with the MOE provisions. In Virginia, officials noted that it was "especially tough on higher education," but not a serious problem with K-12. School-age population and education spending had been growing rapidly enough in Virginia that meeting the 2006 levels of elementary and secondary spending was not a significant difficulty. MOE was even less troublesome in Delaware, where it was deemed to be something to be "mindful" of but not a serious problem.

MOE issues drew attention from accountability and evaluation organizations on a national scale as well. In its bimonthly monitoring reports on the Recovery Act, the Government Accountability Office found that some states had revised their data on 2006 education spending—which formed the basis for the MOE calculations—and provided inadequate explanation for the changes.[11] It recommended that ED enhance its monitoring of state MOE calculations and require more detailed explanations of changes. Similarly, ED's Office of Inspector General (IG) issued a critical report on the department's monitoring and evaluation of MOE data and called for greater scrutiny and oversight of state-reported data and calculations.[12] The department rejected the IG's finding, arguing that it called for actions that went beyond the scope of the statute's requirements and normal departmental practices. Indeed, in its guidance to states on MOE requirements in the SFSF program, the Department of Education stressed that "there are considerable variations in the formulae and other mechanisms that States use in providing support for elementary and secondary education," which necessitated that "the department [provide] states with some flexibility in quantifying that support."[13] Nevertheless, ED did follow up issuance of the IG report with additional guidance and information on state best practices in early 2011.[14]

Operationally, most states' use of SFSF funds for K-12 education proved to be straightforward, both nationally and in our case study states. "We just plugged it into our school funding formula," said a Delaware education official. "It dovetailed into our normal operations, the state aid formula," agreed a Minnesota administrator. In order to document adherence with the program's rules and requirements, however, SFSF funding was coded and tracked separately. "We added 400 codes for the stimulus," said one state budget official, adding that "there was too much focus on dollars and not enough on kids." A Virginia budget official similarly reported that they "gave these funds unique codes from the beginning. We identified it early on as high-risk, one-time funding." This proved to be a wise decision, because Virginia reported having "more IG visits with ARRA than any other program."[15]

This level of accountability proved disconcerting for many states, given what they perceived as contradictory goals and uncertain reporting requirements. "There were lots of conflicting messages—save jobs, spend quick, do reform," said one high-ranking state official. Another compared SFSF implementation with "the wild, wild West in the beginning, trying to figure out the requirements. The feds were trying—everyone was trying and comparing notes from other states."

A common state and local complaint was that "the [federal] guidance was constantly changing." This was particularly challenging, in the states' view, with the federal government's requirement to report on jobs saved or created by the stimulus funds—the so-called 1512 reporting, which was named for the provision of the Recovery Act requiring such information.[16] "The jobs reporting changed more than once," observed an analyst in one state. "It was an ongoing challenge."

Making matters worse, in the recipients' view, was that the jobs reporting was a completely novel requirement. "It's not something that we do," observed a Virginia administrator. Monitoring local reporting of jobs was also viewed as a "shock" to the states. "The locals report jobs directly but the state is responsible for their accuracy," explained this Virginia official. "Yet we have no authority in this area. It's a disconnect."

Network Administration

Field research suggests that established policy and program networks played an important role in implementing the SFSF program and contributing to its accomplishments. The value of these networks was present in multiple contexts and dimensions: laterally—across state administrative agencies; vertically—up and down the chain of federal, state, and local government relations; and horizontally—among the states and their associations.

Most fundamentally, because governors, their staffs, and state budget offices typically lacked direct experience in the implementation of education programs, all the states examined in this report were characterized by close ties between executive office and budget staff, on the one hand, and state departments of education, on the other hand. In a formal sense, this was suggested by the fact that in all states but one the SFSF application was cosigned by the chief state school officer. Less formally, it was manifested in various ways. In Virginia, implementation of SFSF occurred beneath the umbrella of an interdepartmental team created for the implementation of all ARRA programs, including the state's Department of Education and its Office of Management and Budget (OMB). In Delaware, the SFSF was administered jointly by the state OMB and Department of Education. And in Minnesota, collaboration between the state's OMB and Department of Education was aided by an exchange of professional staff.

All states also reported healthy levels of collaboration between the executive and legislative branches. Multiple officials in Minnesota observed that relations between the governor's office and the legislature on SFSF issues were largely cooperative and well coordinated, especially at the leadership level. This included an advisory group of legislative leaders. Virginia officials also highlighted the level of interbranch cooperation, which they felt was essential to the program's initial implementation, given the time pressures involved. Delaware officials agreed that the relations were cooperative in their state as well. In all cases, this cooperation, even across party lines, was deemed to be essential to the early implementation of the program, given the short legislative sessions and need for legislative approval or appropriations.

As noted above, many state and local officials voiced frustrations with the lack of adequate information and guidance from ED early in the implementation of SFSF. Most acknowledged, however, that many problems flowed from the convergence of short legislative sessions and the countercyclical demand for speedy implementation, along with statutory requirements for transparency and new forms of reporting. Virtually all state and local interviewees felt that the federal officials with whom they dealt were trying their best, and they often ventured that ED did a better job of collaborating, sharing information, and trying to provide timely guidance than did many other federal agencies and departments. "They were doing the best they could," said one Minnesota official. "ED did a good job of assisting us," concurred a Delaware budget aide; "they were the best department I dealt with." "Our federal–state interactions were generally good," said another state's official. "There were some early frustrations, but our regular contacts for SFSF funds at ED were very responsive."

This level of vertical collaboration in the intergovernmental system was aided in many states by tapping into strong and well-established vertical implementation networks already present in the education community. Scholars have long noted how the development of strong professional ties between education officials at the federal, state, and local levels improved the implementation of even the most challenging federal aid programs in education.[17] These powerful networks were consciously utilized by states to assist with smoothing the implementation of the SFSF. As one state budget director observed, "It was unusual for us to have interactions with ED. We normally don't have that here, so we tried to preserve the existent relationships they had with the state Department of Education." A Minnesota budget official who had prior experience in the state education department elaborated further on the use of informal networks: "Minnesota ED already has relationships to federal and state partners. When necessary, I was able to use my informal contacts at ED to gather intelligence and feedback." The close collaboration among budget and education staff in Delaware also allowed that state to make use of deep program knowledge and intergovernmental contacts in education as well. Moreover, the state's "strong record of state–local collaboration" was offered up as a major reason for Delaware's selection for an RTTT grant in the first round.

Delaware's experience thus underscores that vertical collaboration involves state–local as well as federal–state relations. Because SFSF funds were heavily used to maintain funding in state aid formulas in K-12 education, state–local relationships were crucial to effective implementation. At the same time, local school districts needed to have clear understanding of the allowable uses and limitations on SFSF funding, accountability and reporting requirements, and the underlying reform objectives associated with the program. To promote this understanding, many states undertook active measures to inform local officials about funding levels and guidelines early in the implementation process. In Minnesota, for example, this included state officials going out to speak to local school officials, presenting seminars on SFSF funding, and working with state education associations to explain the law and its requirements. These state efforts were reinforced at the national level by ED, which also worked with education groups like the National School Boards Association and the National Education Association to explain the law to their members. Both groups developed webinars for their members and invited federal officials to speak about SFSF and other stimulus funding programs at their annual meetings.

Finally, horizontal networks among states proved to be unusually important in the early implementation of the SFSF program. Given the early lack of detailed information about its specific requirements—such as the interpretation of MOE provisions, as well as the evolving nature of the program's reporting requirements—state umbrella associations such as the NGA and NASBO assumed important roles as advocates, conveners, and problem solvers for the states. "NASBO and NGA were very effective," said one state budget director. "They intervened very effectively with OMB and the White House." "The best advice we got" came from NGA and NASBO, agreed another state budget official. "Their webinars and weekly conference calls were very helpful."

Accomplishments

Overall, despite implementation complexities and difficulties, states tended to view the SFSF program as successful. "It was critical assistance," said a Minnesota budget official. "It helped us avoid deeper cuts and tax increases." It "saved us from radical cuts," said another. In Delaware, it "provided relief when we really needed it."

Based on state and local government reporting, the SFSF accomplished its principal goal of protecting instructional and other education-related jobs (figure 3.1). Out of scores of ARRA-funded programs, ED—and the SFSF program in particular—accounted for the largest number of jobs saved or created in every quarterly reporting period from February 2009 until October 2011.[18] Over the entire period of two and a half years, education jobs accounted for 58 percent of all reported jobs, on average, and SFSF accounted for 24 percent to 51 percent of all ARRA reported jobs, depending on the quarter. SFSF averaged 38 percent of all reported jobs over the entire period. Comprehensive data on state and local government employment show that education was hit less hard than total government employment at the state, though not the local, level during the first three years of the Great Recession. At the local level, once virtually all SFSF funds were expended by the fall of 2011, layoffs of teachers and other K-12 education personnel picked up markedly.[19]

Econometric analyses of the employment effects of the stimulus program had mixed assessments, although they typically had difficulty isolating the independent effects of the SFSF program on either overall employment or on the state–local education sector specifically. One study by the economist Daniel Wilson estimated that ARRA spending as a whole created or saved 800,000 state and local jobs, a significant but undetermined number of which were in education.[20] A substantial jobs impact can also be inferred from a

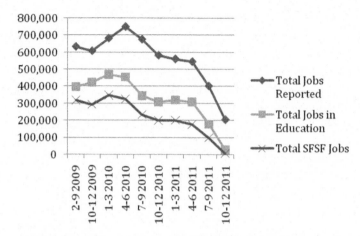

Figure 3.1. State and Local Jobs under the Recovery Act
Source: Recovery Accountability and Transparency Board (www.recovery.gov).

study that focused on the nearest parallel to the SFSF program in the Recovery Act—the temporary increase in the federal matching rate for Medicaid. This research found that "the ARRA transfers to states had an economically large and statistically robust positive effect on employment."[21]

Conversely, an alternative study that attempted to disaggregate the employment effects of different types of federal countercyclical aid to the states questioned the value of flexible assistance such as SFSF. In a paper titled "Did the Stimulus Stimulate?" James Feyrer and Bruce Sacerdote found that "block grants to support local education agencies have very small (and statistically insignificant) impacts on employment" because recipients use it to substitute for state and local funds.[22] They estimated that perhaps 80,000 education jobs would have been lost in the absence of SFSF funding for education.[23] Stronger employment results were found for federal stimulus funds that were targeted to low-income individuals and to infrastructure.

Apart from the program's employment effects, the SFSF program was credited by state officials with some additional accomplishments as well. State interviewees reported that SFSF funds were instrumental in helping them hold down tuition rates at public universities during the recession. Some also stressed the benefits of ARRA's transparency agenda. "We present data better now," reported one state budget official. The program was also praised for furthering the education reform agenda in Delaware, which subsequently received one of two initial grants for the competitive RTTT program.

A Note about the Special Case of Race to the Top

Race to the Top was a unique component of the SFSF program. The $9 billion Government Stabilization Fund and the $39 billion Education Stabilization Fund were distributed by a transparent and predictable formula, and both provided very broad, block grant–like discretion in states' use of funds. In contrast, the RTTT program was a competitive discretionary grant for promoting educational reform.[24] It had a far more elaborate application process and required detailed plans for achieving state educational reforms, including difficult structural reforms, not just broad assurances that certain reform goals would be pursued.

Specifically, the RTTT identified five key reform strategies that state applications were required to address:

1. Adopting more rigorous standards and assessments;
2. Recruiting, evaluating, and retaining highly effective teachers and principals;
3. Turning around low-performing schools;
4. Building data systems that measure student success; and
5. Sustaining education reform through collaboration with stakeholders.[25]

Although the first four strategies are consonant with the overall goals of SFSF, states were required to submit a detailed application outlining how they would approach each strategy in order to receive RTTT funding. ED created a point system with nineteen criteria to evaluate each application, with "over half the points that reviewers may award to states, . . . based on states' accomplishments prior to applying—their successes in increasing student achievement, decreasing the achievement gaps, increasing graduation rates, enlisting strong statewide support and commitment to their proposed plans, and creating legal conditions conducive to education reform and innovation."[26] Forty states plus the District of Columbia submitted applications for the grant in early March 2009, with two initial round winners announced on March 29, 2010. In making the award, Education Secretary Duncan stated, "Two applications stood out above all others: Delaware and Tennessee. . . . Both states have statewide buy-in for comprehensive plans to reform their schools. They have written new laws to support their policies. And they have demonstrated the courage, capacity, and commitment to turn their ideas into practices that can improve outcomes for students."[27]

Because Delaware was an early recipient of RTTT funds (it received $100 million in phase one), its selection for analysis in this study can help to provide some insights into this unique component of SFSF. Those insights are necessarily limited and conditional because this research is confined to a single state for a limited period of time. Nevertheless, Delaware's experience with RTTT does say something about both the selection and implementation processes.

In explaining their success at securing the highly sought-after RTTT funds, state officials in Delaware emphasized what they perceived to be several of their advantages. First, they believed that they had already made significant progress toward the program's stated goals. As a top education official put it, "We had a lot of pieces already in place and had been building our educational system for twenty years. So I think we had a lot of those components and were really able to capitalize on that." External observers agree that Delaware's application was greatly aided by reforms that it had already undertaken or committed to undertake, especially to its system of teacher evaluation and tenure.[28] Consequently, Delaware officials felt that they were poised to make rapid progress that would enable the RTTT program as a whole look successful.

Second, state officials had established a high level of consensus and cooperation on key educational reform goals, including stakeholders from the teachers' unions to the local superintendents: "One of the things cited on multiple occasions for why Delaware's application was so strong was that we had 100 percent statewide participation, which reflects our size and ability to collaborate and our long-standing relationships that we had built. But having every school board, every local union, every district on board—which meant that every single child in Delaware was going to be impacted by Race to the Top—I think that was really one of the key factors."

Such collaboration was attributed in part to the state's small size and the intimate character of its politics. All of the key actors in education and education policy know one another and have a track record of working together, and the political dominance of the Democratic Party enables all actors to interact within a shared umbrella of common values and trust.

Delaware utilized its RTTT funding to implement a broad series of educational reform initiatives and improvements tied to the five federal goals outlined in the RTTT application. For example, in the area of improving student standards and assessments, the state launched new initiatives to improve language training and implement Common Core and "next gen" science standards.[29] To improve teacher quality and evaluation, RTTT funded initiatives for new teacher recruitment and preservice training as well as the deployment of "development coaches" to assess teacher performance and provide mentoring.[30] The program also funded a "data coach" initiative to help teachers, principals, and administrators analyze the increased student performance data being collected.

During the core implementation period, the state demonstrated significant gains in student proficiency and achievement on standardized tests. For example, across all grades, 73 percent of students met standards of proficiency in reading in 2012 (compared with 61 percent in 2011), and 72 percent of students were proficient in mathematics (compared with 62 percent in 2011). These increases in proficiency accrued to all major subgroups of the student population, although significant racial and income gaps remained across grade levels.[31]

Conversely, such gains proved difficult to sustain once RTTT funds were exhausted. For example, between 2009 and 2013, Delaware students showed significant improvements in both reading and math on a different test—a nationwide benchmark for fourth and eighth graders called the National Assessment of Educational Progress. Such gains may well have been aided by the RTTT initiatives. By 2015, however, virtually all these 2013 gains had disappeared, and Delaware students had largely returned to where they were in 2009.[32]

Conclusion

The SFSF was a unique, emergency stimulus program that can provide a useful model for national financial assistance to state and local governments during a future economic downturn. The flexible, block-grant-style program enabled significant amounts of countercyclical fiscal assistance to be disbursed rapidly to the states with remarkably few delays and obstructions. In turn, states, local school districts, and public universities proved generally successful at distributing and implementing the funds quickly and effectively, as measured in terms of preserving public-sector jobs and compensating for the steep decline in state revenues.

Several factors contributed to this relatively successful record of implementation. First, the use of established federal formulas for distributing funds to the states, as well as states' reliance on established systems of educational assistance, allowed funds to be spent rapidly. This approach prevented delays that would inevitably arise from disputes over new formula design or discretionary grant allocation methods. Rapid implementation was also enhanced by the level of state flexibility provided under the program. States and local school districts enjoyed considerable discretion in their use of SFSF funds, particularly under the Government Services Fund, and potentially significant obstacles were ameliorated during both the legislative and implementation processes. The legislative decision to establish 2006 as the base year for MOE calculations, rather than 2008, was enormously consequential for those states suffering the most severe losses of revenues, as was federal officials' accommodation to variations in state educational finance systems. Finally, the education community's reliance on established education finance networks, as well as the development of new (and the restoration of old) channels of communication between top-level budget officials at all levels of government, contributed measurably to effective program implementation and stronger intergovernmental cooperation.

Notes

1. This is PL 111-5, Title XIV.

2. US Government Accountability Office, *Recovery Act: Funds Continue to Provide Fiscal Relief to States and Localities, while Accountability and Reporting Challenges Need to Be Fully Addressed*, GAO-09-1016 (Washington, DC: US Government Accountability Office, 2009), 42, www.gao.gov/assets/300/295645.pdf.

3. US Department of Education, "Guidance on the State Fiscal Stabilization Fund Program," April 2009, 2.

4. In South Carolina, Governor Mark Sanford signed "under duress" and indicated his opposition to the Recovery Act. As allowed under the statute, the state legislature directed the state's acceptance of ARRA funding.

5. US Department of Education, "State Grants under the State Fiscal Stabilization Fund," www2.ed.gov/programs/statestabilization/resources.html.

6. For some perspective on the impact of the Great Recession on state revenues and finances, see Donald J. Boyd and Lucy Dadayan, "State Tax Decline in Early 2009 Was the Sharpest on Record," *State Revenue Report*, Rockefeller Institute, July 2009.

7. This and all other unattributed quotes appearing in this chapter are derived from the author's interviews with federal, state, and local officials involved in designing or implementing the State Fiscal Stabilization Fund, as well as knowledgeable participants in related professional and trade associations. Pursuant to the study's Institutional Review Board protocol, interview subjects were given assurances of confidentiality. Twenty-seven interviews were conducted between April 2010 and August 2011 in Dover, Delaware; Saint Paul; Richmond; and Washington.

8. Center for Education Policy, *An Early Look at the Economic Stimulus Package and the Public Schools: Perspectives from State Leaders* (Washington, DC: Center for Education Policy, 2009), 14.

9. Center for Education Policy, *More to Do but Less Capacity to Do It: States' Progress in Implementing the Recovery Act Education Reforms* (Washington, DC: Center for Education Policy, 2011), 6.

10. Noelle M. Ellerson, "Schools and the Stimulus: How America's Public School Districts Are Using ARRA Funds," American Association of School Administrators, August 2009, 3.

11. US Government Accountability Office, *Recovery Act: One Year Later, State Uses of Funds and Opportunities to Strengthen Accountability*, GAO-10-437 (Washington, DC: US Government Accountability Office, 2010), 38–40.

12. US Department of Education, Office of Inspector General, *American Recovery and Reinvestment Act of 2009: The Department's Implementation of the State Fiscal Stabilization Fund Program—Final Audit Report*, ED-OIG A19J0001 (Washington, DC: US Government Printing Office, 2010), 5–9.

13. US Department of Education, *Guidance on the Maintenance-of-Effort Requirements in the State Fiscal Stabilization Fund Program*, OMB 1810-069 (Washington, DC: US Government Printing Office, 2010), 2, www2.ed.gov/policy/gen/leg/recovery /statutory/moe-guidance.pdf.

14. US Department of Education, "State Fiscal Stabilization Fund: 2011 Updates," unpublished webinar, February 1, 2011.

15. See, e.g., US Department of Education, Office of the Inspector General, *American Recovery and Reinvestment Act: Virginia—Use of Funds and Data Quality for Selected American Recovery and Reinvestment Act Programs, Final Audit Report*, ED-OIG A03K0008 (Washington, DC: US Government Printing Office, 2011).

16. See, e.g., Peter R. Orszag (director, US Office of Management and Budget), "Memorandum for the Heads of Executive Departments and Agencies: Updated Guidance on the American Recovery and Reinvestment Act—Data Quality, Non-Reporting Recipients, and Reporting of Job Estimates," M-10-08, December 18, 2009, www.whitehouse.gov/sites/default/files/omb/assets/memoranda_2010/m10-08.pdf; and US Department of Education, "Clarifying Guidance on the American Recovery and Reinvestment Act of 2009 (Pub. L. 111-5) (ARRA, Recovery Act)," August 26, 2010, www2.ed.gov/policy/gen/leg/recovery/section-1512.html.

17. See, e.g., Michael Kirst and Richard Jung, "The Utility of a Longitudinal Approach in Assessing Implementation: A 13-Year View of Title I, ESEA," *Educational Evaluation and Policy Analysis* 2, no. 5; and Paul E. Peterson, Barry G. Rabe, and Kenneth K. Wong, *When Federalism Works* (Washington, DC: Brookings Institution Press, 1986).

18. Author's calculations, based on job data reported in "ED Recovery Act Report: Summary of Programs and State-by-State Data," www2.ed.gov/policy/gen/leg /recovery/spending/index.html; and at www.Recovery.gov.

19. See Center for Education Policy, *Teaching Jobs Saved in 2009–10, but Teacher Layoffs Loom for Next School Year* (Washington, DC: Center for Education Policy, 2010); and Phil Oliff and Michael Leachman, *New School Year Brings Steep Cuts in State Funding for Schools* (Washington, DC: Center for Budget and Policy Priorities, 2011).

20. Daniel J. Wilson, "Fiscal Spending Jobs Multipliers: Evidence from the 2009 American Recovery and Reinvestment Act," *American Economic Journal: Economic Policy* 4, no. 3 (August 2012): 278.

21. Gabriel Chodorow-Reich, Laura Feiveson, Zachary Liscow, William Woolston, and William Gui, "Does State Fiscal Relief during Recessions Increase Employment? Evidence from the American Recovery and Reinvestment Act," *American Economic Journal: Economic Policy* 4, no. 3 (August 2012): 121.

22. James Feyrer and Bruce Sacerdote, "Did the Stimulus Stimulate? Real Time Estimates of the Effects of the American Recovery and Reinvestment Act," Working Paper 16759 (Cambridge, MA: National Bureau of Economic Research, 2011), 19, www.nber.org/papers/w16759.

23. Ibid., 20.

24. On the importance of this change in policy instruments, see Paul Manna and Laura L. Ryan, "Competitive Grants and Educational Federalism: President Obama's Race to the Top Program in Theory and Practice," *Publius: The Journal of Federalism* 41, no. 3 (Summer 2011): 522–46.

25. White House, "The Race to the Top: Promoting Innovation, Reform, and Excellence in America's Public Schools," fact sheet, November 4, 2009, 1–2, www.whitehouse.gov/the-press-office/fact-sheet-race-top.

26. US Department of Education, "Overview Information: Race to the Top Fund—Notice Inviting Applications for New Awards for Fiscal Year (FY) 2010," *Federal Register* 75, no. 71 (April 14, 2010): 19510.

27. Arne Duncan, "US Secretary of Education Arne Duncan's Statement on Race to the Top Phase 1 Winners," US Department of Education, March 29, 2010, www.ed.gov/news/speeches/us-secretary-education-arne-duncans-statement-race-top-phase-1-winners.

28. See, e.g., Patrick McGuinn, "Stimulating Reform: Race to the Top, Competitive Grants and the Obama Education Agenda," *Educational Policy* 26, no. 1 (2012): 146–47.

29. See Delaware Department of Education, "Delaware Education Plan Overview," December 2010, www.doe.k12.de.us/cms/lib09/DE01922744/Centricity/Domain/87/De_Ed_ReformPlanOverview.pdf.

30. Delaware Department of Education, "Race to the Top: Detailed Overviews on Initiatives," www.doe.k12.de.us/Page/1427.

31. Delaware Department of Education, "State End-of-Year DCAS Performance Summary 2012," www.doe.k12.de.us/Page/1041.

32. See "Delaware Scores Slip on National Exam," Newsworks, October 28, 2015, www.newsworks.org/index.php/local/delaware/87666-delaware-scores-slip-on-national-exam; and National Center for Education Statistics, "State Profiles," http://nces.ed.gov/nationsreportcard/states/.

4

The Rush to Pave

ADAPTING THE FEDERALLY AIDED HIGHWAY NETWORK TO ARRA

Sheldon M. Edner and Matthew J. Critchfield

THE AMERICAN RECOVERY AND REINVESTMENT ACT (the Recovery Act, or ARRA) added more than $40 billion per year for fiscal years (FYs) 2009 and 2010 to the Federal-Aid Highway Program appropriations, growing the program to a total of more than $106 billion across those two FYs.[1] This represented a steep increase, given that the Federal Highway Administration (FHWA) was appropriated nearly $42 billion in FY 2011 and requested $51.3 billion for FY 2016.[2] Further, the Recovery Act legislation specified that funds should be used for projects that can be "started and completed expeditiously,"[3] with a priority placed on projects that have a projected completion date within three years of enactment or projects that are located in "economically distressed areas."[4] In general, the implementation of ARRA by the FHWA, working with its state partners, proceeded relatively smoothly. Congress did not fundamentally alter highway funding and implementation with the passage of the Recovery Act but rather maintained its basic relationships and processes. With such continuity, existing networks were largely able to absorb the increased workload and new requirements by selectively prioritizing appropriate projects, using existing staff talent wisely, adopting somewhat minor additions of rules and oversight, and collaborating actively and consistently with the federal establishment, the states, and, where necessary, local government entities.

The FHWA has the responsibility of administering the Federal-Aid Highway Program (FAHP) jointly with the states.[5] The Surface Transportation Program (which includes highway, transit, safety, motor carrier, rail, and ferry funding) is periodically reauthorized for five to six years.[6] During the past twenty years, as current authorizations have expired, Congress has found the timely reauthorization of the legislation challenging due to interest in restraining overall federal spending, questions about whether the program should be devolved to the states, and reduced revenues from the federal gas tax. Congress has instead extended the program through temporary reauthorizations and continuing resolutions until a legislative consensus on reauthorization could be achieved. These temporary extensions have persisted for multiple years in some cases. At the time of ARRA's enactment, the FAHP was operating under such a temporary reauthorization.

The research for this chapter was based on participant observation and interviews conducted with US Department of Transportation (USDOT), the FHWA, and state department of transportation (SDOT) personnel. Interviews were conducted with key FHWA personnel at the headquarters and field levels to explore and more fully understand the agency's strategy for program implementation. In addition, fieldwork was conducted in the states of Washington, West Virginia, and Virginia to understand some of the responses to and implementation of the act. Virginia was commonly selected by all members of the research team and across all programs. West Virginia and Washington were selected for analysis in this chapter based on discussions with FHWA staff working on the ARRA program. These states were seen as presenting useful implementation examples and as generally characterizing the experience across all states. The FHWA's division administrators and SDOT officials charged with the implementation of ARRA at the executive and middle-management levels provided responses to questions focusing on their experiences with ARRA implementation. In total, more than forty respondents were interviewed in the course of this research.

The FHWA Highway Program and ARRA

Funding for the regular FHWA program is made available to the states on an annual basis as an apportionment for projects chosen by the states. The apportionment notice, often referred to as the state "federal checkbook for highway infrastructure," allows a state to obligate funding for projects it has chosen. An individual state may have hundreds, if not thousands, of projects that it is managing (initiating, constructing, and completing) in a given year. Hence, ensuring the flow of federal funds to eligible projects is an annual management challenge. From a financial perspective, states must carefully manage their overall federal funding to avoid overdrawing their balances or allowing funds to lapse.[7]

The Recovery Act emphasized the physical improvement of infrastructure, including roads, highways, and bridges throughout the country. To accomplish its share of the infrastructure improvements, the FHWA was authorized and appropriated $27.5 billion. Of this amount, $26.6 billion was added to the existing FAHP. By the end of 2012, funding had been committed for the completion of more than 12,000 projects scattered throughout all fifty states, the District of Columbia, Puerto Rico, and the Pacific Trust Territories.[8] Approximately $1 billion was dedicated to projects on Native American reservations and federal property, to the construction of ferryboats and terminals, and to administrative costs.

ARRA's support for highways followed the basic structure of the preexisting highway funding and management process but with an overlay of unique requirements. Specific requirements under the Recovery Act were grafted onto the existing highway program and included most notably the need for "shovel ready" projects, spending timelines, reporting requirements, increased audit oversight and accountability, and targeted funding to high-priority areas, as identified by the Economic Development Administration (EDA). The standard state matching requirement for highway projects (90 percent federal and 10 percent state) was eliminated for ARRA-funded projects, and all projects were funded at up to 100 percent with federal dollars. ARRA also added a maintenance-of-effort requirement that directed states to maintain prior-year levels of state funding for their highway programs. Additionally, the interest of the White House and Congress in seeing ARRA money expended quickly, in being able to shape how projects were selected, in ensuring transparency, and in counting jobs in a geographically specific way challenged administrators in the preexisting program structure. In general, however, administrators were able to meet these challenges successfully.

Managing Federal Highway Dollars under ARRA

From the additional $26.6 billion ARRA funding for the FAHP, new monies were allocated to the states based on their current funding formula. These new funds had to be obligated by March 1, 2010. Hence, the first challenge for most states was to utilize ARRA funding by increasing the number and flow of projects in their programs. The identification of these additional projects had actually begun late in 2008, before the passage of ARRA. The principal state advocate for federal highway funding, the American Association of State Highway and Transportation Officials, had asked its members to identify lists of projects that could be funded as part of an overall economic stimulus package. These lists were provided to Congress as examples of infrastructure work that could help stimulate economic growth if Congress were to enact a program.

Thus, when ARRA was signed, the states generally were poised with additional funding opportunities and could begin obligating funds immediately. Each state, however, chose a mix of projects that reflected its unique needs and complied with the fast-tracking expectations of ARRA. For some states, this meant an emphasis on maintenance and rehabilitation projects that required relatively less preconstruction work. In other cases, a state's needs might mean supplementing already-funded projects that required additional monies to accelerate later project phases or reduce funding shortfalls produced by cost increases. For other states, a mix of maintenance and new, ready-to-go projects worked. For any given state, its ARRA strategy might mean a combination of all these options.

The large infusion of Recovery Act funds placed an increased risk and burden on the capabilities of state and local agencies. The collaboration between SDOTs and the FHWA can potentially involve a variety of subrecipient agencies at the local level of government. The states are responsible for program stewardship and oversight for projects implemented both by themselves and also by local public agencies. SDOTs routinely deal with the federal conditions of aid and are well schooled in satisfying them. Local entities, however, may not receive FHWA funding very often and have little or no prior experience with federal requirements, which presented a steep compliance learning curve and often added to the time needed to implement an FHWA-funded project.[9]

Where SDOTs managed projects directly, accommodating the financial management challenges was within state control. However, where projects were funded through sub-awards to local entities, the SDOTs and these entities had a shared responsibility to track state funding balances. All local entities receiving funding were required to e-mail customized financial reports to their respective SDOTs on a monthly basis.[10] This ensured that states were able to follow their balances closely and recognize any discrepancies that needed correction quickly. Cost increases or decreases on locally administered projects could have an impact on the state's ability to meet its March 1, 2010, obligation deadline (and thus, giving inexperienced local governments project-management responsibility was very risky).

With more than 12,000 projects chosen by the fifty states, Puerto Rico, and the District of Columbia, the financial challenge of obligating ARRA highway funding was significant. Working aggressively with the states, the FHWA was able to successfully meet the obligation deadline on February 27, 2010.[11] At the point of ARRA's enactment, the recession was in full effect and infrastructure contractors were hungry for work. States experienced a significant reduction in estimated project costs as bids were received, reflecting the economic status of the construction industry and the intense competition for new work. The good news for the federal and state governments was project savings, which meant more projects could be funded, at least until February 27, 2010.

Choosing Projects

For the purposes of timeliness and impact, ARRA required federal funding recipients to move quickly to implement projects. In some states, ARRA projects were already included within federally accepted plans and programs. In others, these plans and programs had to be amended to include additional projects for ARRA funding. Such potential delays were perceived as obstacles to be avoided. On a practical level, the term "shovel ready" was utilized to operationalize the criterion of moving quickly to implement projects. From a politician's or layperson's perspective, this might mean the immediate scheduling of the ceremonial turning of the first shovelful of dirt. In point of fact, and for the FHWA infrastructure program, the term lacks practical meaning. Under the traditional federal highway program, the focus of federal oversight and control is not on the individual project but rather on management of an overall flow of federal funds across all projects managed by a state. For ARRA, conversely, the unit of analysis for federal accountability is the individual project.

A key issue was that infrastructure projects in many cases take years to construct and are often, especially for truly large-scale projects, authorized in phases. In some cases, only the first phase of a project—which usually included completion of final design, environmental analyses, construction contract bidding, and so on—could be considered close to immediate shovel readiness. As the initial phase was constructed, subsequent project phases proceeded to final design and completion of all required preconstruction work for those phases. As a result, states either bypassed using ARRA funding for large infrastructure projects or funded a particular stage of such projects. As an example, the state of Washington chose to use ARRA funds to accelerate projects already under way by completing phases of projects earlier than planned so that the state did not have to wait on the flow of future state revenues and funding to construct later phases.

Another issue with the ambiguity of "shovel readiness" involved the point of "project initiation." For projects funded through the traditional FHWA program, federal authorization to initiate a project is required only for "major projects."[12] Determining when minor projects begin is usually not a matter of day-to-day concern for the FHWA. Indeed, the FHWA typically recognizes initiation and implementation of minor projects in the form of reimbursement requests in which the state is often recovering funds it spent

several months previously. For ARRA funding, the point of project initiation did matter. For purposes of ARRA reporting, the FHWA chose to use
the point at which the implementing agency issued a "notice to proceed" to its
contractors as the point at which the project technically was initiated.

In summary, project funding and initiation under the ARRA's "shovel
ready" timeline caused the states and the FHWA to substitute some new management strategies for the purposes of demonstrating an efficient utilization
of ARRA funding and compliance as well as meeting the reporting expectations of the act. For shovel ready purposes, many states chose to implement
minor projects that could issue a notice to proceed quickly—for example, repaving and maintenance work. These projects were operationally ready to initiate
work. Some major projects were chosen for ARRA funding if a future phase of
an existing project could be implemented immediately with ARRA monies.
In other cases, new projects were added to existing plans and programs.

USDOT's Oversight of the Federal-Aid Highway Program under ARRA

Typically, the FHWA administers the FAHP on a day-to-day basis without
direct operational oversight from the Office of the Secretary (OST). Although individual projects might provoke the OST's attention for a number
of different reasons (environmental impact, financial effects, political controversy, etc.), the FHWA is primarily responsible for the FAHP. The OST
has oversight for the FHWA's budget proposals to Congress and for the reauthorization of its program, but operational responsibility for grant-making
activity is the responsibility of the FHWA administrator.

Under ARRA, however, the political stakes and visibility of the program
and the responsibility for weekly reporting were centralized in the hands of
the OST and the senior accountable officials (SAOs)—the deputy assistant
secretary for budget and programs and the deputy assistant secretary for policy. Consequently, OST formed a "TIGER (Transportation Improvements
Generating Economic Recovery) Team" composed of representatives of the
ARRA-affected DOT agencies.[13] This team met weekly, or more often as
needed, to provide OST with status updates on ARRA's program implementation and to troubleshoot implementation issues such as generating grant
reports, targeting projects to EDA areas, and obligating and expending grant
dollars. Cochaired by the two SAOs, the team typically met Monday after-
noons after the Monday morning ARRA briefing for the secretary of transportation and his team of modal administrators and senior political appointees. The secretary was briefed on implementation issues and progress so
that he was up to date on program status and able to respond to calls from

the White House and its ARRA Team, which was headed by Vice President Joseph Biden.

Typical issues handled by the TIGER Team and/or the secretary's team might be politically controversial project issues, rates of grant obligations and expenditures, definition of key terminology affecting program administration, new guidance from the Office of Management and Budget, and the like. As issues were identified, the affected modes of transportation and their senior political and executive team members would be asked to respond as appropriate. From time to time, congressional offices would issue reports on funded projects critiquing selections made, dollars involved, and other project attributes.[14]

Representative Jim Oberstar, chair of the House Committee on Transportation and Infrastructure, added specific reporting and program implementation requirements, contained in Section 1200 of ARRA, which directed DOT's modal agencies to provide independent reports and schedules of reporting on projects funded. Oberstar's provisions reflected not only his power as chair but also the committee's oversight and authorization of the surface transportation program.[15] He wanted to make sure that the contribution of ARRA funds to the ongoing authorization of the program was positive and recognized. The DOT TIGER Team and secretary's team were called on to provide testimony to both Oberstar's committee and also to other congressional committees. The TIGER Team also reconciled the sometimes-competing implementation oversight issues produced under the general ARRA legislative provisions and Section 1200 of the legislation.[16]

The FHWA's Oversight of ARRA Highway Program Funds

Under ARRA, the FHWA deemed it necessary to enhance its financial oversight activities. This decision was driven by the substantial infusion of additional federal funding; the legislative and executive insistence that the ARRA spending be highly transparent; and the concern with potential fraud, waste, and abuse. Additional incentives were provided by the extra ARRA funding provided to agency inspectors general ($20 million for the USDOT alone) and the specialized audit mandate to the US Government Accountability Office (GAO). In an effort to reduce the risk of errors, the FHWA asked its state partners to adjust their annual stewardship agreements with its field offices to include enhanced federal oversight generally as well as in-depth federal engagement for large and expensive projects that might strain state and local administrative resources. In addition, the FHWA's executive director charged its division administrators (i.e., its state-level field offices) to direct their staffs to closely monitor states' utilization of ARRA funding.

This monitoring was aimed at facilitating state utilization of the funds, expeditious implementation of projects, and compliance with federal require- ments. The FHWA's administrator and executive director would meet and/or hold video conferences periodically with the division administrators to en- courage state diligence in the obligation and expenditure of funds and the effective oversight of federal requirements.

In addition, the FHWA established a national-level review team that visited individual states (in some cases five or more times) on a rotating and continuous basis to monitor the FHWA's implementation of ARRA.[17] This team, composed of field and headquarters managers, reviewed program im- plementation by the FHWA field offices and the states to ensure compliance, anticipate issues, and identify best practices for adoption by the FHWA and other states.

State transportation agencies and local implementers also were encour- aged by the FHWA to take a stronger approach to project monitoring. Track- ing programs were implemented to follow the status of individual projects within a state, regardless of which agency was responsible for its implemen- tation. In anticipation of the ARRA's grantee reporting requirements, the FHWA created a Recovery Act Data System (RADS) that allowed the states to collect and report information on ARRA-funded projects. The FHWA maintained the system and the states entered project data into it. At the point of required quarterly reporting under Section 1512 of ARRA, the states were able to use RADS to produce their 1512 report, which they uploaded to FederalReporting.gov, the national-level reporting system required by ARRA. For the purposes of Section 1512 reporting, the states were assumed to be the primary recipients of ARRA funding, and subgrantees were assumed to be the secondary recipients.

"Programmatic performance measures" were used to ensure that proj- ects were on time and following budget restraints.[18] This system allowed SDOTs and local entities to increase oversight for projects that were not meeting goals, sometimes resulting in drastic administrative alterations to the projects.

Implementation in the States

All three states examined in this study were able to obligate their ARRA funding to projects within their respective metropolitan, suburban, and rural areas. Washington awarded grants to 225 projects, totaling more than $491 million; West Virginia awarded grants to 155 projects, totaling $212 million; and Virginia awarded grants to 141 projects, totaling $635 million.[19] However, they took different approaches to project funding and oversight of project implementation, reflecting each state's unique operating circumstances and the regular highway program logic.

Project Choice and Priorities

As discussed above, the ARRA program imposed some broad conditions for funding projects, specifically those projects that were (1) ready to proceed to construction, (2) largely within EDA areas, and (3) could be finished relatively quickly. As discussed above, in many states the first and third of these conditions were satisfied by selecting relatively minor projects that could be implemented quickly, such as repaving, reconstruction, and safety improvements. Projects of this character not only could be implemented quickly but also reflected the nature of many state road programs, where maintenance and rehabilitation constituted the bulk of state needs. An additional advantage was that lower costs for these kinds of programs allowed the distribution of funding to be spread relatively evenly across the state (a "peanut butter" approach).

It was less difficult for West Virginia to satisfy the EDA's requirements than its peers because almost the whole state is economically disadvantaged. In addition, West Virginia made a conscious policy choice to distribute its funding mostly to maintenance and rehabilitation of facilities. As a matter of policy, it also made sure that at least one new construction project was undertaken in each of its three congressional districts. Maintenance and reconstruction funding was distributed in the same fashion.[20]

Washington State chose to use ARRA funding to support a mix of maintenance and rehabilitation projects and construction projects that were already under way. The 100 percent federal funding allowed it to supplement existing projects for which insufficient state or federal funds were available, including advancing planned later stages of a project much earlier. The 100 percent funding also allowed the state to manage its funding flows more smoothly because it could apply for reimbursement quickly, allowing state funds to be managed more efficiently.

Before the passage of ARRA, Virginia faced a major downturn in projected state transportation revenues and had to downsize its overall program (by $1 billion from 2008 to 2009, and by $3.5 billion from 2009 to 2010).[21] The ARRA funds made this process play out more smoothly and with less political consequence and intensity. However, Virginia had to reduce the overall size of its program in such a way that it could meet the spending requirement built into ARRA. The FHWA worked with the state to achieve this outcome in a fashion consistent with the ARRA maintenance-of-effort requirement.

Expending ARRA Funds

The political logic of ARRA was that quickly spending federal funds would improve the economy. But accounting technicalities in showing when reimbursements became federal expenditures made this hard to track.

The regular highway program operates as a reimbursement funding process, which created a reporting and transparency issue under ARRA. States and their local partners had to expend their own funds first (which they reported as expended in the Recovery Act Transparency Board's reporting solution). The federal fund expenditures did not book as expended until the reimbursement request from the state was honored by the FHWA. If a state was timely with the request, the difference in reporting dates could be minimal. However, if a state was not pressed because it was blessed with a good cash flow, the reimbursement request could lag by months, creating what appeared as a very slow federal expenditure of ARRA funds and a mismatch in reported state and federal dollars. All three states in our case studies processed reimbursement requests in a timely fashion.

As noted above, the FHWA met the deadline to obligate ARRA on February 27, 2011. This success was a product of all states meeting the deadline to obligate their share of the funding. The irony here is that the apportionment of funds to the states in early 2009 did not constitute a "grant" to them. Grants were not considered awarded until the states identified a project to which they would commit federal funds. In circumstances where a local government project was chosen and that government sought to implement the project, rather than having the state do it for them, the local government would need to expend its own funds and then seek reimbursement from the state, which would then seek reimbursement from the FHWA. ARRA funds were considered obligated at the point a project agreement had been executed by the state and the FHWA, and the funds had been committed to the project in the FHWA's Fiscal Management Information System. However, funds were not booked as "expended" by the FHWA until the state sought reimbursement, at which point the obligation was liquidated and treated as an expenditure. The states varied in terms of how quickly they processed reimbursement requests.

The two-year expiration of ARRA funds also influenced the selection of local versus statewide projects, giving preference to those that could be implemented quickly. Many local governments own and maintain roads, but the total share of road ownership varies from state to state. West Virginia owns roughly 92 percent of its total road miles in the state, while Virginia owns about 68 percent.[22] In Washington, the state owns closer to 30 percent of its total mileage, but this share accounts for a significant percentage of total traffic volume. Each of these states has a completely different experience with local government involvement in federal funding. Both West Virginia and Virginia have traditionally dominated project implementation, while Washington shares responsibility with local governments. Because ARRA did not change the basic federal–state–local relationships that existed in the highway program, each state followed its existing programmatic approach. Local governments experienced with federal funding had a better shot at receiving ARRA funding.

Federal–State Operational Relations under ARRA

All three states and their respective FHWA division offices expressed a common sentiment: that ARRA had improved and fostered the working relationship between federal and state officials. The pressure of hard deadlines, the incentive of additional funding, and the novelty of new requirements served as spurs to make things work. Further, the gravity of the economic recession and the priority given ARRA by the new administration and Congress clearly created a situation in which no agency wanted to be identified as the impediment to success. And even more important, every state had a backlog of projects. No SDOT wanted to forgo money that would make positive improvements in its transportation system.

Three additional factors further enhanced the working relationship between the state and federal partners: increased oversight, transparency, and novelty. In terms of oversight, the additional $20 million in funding given to the USDOT Inspector General's Office and the congressional tasking of GAO to report multiple times on ARRA implementation clearly signaled that mistakes, if any, would not be hidden. Further, the addition of new reporting requirements and deadlines clearly constituted changes to status quo processes and introduced new "risks" in program implementation. In creating its audit plan, GAO went so far as to identify a list of sixteen states for special attention to target their oversight. Overall, this increased "audit" environment spurred a mutual dependency between state and federal agencies: They were in it together and would succeed or fail jointly.

As a result, the FHWA directed its field offices to pay increased attention to risk management concerns and work with the states to reduce chances of fraud, waste, and abuse, and also bureaucratic inefficiency. The division offices reviewed annual work plans and stewardship agreements with an eye to reducing the risk of project and ARRA failure. Some division offices moved to 100 percent review of project plans and specifications. Others moved from selective project inspections (focusing only on high-risk projects) to 100 percent inspection rates. Each division office negotiated a state-specific strategy that would reduce risk and ensure effective oversight of ARRA projects. This increased federal oversight might have been more contentious in prior years but was expedited and smoothed by the mutually recognized codependency of the federal and state partners.

The high expectations and deadlines for ARRA project implementation drove both the federal and state agencies to get the work done with existing staff. The acknowledged lag in hiring additional, new government workers, the hard implementation deadlines of the act, and the novelty of the ARRA program mutually supported getting the work done with existing rather than new staff. Indeed, each of the states interviewed here was experiencing its own version of a "graying workforce" and needed to modify its business processes and staffing patterns to change with the times. West Virginia used the ARRA experience to empower many of its existing mid-level managers and make them key players in the new work activity. The novelty of the new programmatic activity was a motivating force for these managers and added a significant positive new experience to the routine activity. All three states created internal programmatic meetings, which brought key office directors and senior executives together on a weekly or biweekly basis to troubleshoot program and project implementation. Washington found that its already-existing expedited design process could be further accelerated given the ARRA deadlines. The novelty and transparency of the ARRA's highway program was an absolute spur to change internal management processes, particularly where such initiatives were already under way. At the same time, expedited project implementation efforts required reliance on routine private-sector contracting for construction.

The Political Process's Impact on ARRA and State Programs

Each state had a different experience with ARRA, depending on the status of its existing state program. Universally, new money brought new attention from federal and state legislators. As indicated above, Representative Oberstar's insertion of special, independent monitoring and reporting processes gave the House Transportation and Infrastructure Committee and the US Congress a front-row seat for program implementation, even though it added to the overall reporting burden as a separate process with independent data items and time frames. Additionally, the role of "loyal opposition" assumed by congressional Republicans led to intense legislative scrutiny and reporting. There were multiple hearings at which federal and state political and career officials were invited to testify, with some members of Congress taking the initiative to do their own investigation of where the money was going.

At the state level, the new ARRA funding in many cases doubled state program levels over normal levels. The likelihood of intense legislative engagement was recognized and dealt with early in each of the cases reported here. The secretary of the West Virginia Department of Highways worked closely with the governor's office and the state legislature to ensure that ARRA investments were distributed across the state in a balanced way (similar dollars, similar types of work, and one major new project per congressional district). In Washington, the context of two major gas tax increases in prior years had already energized legislative engagement, and the ARRA funding went to existing lists of projects already planned or under way in the state. The Virginia case of reduced program funding invited a leveling process that spread the money throughout the state to meet already-existing needs and reduce the sting of funding cuts.

In general, the context of a recession and new money meant that politics would be a clear factor. Executive and administrative entities chose a proactive process to reduce unpredictable political oversight and intervention and allow for the smooth implementation of projects in compliance with ARRA deadlines. Protracted political wrangling would add delays and hamper compliance with program requirements. Also, post-ARRA, the political process would still be there and have to be dealt with in the routine process of highway funding and project implementation. Thus, it would not be prudent to leave a negative legacy for the future.

Public Involvement and Transparency

The perception of those interviewed regarding transparency and reporting was typically positive. The additional "sunlight" shone on the ARRA effort through reporting supported the overall sense that the work being done was for a legitimate public purpose. Further, though the additional reporting was burdensome, it was perceived as giving the highway program additional credibility for its ability to get things done quickly while at the same time managing the existing "regular" program.

Some of this positive perception was associated with the process of public involvement begun in the 1990s, which opened the "backrooms" of highway planning and project selection to more participants and the public generally. Additionally, the continuing struggle to get congressional attention for reauthorizing the highway program may have received a positive boost from the ARRA's success story. An additional benefit for the ARRA's reporting expectations was translating highway project descriptions into layperson's English. For example, a "five-mile chip sealing and roto-milling/ bituminous overlay between mileposts 51 and 56 on State Route 21" had to be translated into everyday English as "repaving State Route 21 between the intersections of Route 5 and Route 10."

Implications for Federal and Nonfederal Managers

The most cogent and obvious ARRA story from the highway program is that the existing management network that preexisted ARRA adjusted, adapted, and made ARRA work. There were no start-up delays or huge process revisions, and no new major program risk issues emerged. The network created around the "grant tool" at the core of the highway program absorbed the challenge and used the money to meet existing needs. The regular program went on, managed in parallel with the ARRA effort. Existing staff, not new staff and organizations, got the job done. Some of this may have been a reflection of the institutionalized relationship that had evolved vis-à-vis transportation over the preceding more than fifty years. The existence of substantial, unmet needs and a system eager for additional funding may have also contributed.

The highway program did not experience a substantial retreading of its content to serve ARRA's policy goals. It was essentially utilized as is, with some minor addition of rules and oversight. It responded by making necessary adaptations for new requirements and absorbing the new funding directly into ongoing activity. Existing collaborative relationships between network players made it possible to convene problem-solving solution teams and to work through things cooperatively and quickly. There were only a minimal number of the "getting-to-know-you" courtship dances typically experienced in new organizations and processes. Where challenges emerged, they involved tensions between the routine highway community and the increased engagement of central political officials. Depending on the state, the governor's office may not have been routinely involved in highway funding decisions (a tendency reflected also in the FHWA–secretary of transportation relationship). The White House's interest in ARRA's success increased the political intensity of funding decisions and had an impact on routine relationships, sometimes by adding unwanted time and turbulence.[23]

The Obama administration's insistence that the governors should play a central role in the reporting and oversight of ARRA programs did offer a slight challenge to most states. The functional transportation "picket" of highway program administration typically did not have day-to-day involvement of the governor and/or the governor's staff. Centralized reporting encouraged by the Office of Management and Budget raised some technical definition issues (e.g., when was federal money expended in a reimbursable program) and forced some new working relationships between SDOTs and central administrations. Yet the highway officials appeared to adjust and adapt without creating new working tensions with the governors or legislatures. Some of that adaptability may reflect the reality of needing more political support for future program reauthorizations and appropriations.

From a big-picture perspective, the highway network adapted and utilized its institutionalized strength to adjust to a short-term intrusion on its routine practices. New monies were absorbed and put to work, mostly on existing projects and priorities. Increased visibility and new players were tolerated and worked into decision-making processes. Short-term pressure to spend new money was met, and things returned to "normal" shortly afterward. There may have been some positive effects on reauthorization, but to date nothing has manifestly restructured network processes, relationships, or politics. The search for a new rationale for a federal highway program in the reauthorization process and new funding sources is likely far more important in the highway world.[24]

At the federal level, the DOT secretary viewed ARRA as a legacy benchmark for a new administration. The act's passage early in 2009 came when few political appointees for the new administration were in place, and thus it fell to the career staff to take the lead. As a result, the appointees who were in place and those who came shortly after had a unique opportunity to "bond" with the career staff around the ARRA effort. The bonding proceeded faster than it might in a more typical transition and pushed careerists and new political appointees to step up to the task assertively. Thus, it is not surprising that USDOT's OST found FHWA positioned to play a constructive role in successfully implementing ARRA.

Some federal and state officials perceived the focus on "jobs created" as the biggest flaw in the ARRA effort. The meaning of a job—its nature, longevity, and geographic location—were all confounded in the simple counting exercise expected in ARRA reporting. Construction jobs are not inherently long lasting in a given geographic location, but the continued availability of work may make it possible for a firm to move from one geographic location to another in pursuit of new contracts. Further, the locational proximity of project place and jobs may not be the same. The FHWA undertook a handful of pilot efforts to track jobs associated with projects and found that in some cases jobs were created nationally and regionally in terms of where successful bidders were located and not always in the immediate proximity of construction work.[25]

Both DOT SAOs observed that the DOT secretary's support and personal commitment were a clear factor in DOT's success. Further, one can infer that because ARRA went into effect so early in the process of recruiting new political policy leaders, the secretary could count on modal administrators to follow his lead. Experience suggests that as an administration's tenure drags on, individual political appointees gain more independence in their decision making and performance, especially because the secretary does not have a direct decision role in many modal affairs.

This last point underscores one of the key points about the utilization of an existing network to do new things. Where a program is utilized substantially "as is" to do new things, these things will likely be done in a timely and expeditious manner. But where there is no administrative infrastructure or program, the start-up and building processes needed to create them will take substantial up-front time and resource commitment. Results, consequently, may be far less predictable or clear. Additionally, institutionalized existing networks can adapt to significant changes in the short term without overwhelming stress or operational effects. The consequences for the long term would require longitudinal research that accounts for the characteristics and sources of multiple changes and forces.

Did the ARRA experience portend future shifts in the federal role for the major federal highway and transportation programs? ARRA provided for greater federal attention when compared with the normal highway program and may have presaged a similar federal role in performance expectations in subsequent highway and transportation bills. A quick review of the 2012 highway reauthorization, Moving Ahead for Progress in the 21st Century Act (known as MAP-21), confirms the clear addition of a performance-based justification process for project choices but no greater federal role in project selection. Recent reports by the USDOT inspector general do recommend that the FHWA's oversight role for funded programs and projects should be strengthened as a result of the ARRA accountability experience.[26] The December 2015 reauthorization, Fixing America's Surface Transportation (FAST Act), retained the changes of its predecessor.

Conclusion

The FHWA successfully adapted its management strategy and network to the context of ARRA. Relying on an intensified risk-assessment process for its activities and its network partners, the FHWA pursued a risk management strategy more aggressively. Commensurate with the heightened stakes for top federal officials, both the OST and FHWA increased their roles in overseeing ARRA's implementation compared with normal program responsibilities. The significant role played by the vice president himself radiated down through the federal bureaucracy, prompting both political and career federal officials to rise to the occasion, knowing that their own program decisions were being scrutinized as never before. The network did not change institutionally or behaviorally but rather adapted to the added expectations of ARRA. Newly appointed policy leaders in the OST were drawn in to the ARRA process and became key spokespersons for the ARRA effort and defenders of the DOT and FHWA administrative processes.

At the state and federal levels, the states realized that there was a positive outcome to being key players in the ARRA program. They were clearly benefiting from the additional money and were in the driver's seat regarding how to use the funds. Transparency, though an additional burden, was not perceived as a major irritant. Indeed, some state administrators saw it as a precursor of other new initiatives and working conditions. Being early adopters in the context of ARRA might bode well for future reauthorization and public support for surface transportation investments. Being able to absorb the additional work with existing staff and bending that adaptation to their current management needs was a net positive for network players. An additional benefit was the widespread recognition that the codependency of all partners meant that they must focus on a supportive rather than contentious approach.

In sum, the lesson of ARRA that can be drawn from the highway program is that rapid implementation is facilitated by a reliance on existing collaborative relationships and institutions built up over many years to manage similar projects and activities. New programs benefit by borrowing strength from the expertise and stability embedded in established networks and institutions. Although preexisting networks help smooth the implementation of major new domestic policy initiatives, they also work to limit and constrain the breadth and scope of innovation. Changes in outcomes and processes can be expected to follow incremental paths featuring modest shifts in resources and priorities as existing network actors work mightily to channel new policies and funding into familiar and stable routines and patterns. Such outcomes worked well in an area like highways, where established models and expertise were sufficient to deliver benefits for the economy and for infrastructure development. However, such a model may prove to be wanting for emerging new policy areas, where innovation and experimentation are most important to advance federal policy goals.

Notes

1. Federal Highway Administration, "Financing Federal-Aid Highways, March 2007; The American Recovery and Reinvestment Act of 2009, Title XVI, Section 1601."

2. Federal Highway Administration, "Testimony of Deputy Administrator Gregory Nadeau before the House Subcommittee on Transportation, Housing and Urban Development, and Related Agencies," House Appropriations Committee, March 19, 2015; Federal Highway Administration, "Distribution of Federal-Aid Highway Program Obligation Limitation for the Period Beginning on October 1, 2015, and Ending on November 20, 2015, Issued November 6, 2015."

3. *The American Recovery and Reinvestment Act of 2009*, Title XVI, Section 1602.

4. Federal Highway Administration, "Summary of ARRA Provisions for FHWA (PL 111-5)."

5. This is found in 23 USC Sec. 145.

6. The most recent reauthorizations were the Intermodal Surface Transportation Act of 1991 (known as ISTEA); the Transportation Equity Act for the 21st Century of 1998 (TEA-21); the Safe, Accountable, Flexible, Efficient Transportation Equity Act: A Legacy for Users of 2005 (SAFETE-LU), PL 112-141; the Moving Ahead for Progress in the 21st Century Act (MAP-21), signed into law on July 6, 2012; and the Fixing America's Surface Transportation Act (FAST Act) signed into law December 4, 2015.

7. As projects grow or shrink in cost due to unanticipated expenses or project savings, the checkbook balance is affected. Regular annual apportionments remain available for use until they are completely obligated and lapse at the end of the fourth fiscal year. Changes in project estimates draw on or return funds to the checkbook balance.

8. Federal Highway Administration, *The American Recovery and Reinvestment Act of 2009*, www.fhwa.dot.gov/economicrecovery.

9. US Department of Transportation, "Memorandum: ARRA Guidance on Federal-aid Program Stewardship and Oversight," April 6, 2009.

10. Federal Highway Administration, "Questions & Answers to ARRA Lapsed Funding GuidanceSeptember 2, 2010 (Updated January 15, 2013)," www.fhwa.dot.gov /economicrecovery/lapsedqandas.htm.

11. Federal Highway Administration, "American Recovery and Reinvestment Act."

12. The FHWA defines major projects as significant infrastructure projects that cost more than $500 million or projects of a significant cost that attract a high level of public attention or political interest because of substantial direct and indirect impacts on the community, environment, and state budgets, exceeding a total project value of $1 billion, which are subject to federal review and authorization. See J. Richard Capka, "Megaprojects: They Are a Different Breed," *Public Roads*, July–August 2004.

13. These included the FHWA, the Federal Transit Administration, the Federal Railroad Administration, the Maritime Administration, and the Federal Aviation Administration as well as key OST offices such as policy, public affairs, and budget.

14. E.g., Senator McCain and Senator Coburn issued a series of reports on "wasteful projects" that in their judgment cost the American people too much money. The

reports identified projects that were dubious in terms of the jobs created, public purpose served, and funds spent. The TIGER Team would ask each DOT modal office to review the listed projects to identify any that they had funded (the lists covered all ARRA projects). The review would validate the project and its purpose, benefits, and location. Factual clarification and descriptions would be issued by the agencies as appropriate. Modal representatives often found inaccurate descriptions, non-ARRA projects, or poorly named projects. An example was the "Wine Train," which was an economic development project for the Napa Valley funded by another federal agency (it had been erroneously identified as a Federal Railroad Administration project) to provide enhanced tourism and promote wine sales for California vintners by transporting tourists into the California wine country. It turned out to be a Corps of Engineers flood-control project that relocated multiuser tracks to reduce flood damage. One of the track users was a tourism train that accessed the wine country.

15. See the South Carolina DOT listing of all ARRA Recovery Reporting requirements at www.scdot.org/inside/pdfs/reporting_requirements.pdf. Another summary of reports, produced by the state of Iowa, is at www.iowadot.gov/recovery / . . . /ARRA Report Titles (3).pdf.

For the legislative wording, see www.gpo.gov/fdsys/pkg/BILLS-111hrlenr/pdf /BILLS-111hrlenr.pdf.

16. Section 1201 required reporting of highway and transit project sponsors to the USDOT which provided it to Representative Oberstar's Committee. Section 1512 required reporting to an independent reporting by grantees to a reporting solution created by the Recovery Act Transparency Board.

17. The FHWA developed an overall risk assessment, which was made available at www.fhwa.dot.gov/economicrecovery/riskmgmtesumm.htm. See USDOT, "Inspector General Report on the National Review Team Process," www.oig.dot .gov/sites/dot/files/FHWA'S_National_Review_Teams-_Final_Report.pdf; and GAO, "Recovery Act: Grant Implementation Experiences Offer Lessons for Accountability and Transparency," GAO-14-219, January 2014, 25.

18. US Department of Transportation, "Memorandum: ARRA Guidance."

19. See the website www.recovery.org.

20. See the reference to reporting requirements cited above.

21. Interview with Virginia DOT staff member, October 2011.

22. Interviews with state DOTs.

23. GAO, "Recovery Act: Grant Implementation Experiences Offer Lessons for Accountability and Transparency," GAO-14-219, January 2014, 16.

24. Ibid., 52.

25. The economic stimulus effects of public infrastructure spending continue to be debated. A part of the debate revolves around "when" they occur. A recent article found that the effects are bimodal, with the largest effects found in the first two years and a subsequent "bump" eight years out. The economic effects of such spending return to normal about ten years out. Sylvan Leduc and Daniel Wilson, "Roads to Prosperity or Bridges to Nowhere? Theory and Evidence on the Impact of Public Infrastructure Investment," *NBER Macroeconomics Annual* 27, no. 1 (2012): 89–142.

26. Federal Highway Administration, "Lessons Learned from ARRA Could Improve the Federal Highway Administration's Use of Full Oversight," Report MH-2013-075, May 7, 2013; Federal Highway Administration, "FHWA Has Opportunities to Improve Oversight of ARRA High Dollar Projects and the Federal-Aid

Highway Program," Report MH-2013-012, November 14, 2012; Federal Highway Administration, "Most FHWA ARRA Projects Will Be Closed Out before Funds Expire, but Weaknesses in the Project Close-Out Process Persist," Report ST-2015-029, March 2, 2015; Federal Highway Administration, "Lessons Learned from ARRA: Improved FHWA Oversight Can Enhance States' Use of Federal-Aid Funds," Report ZA-2012-084, April 5, 2012.

5

Oh What a Tangled Web

IMPLEMENTATION OF BROADBAND ASSISTANCE GRANTS

Priscilla M. Regan

CONSISTENT WITH THE GOALS of job creation and economic development, the American Recovery and Reinvestment Act (the Recovery Act, or ARRA) provided $7.2 billion for broadband internet access grant and loan programs to be administered by both the Department of Commerce, through the National Telecommunications and Information Administration (NTIA), and the Department of Agriculture, through the Rural Utilities Service (RUS). The NTIA initiative, the Broadband Technology Opportunity Program (BTOP), was appropriated $4.7 billion for a competitive broadband grant program.[1] The RUS program, the Broadband Initiatives Program (BIP), was appropriated $2.5 billion to be divided between grants and loans as RUS saw as appropriate.

Enhancing broadband development was a perfect fit with ARRA's overall economic recovery goals, for not only would jobs immediately be created in the process of expanding broadband deployment but private investment in broadband would also be stimulated. In addition, expanding high-speed broadband access would close the digital divide and spread access to schools, universities, libraries, community centers, job training centers, hospitals, and public safety personnel. Increased demand for and use of broadband was seen as an infrastructure improvement that would stimulate overall economic recovery.

In terms of the initial implementation of ARRA, both NTIA and RUS were basically dealing with new programs, new rules, unprecedented budgets, and an eighteen-month compressed time frame in which to make awards. Although both agencies faced enormous challenges in starting up their ARRA programs, NTIA faced the larger challenge in that it had to establish the

BTOP "from scratch" while RUS had existing long-term programs that needed to be significantly scaled up.[2] Unlike several of the other ARRA programs discussed in this book—such as highways, education, and the New Market Tax Credit—there were no existing broadband networks to absorb these challenges. Instead, the federal government was initiating new relationships with state agencies, nonprofit agencies, and businesses in order to identify opportunities, review and award grants, and implement and oversee funded projects.

To provide an understanding of the federal government's role in working through networks to implement the goals of ARRA's broadband programs, relevant government documents, research reports, and media coverage were reviewed. In addition, interviews were conducted with more than twenty federal and state officials as well as with nonprofit actors. As in the other chapters in this volume, three states were selected for rather extensive coverage: California, Florida, and Virginia. Virginia serves as a common state for all the chapters. California and Florida were both selected as populous states with mixed urban, suburban, and rural areas. During most of ARRA's implementation, California had a Democratic governor and Florida had a Republican governor. Additionally, both states are examined in other chapter analyses—California in the New Markets Tax Credit Program and in accountability, and Florida in accountability.

Pre-ARRA Federal Broadband Activity

Before the Recovery Act, the federal government had generally played a hands-off role regarding broadband development. The private sector assumed the lead role, with the FCC ensuring that the market remained competitive and open, as outlined in its Broadband Policy Statement of 2005.[3] Two broadband areas of policy concern to the federal government were, first, the "digital divide," the effect that socioeconomic status and education had on broadband access and interest; and second, national broadband deployment, whether telecommunications generally and the internet in particular, were available to all geographic and economic areas of the country.

Because of particular concern about the slow pace of broadband development in rural areas, in 2001 and 2002 Congress funded pilot broadband loan and grant programs to be managed by the RUS. These pilot programs became the only two ongoing federal programs funding broadband deployment before ARRA: the Rural Broadband Access Loan and Loan Guarantee Program, with an annual budget of $15 million; and the Community Connect Grant Program, with an annual budget of $12 million.[4] Since the RUS programs began in 2001, there have been a number of criticisms of them, including the complex and burdensome loan application process; the low rate of approval for loan applications; the lack of clarity in the eligibility criteria, so that it is difficult to distinguish between rural and suburban communities; and loans being issued to communities that had existing broadband providers.[5]

Before ARRA, NTIA did not play a role in broadband deployment, but it did have two programs related to broadband uses: the Public Telecommunications Facilities Program, with an average annual budget of $23 million, which provided grants for using broadcast and nonbroadcast telecommunications technologies for educational and cultural programs; and the Telecommunications Opportunities Program, with an annual budget of $24 million, which made grants for model projects demonstrating innovative uses of network technologies. NTIA, along with the Department of Homeland Security, had also administered the Public Safety Interoperable Communications Program, which had a one-time appropriation of $1 billion.[6]

Broadband ARRA Implementation Framework: Awards Phase

In two rounds of ARRA funding, NTIA awarded 233 BTOP projects, totaling $3.9 billion, and RUS awarded 320 BIP projects, totaling $3.6 billion (see table 5.1 for a breakdown by states).[7] Job creation for both programs took off rather slowly but became more successful over time. For example, recipients of NTIA awards funded 20 jobs in the first quarter of 2010, 1,598 jobs in the first quarter of 2011, and 4,273 jobs in the first quarter of 2012. A similar trajectory exists for RUS awards, with no jobs reported in the first quarter of 2010, 1,574 in the first quarter of 2011, and 3,799 in the first quarter of 2012.[8]

Unlike other ARRA programs, the broadband initiative had a broader purpose than immediate job creation alone—to build the longer-term national communications infrastructure. In May 2012 the NTIA assistant secretary testified to a House committee that BTOP recipients had deployed or upgraded more than 56,000 miles of broadband infrastructure; had connected more than 8,000 anchor institutions to high-speed internet networks; had installed more than 30,000 workstations in public computer centers; and had generated about 350,000 new broadband internet subscribers.[9] At the same hearing the RUS administrator reported that the RUS awards would connect nearly 7 million rural Americans, more than 360,000 businesses, and more than 30,000 critical community institutions to new or improved broadband service.[10] The 2014 Council of Economic Advisers' final report to Congress noted that broadband access rose substantially through ARRA broadband grants; more than 110,000 miles of broadband infrastructure were added or

Table 5.1. State-by-State Distribution of All BTOP, SBDD, and BIP Awards

State or Jurisdiction	Number of Awards	Total Amount of Grants and Loans (millions of dollars)
California	29	444.3
Kentucky	20	315.0
Texas	32	312.8
North Carolina	18	278.6
Oklahoma	27	277.6
Missouri	20	263.5
Michigan	18	245.7
Washington	17	244.3
Minnesota	29	242.3
Illinois	18	239.6
Tennessee	16	233.9
Pennsylvania	13	215.9
Ohio	20	202.4
Louisiana	10	189.8
New Mexico	17	184.5
West Virginia	10	184.3
Vermont	7	174.0
Wisconsin	23	171.4
Georgia	17	170.7
Iowa	20	166.9
New York	20	160.7
Virginia	16	154.5
Colorado	13	146.5
Kansas	14	144.9
Alabama	15	142.5
Alaska	9	138.8
Montana	8	133.4
Arkansas	8	128.5
Mississippi	10	127.3
Florida	13	126.5
Maryland	6	125.0
Arizona	14	113.0
Connecticut	2	97.6
North Dakota	11	96.1
Massachusetts	9	94.5
American Samoa	2	92.9
Virgin Islands	4	67.5
Nevada	12	66.7
Indiana	10	63.5

Table 5.1. (*cont.*)

State or Jurisdiction	Number of Awards	Total Amount of Grants and Loans (millions of dollars)
New Hampshire	7	54.5
South Dakota	8	53.4
Oregon	15	52.7
New Jersey	3	49.7
Utah	9	48.9
South Carolina	7	45.4
Maine	7	42.6
Puerto Rico	3	41.1
Hawaii	5	40.4
Nebraska	6	31.6
Idaho	13	30.5
District of Columbia	4	27.2
Rhode Island	3	24.9
Wyoming	3	14.8
Guam	2	7.5
Delaware	2	5.0
Northern Mariana Islands	2	3.4

Note: State Broadband Data and Development (SBDD) grants are included in these calculations as part of the Broadband Technology Opportunities Program (BTOP) awards; BIP stands for the Broadband Initiatives Program. These grants totaled $293 and were distributed to each of the fifty states, five territories, and the District of Columbia.

Sources: National Telecommunications and Information Administration, "The Broadband Technology Opportunities Program: Expanding Broadband Access and Adoption in Communities Across America—Overview of Grant Awards," December 2010, www.ntia.doc.gov/reports/2010/NTIA_Report_on_BTOP_12142010.pdf; Lennard G. Kruger, "Background and Issues for Congressional Oversight of ARRA Broadband Awards," Congressional Research Service Report R41775, March 14, 2012, 17–18.

improved, and high-speed connections were made available to about 20,000 community institutions.[11]

The two programs had slightly different mandates. NTIA's primary focus was to establish broadband expansion to "unserved and underserved areas" through projects with the highest possible speed for customers. Notably, federal NTIA officials were required to consult with states to identify these areas and the appropriate allocation of grants within the state and to limit the federal share to 80 percent of the project cost.[12] For the RUS program, ARRA specified that at least 75 percent of the areas served by a project had to be rural areas without sufficient access to high-speed broadband, that priority be given to projects that gave users a choice of broadband providers and also to former borrowers of rural telephone loans, and that no project could also receive funding under NTIA's BTOP.

Managing the Start-Up Workload

The quick start-up presented enormous staffing issues for both agencies. In spring 2009, NTIA established a BTOP program office with approximately forty staff members and gave them grants training.[13] Both NTIA and RUS contracted with private-sector agencies. NTIA contracted with Booz Allen Hamilton for assistance with evaluating applications and overseeing the implementation of the grants, including audits and site visits; the cost of the contract was about $99 million, and at times of heaviest work the contract provided about two hundred additional staff members.[14] NTIA also used unpaid volunteers during the review of the first round of awards to help examine and score applications. RUS contracted with ICF International to assist in the application review process and the development of postaward oversight; RUS did not use outside volunteer reviewers.[15]

There were two rounds of ARRA broadband funding, and the two agencies sought to collaborate where possible. In the first round, both NTIA and RUS used the same definitions for "unserved," "underserved," "broadband," and "rural area." NTIA was allowed to make awards for applications submitted to RUS after RUS reviewed the application and decided not to fund it. Both agencies used a two-stage process, first scoring all applications on the project's purpose, benefits, viability, budget, and sustainability. Those who scored highest were asked for further documentation. Recommendations, or priority listings, from the states were also considered. NTIA used outside, volunteer "expert reviewers" to score applications during the first stage; RUS used its staff and contractors.

During the first round, NTIA and RUS received more than 2,200 applications requesting nearly $28 billion; applications were received from all states, the five territories, and the District of Columbia. NTIA awarded 82 BTOP projects, totaling $1.206 billion, and RUS awarded 68 BIP projects, totaling $1.069 billion. As discussed below, the states did not play a role in approving applications, nor did the ARRA broadband funds go through the states. The states did have the option of ranking applications from their states, and in most cases states did avail themselves of this opportunity.

The second round of funding was announced on January 15, 2010. In response to agencies' experiences during the first round and to public comments, both agencies simplified the applications process and made some substantive changes, including giving applicants the option of applying to either program, with the NTIA projects focused on the middle mile and RUS projects on the last mile of broadband service, offering RUS projects a standard 75 percent grant / 25 percent loan combination.[16] NTIA and RUS received 1,643 applications in the second round, requesting $22.2 billion. NTIA awarded 151 BTOP projects, totaling $2.694, and RUS awarded 262 BIP projects, totaling $1.625 billion.

Building an Implementation Network: Growing Pains

The initial implementation posed challenges for coordination among the federal counterparts and with state, private-sector, and nonprofit parties. Most prominent among these challenges were (1) the need to start the programs quickly, (2) the lack of clear guidance regarding key criteria to be used in making awards, and (3) the reality of the administrative tasks and coordination required.

FEDERAL PARTNERS: LEARNING AS THEY GO

Before the Recovery Act, the federal entities involved in broadband (NTIA; RUS; and the Federal Communications Commission, FCC) worked together sporadically in ad hoc relationships with relatively low stakes and little need to coordinate their activities. Given the political necessity of starting the NTIA and RUS broadband programs quickly and because of the on-the-ground learning that was taking place, this ad hoc arrangement largely continued as the working model among the federal agencies during the time of ARRA funding. Before the first round of funding, NTIA and RUS issued a joint request for information and a notice of public meetings in March 2009 to get input on implementation issues, including role of states, eligibility criteria, grant mechanics, coordination of the two programs, and definition of some key terms (including "underserved," "unserved," and "broadband"). NTIA and RUS then worked together on a joint Notice of Funds Availability, which was released in July 2009.[17] In response to their experiences with the first round of funding and public comments submitted in November 2009, NTIA and RUS issued separate Notices of Funds Availability for the second round of funding and modified some of the requirements and processes. For example, the requirement that projects were to be awarded to "unserved" or "underserved" areas was dropped, and instead this was to be considered as one of several factors in an application evaluation.

ARRA also carved out a role for the FCC, requiring it to develop a long-term "National Broadband Plan" with a detailed strategy for affordable broadband access for all Americans.[18] The FCC was also directed to evaluate the progress of BTOP grant projects. Finally, the FCC and NTIA were required to coordinate on the development of "non-discrimination and network interconnection obligations," often referred to as "net neutrality" or "open access." This required the agencies to ensure that market forces drove the relationships between grant recipients and broadband customers and that grant recipients not give preference to any particular internet applications or content.[19]

STATES WORK TO MAKE THE MOST OF THEIR LIMITED ROLE

With respect to state governments, neither NTIA nor RUS had formal, ongoing interactions with state governments on broadband issues. Although the federal government had been taking on a leadership role in addressing the broadband digital divide and advocating for the critical role broadband deployment played in economic development, this did not lead to ongoing working relationships with state agencies, as were typical for education or highways. Instead, the funding relationships with states were more project-driven and responsive to grant proposals or, in the case of RUS, were based on loan applications from nonstate agencies.

ARRA required more systematic state involvement, particularly with respect to the NTIA/BTOP program, where NTIA was required by statute to consult with states to identify the areas of need and the appropriate allocation of grants within the state. In the NTIA/BTOP application review process, states were formally involved in the second step, following the initial screening by NTIA staff and the first step review and ranking by independent reviewers. During this second stage, state governors' offices had an opportunity to rank the applications from their state and/or affecting their state. It is important to point out that the governor's office received these applications from NTIA, not from the applicants themselves. The states, therefore, entered the process somewhat on the back end rather than the front end.

From a network management perspective, the point of contact between NTIA and the states was the governor's office. This meant that the governor's office became the pivotal organizing unit within state governments and that the governor's office had the responsibility and control for managing the state's response for ARRA broadband. The contact was centralized rather than decentralized and required the governor's office to oversee and coordinate activities within the state. Given the importance of broadband to economic development generally, many states had existing formal broadband task forces, often operating within the governor's office, or had bureaus within line agencies that had been promoting broadband development. The states, which did have formal broadband organizations in place when ARRA funding was announced, were in a better position to organize within the state and with private and nonprofit groups than those that did not have formal organizations in place. Existing state organizations became the nucleus for the ARRA broadband group and served as a way of involving knowledgeable and experienced people from state agencies, private-sector companies, and nonprofit groups. All the states were very conscious of the tight time frame for ARRA broadband grant opportunities, and all tried to use existing personnel and state agencies. Given the importance of the effort, many states designated their best staff, the "A team," to take the lead on ARRA broadband efforts.

Among the three states examined in some detail for this case study, experiences varied. California established a Broadband Task Force in 2006, which conducted a voluntary broadband mapping in the years 2006–7, issued a report in 2008, and established the California Advanced Services Fund as a state broadband infrastructure grant program within the California Public Utilities Commission (PUC). These activities positioned California well for ARRA both because there was something of a plan in place and because there was a well-connected network of interested parties who had been on, or staffed, the task force.[20] In 2010 the California Broadband Council was established by statute, with the PUC providing most of its staffing. Before ARRA, oversight and coordination of broadband were conducted through the PUC. With the passage of ARRA, coordination moved directly to the governor's office and the establishment of the ARRA Task Force to coordinate all stimulus funding and deal with the reporting requirements. The California Technology Agency took the lead on broadband. The ARRA Task Force, whose members were all appointed by the governor, was successful in establishing new lines of communication, involving new people at higher levels, and educating them quickly as to the processes and opportunities. The governor and the task force were able to catalyze involvement of other state agencies as a force multiplier. For example, highway projects could be required to facilitate the laying of broadband cable during construction to facilitate both efforts in a more cost-effective way.

Virginia initiated broadband task forces beginning in the late 1990s and viewed the internet as a "leveragble asset" and important infrastructure for economic development. When the tobacco settlement monies became available in early 2000, broadband deployment was viewed as a key component of economic redevelopment plans, particularly in southern Virginia; by 2008 the Virginia Tobacco Commission had invested $85 million in fiber optic infrastructure in south and southwest Virginia.[21] Interest in broadband further intensified after the September 11, 2001, terrorist attacks, as the telecommunications system was clearly viewed as critical infrastructure and as the state took on the task of broadband mapping. In Virginia the Office of Telework Promotion and Broadband Assistance, created in 2006 and located in the Center for Innovative Technology in the office of the secretary of technology, has been the lead state agency coordinating broadband activities, and it took on this responsibility under ARRA as well. A Broadband Advisory Council within this office has representation from the legislative and executive branches as well as from the private and nonprofit sectors. Because of the existing relationships that had been established through these various activities and groups and because of the informational resources—including the maps, tool kit, and website—the "timing of ARRA was good" for Virginia, as it was "years ahead" of some states in its activity.

Florida viewed broadband as infrastructure for economic development and the quality of life, but before ARRA it had not organized a state task force specifically on broadband deployment. After the passage of ARRA, the Florida Office of Economic Recovery formed an ARRA Broadband Strategy Working Group to develop an ARRA broadband plan, collaborate with various stakeholders inside and outside government, and coordinate Florida's grant proposals. This small group of six to seven served as a multidisciplinary review committee in the governor's office and made recommendations on the Florida applications. The group "had not worked together before" and included people from economic development agencies, universities, K-12 education, health agencies, and the data network provider. The Department of Management Services, working with SUNCOM within the Division of Telecommunications (DivTel), became the primary state agency for the Broadband Florida Initiative. Additionally, the North Florida Broadband Authority was established as a governmental entity for the purpose of pursuing and sustaining broadband resources, infrastructure, and services for the region; it received the only grant awarded to Florida in the first round of broadband funding.[22]

All the states, including those examined in depth here, took their new leadership roles seriously, but with differing processes and outcomes. States focused on disseminating information to potential applicants through workshops and websites and made sure applicants knew how to fill out the applications. Most states did rank applications, although processes for ranking applications varied, with the governor's office taking the lead in some states, the state PUC in others, and in some states an independent third party.

Two aspects of this process seem important from a network and collaboration perspective. First, in some cases but not all, states knew which proposals were being submitted to NTIA; this occurred primarily because of the state's outreach regarding ARRA broadband opportunities and because of proactive steps to assist those interested in submitting grants. But in several cases entities submitted grants without the knowledge of the governor's office. Second,

NTIA asked states to "rank" the ARRA applications from their state. Most states, including California and Florida, ranked the applications received for NTIA. In California the governor's office set up a process for getting requests from various players (PUCs, industrywide associations, government agencies) for an overall sense of what the priorities should be. In general the priorities from the 2008 report, with infrastructure as the top concern, were accepted by all. There was then an attempt to communicate these priorities to those who were likely to submit. However, Virginia did not rank the applications, in part because the award criteria (e.g., what was an "underserved" area?) were not entirely clear, but instead wrote letters of support for those applicants using companies in Virginia and bringing or keeping jobs in Virginia.

Some states viewed NTIA as something of a "black hole" because states were frustrated by a lack of timely feedback and information that did not always seem complete or understandable. State-level people involved in broadband had not really worked with NTIA before, and they were not clear on how best to proceed in dealing with this federal agency. This uncertainty was complicated by the fact that there was a lack of clarity on some key NTIA criteria (e.g., what did having a project "substantially completed" in two years mean?).[23] Moreover, the states themselves, as well as both NTIA and RUS, did not have adequate, reliable, and timely data about current broadband deployment within their states. Part of NTIA's ARRA funds were targeted to broadband mapping, which would ultimately provide such information, but the perception among the states was that in a perfect world, this mapping would have been done first. In many cases, states themselves "scrambled" to collect this information quickly at the same time as they were also doing outreach to potential applicants within the state. In some states, existing areas had been designated as in need of increased broadband deployment; in Florida these were termed Rural Areas of Critical Economic Concern (RACEC). In Virginia the areas hit hardest by the withdrawal of the tobacco industry were viewed as areas in need of economic development and areas that generally met the rural requirements. Although states played an advisory role in the application review process, NTIA was not required to follow the states' recommendations—and sometimes it did not, which added to the perception that NTIA was a "black hole."

PRIVATE-SECTOR COMMUNICATORS ARE WATCHFUL OBSERVERS IN ARRA'S BROADBAND ROLLOUT

It is important to note the role of the private-sector firms in the ARRA broadband implementation process. In general, states did not have existing relationships with private-sector broadband firms other than their involvement in awarding competitive contracts for state operations and then overseeing those contracts. But states generally did not play a role in "championing" particular state firms or lobbying on their behalf. Indeed, most broadband companies were national in scope, not state based. Within state governments, there was a lack of experience working cooperatively with these firms, and therefore there was not a basis for immediately collaborating on ARRA broadband funding.

A range of private-sector firms viewed themselves as affected by ARRA broadband activities. Broadband can be delivered by fiber, wire, cable, wireless, cellular, and satellite—and those companies, both large and small, were potential partners in broadband grant and loan applications. In the broadband area, industry trade associations are prolific, powerful, and well-financed. They include the United States Telecom Association, the trade association representing service providers and suppliers for the telecommunications industry; the National Exchange Carrier Association, a not-for-profit association of incumbent local exchange carriers; COMPTEL, an industry association representing competitive communications service providers and their supplier partners; the National Telecommunications Cooperative Association, the trade association representing rural telecommunications providers; the Organization for the Promotion and Advancement of Small Telecommunications Companies; the Coalition for Rational Universal Service and Intercarrier Reform; the Rural High-Cost Carriers, a cross-section of rural incumbent local exchange carriers;[24] and the National Cable and Telecommunications Association.

Although private-sector firms were potential applicants, they were also concerned that ARRA projects would compete with their planned deployment efforts or with their existing broadband infrastructure. At the same time, private-sector suppliers of end-user equipment, particularly computers, would be advantaged by more deployment of broadband to unserved or underserved communities.

Larger private-sector players were reluctant to get involved in the first round of ARRA funding because they did not necessarily want to reveal so much of their proprietary information and were worried that they might be exposed to net neutrality rules in unexpected ways. This "shrunk the potential applicant pool and had a negative impact" in some states. The private sector's disinterest is reflected in the number of awards made by sector, with the for-profit sector receiving 55 of the 233 NTIA awards (24 percent); this was the first time that NTIA had made such awards to private-sector companies. For-profit corporations, however, secured 202 of the 297 RUS awards (68 percent), with most of these going to small local companies.[25]

THE NONPROFIT SECTOR BECOMES AN ALLY OF
ARRA-FUNDED BROADBAND NETWORKS

The nonprofit sector was involved in the ARRA broadband process as applicants for grants and loans either in partnership with others or alone and, if successful, as implementing entities. A quarter of the NTIA/BTOP awards were made to nonprofit organizations, for a total of 58 awards out of 233. Only a small number of RUS/BIP awards, 8 out of a total of 297, went to nonprofits.[26] In some states nonprofit organizations, such as community health care organizations and community colleges, had long recognized the importance of broadband service for economic and community development. For example, in southeastern Massachusetts, in 2006 a group of nonprofit organizations organized a consortium of government, business, educational, and nonprofit organizations, which was then, as a 501(c)(3) called OpenCape Corporation, poised to submit a $40 million NTIA application.[27]

California had a nonprofit organization, the California Emerging Technology Fund (CETF), which had been established in 2005 as a result of the merger activities between AT&T and Verizon. Originally focused on bridging the "digital divide," CETF's activities broadened to include telehealth, getting broadband to new schools and new homes, training, distance learning, and policy advice. Some in California saw CETF as playing a role in "absorbing some of the broadband coordination beyond ARRA." Florida was somewhat unique in that one of the two primary broadband implementing organizations was a nonprofit, the Florida Rural Broadband Alliance, which was created by two nonprofit economic development organizations: Florida's Heartland Regional Development Initiative, a development unit of RACEC, and Opportunity Florida. The other implementing organization was the North Florida Broadband Authority, a government entity, discussed above. In Virginia, the Center for Innovative Technology (CIT) was created by the General Assembly in 1984 as a nonprofit corporation to enhance the research and development capability of the state's research universities in partnership with industry; telecommunications and broadband specifically had been a key priority of CIT since its inception, and CIT took on a major role in ARRA, including coordinating activities and applying for grants itself.

Continuing Implementation Challenges: Post-Award Initiatives

With the awards phase completed as of October 1, 2010, efforts shifted to monitoring and overseeing the awards to ensure that projects were moving forward in a timely fashion and that award monies were being spent responsibly. NTIA

and RUS both required quarterly reports on financial and programmatic activities from grant recipients, and NTIA reports every ninety days on the
status of BTOP to congressional appropriations and commerce committees.
NTIA also conducted site visits to monitor progress and offer advice, as well
as individual and conference calls to assess progress. The secretary of agriculture was similarly required to submit detailed reports to the congressional
appropriations committees on spending and obligations for RUS broadband
programs. The RUS general field representatives served as the primary contact point for awardees and collected information on the projects in order to
submit monthly progress reports.[28]

In terms of transparency, NTIA was required by the Recovery Act to
provide information to the public on its broadband grant activities. Accordingly, it maintained a website that provided detailed information on all projects, including their quarterly reports. RUS, however, was not tasked by the
Recovery Act with any specific transparency requirements, and it released
only brief project summaries on its website.[29]

In order to carry out post-award functions, the absence of adequate staffing
at both NTIA and RUS continued to raise problems. Early on, the Department
of Commerce's Office of the Inspector General (OIG) and the Government
Accountability Office (GAO) both pointed out that funding for the BTOP office would expire in December 2010 and recommended that NTIA develop alternative oversight strategies based on possible funding scenarios.[30] Given that
NTIA did not have a grants management office, NTIA had established mem-
orandums of understanding (MOUs) with other Commerce bureaus—the National Institute of Standards and Technology (NIST, $2.23 million) and the
National Oceanic and Atmospheric Administration (NOAA, $4.15 million)—
but the Department of Commerce's OIG noted that the MOUs needed to be
clearer regarding roles and responsibilities, especially as "only the grants officers at NOAA and NIST can approve or issue amendments to grant awards."[31]
RUS hired additional general field representative staff to assist with monitoring the broadband projects and contracted with ICF International to review
technical and financial materials.[32]

Challenges in Delivering Projects on Time

A major challenge involved the spending rate of the awards. NTIA projects
were to be 67 percent complete within two years of the grant and fully complete within three years. Although in September 2011, NTIA grant recipients had spent only about 19 percent of total funds,[33] by March 1, 2015, BTOP
grant recipients had drawn down 91 percent of ARRA funds ($3.71 billion)
and had completed 213 projects, with the remaining 12 close to being com-

pleted by the September 2015 deadline.[34] Under ARRA, all RUS awards required that loan/grant funds had to be advanced by September 30, 2015, or they would be rescinded by RUS and returned to the Department of the Treasury. In June 2014 GAO concluded that about 85 percent of RUS projects, 216 of 255, were incomplete.[35] As of March 31, 2015, of the 297 RUS loans and grants, 42 (14 percent) were rescinded and $325 million was returned to the Treasury. Of the remaining 255 active projects, 68 were fully operational or complete, 180 were partially operational, and 7 were under construction; $2.56 billion of the $3.1 billion awarded to RUS for active projects was advanced by March 31, 2015.[36] A July 2015 *Politico* investigation reported that about half of the RUS-funded projects had not yet drawn down the full amounts awarded and that more than 40 RUS projects had never started.[37]

During the course of ARRA broadband implementation, congressional committees were concerned about funding rates and the likelihood that projects might not be completed on time. For example, the Subcommittee on Communications and Technology of the House Committee on Energy and Commerce held a hearing in May 2012, stating in their hearing announcement that

recipients of 233 National Telecommunications and Information Administration awards worth $4 billion have spent just $1.6 billion of it so far. Less than a dozen of the projects have been completed. Six of the awards worth $124.5 million have been returned or revoked. Recipients of 320 Rural Utility Service Awards worth $2.4 billion have spent $968 million. Five projects have been completed. As of July 2011, $124 million in grants and $35 million in loans have been rescinded or revoked.[38]

Completing projects in the time frame required by ARRA would have been difficult under the best of circumstances, but it was made even more problematic by the usual delays experienced by large projects that involved multiple contractors and subcontractors and required complicated and multilevel approval processes. Some projects did not meet their initial grant requirements and were declined before they were begun.

In testimony to a House hearing in May 2012, the Inspector General for the Department of Commerce reported that as of April 2012, "the total number of BTOP grants decreased from 233 to 228 due to grant cancellations, modifications, and terminations, which resulted in approximately $127 million returned" to the Treasury.[39] He went on to acknowledge that "slow awardee spending could result in unfinished grant projects" and that "spending—particularly with infrastructure projects—continues to lag."[40] He also noted that NTIA oversight was successful in identifying projects that were falling behind schedule and that eight projects had returned or de-obligated $125 million in federal funds and that one grant had been terminated for failure to comply with the terms of the grant.[41] At the same hearing the RUS administrator reported that "tough calls" had been made as they managed awards, resulting in the rescission of thirty-six BIP awards and the return of approximately $266 million to the Treasury.[42]

Each of the three states examined in some detail here had grants that were identified as being in trouble in reaching financial goals. In Florida, for example, the North Florida Broadband Authority, which received a $30 million grant in BTOP's round one funding, had spent only $7 million and completed zero miles of route as of September 2011, and so it was suspended by NTIA[43] because of waste and conflict of interest issues.[44] The project was restarted in late spring 2012 after two of the subcontractors resigned and the authority was reorganized.[45] In California, the Department of Commerce's OIG investigated a $50 million BTOP grant for the San Francisco Bay Area Wireless Enhanced Broadband Project, with particular attention to project readiness and governance structure.[46] In Virginia, the Lenowisco Planning District returned a $20.2 million award to RUS because the partners could not agree on the revenue split and the repayment on the loan portion of the award.[47]

Environmental Reviews Challenge Federal and State Managers

The delays noted above were exacerbated by environmental review requirements pertaining to many broadband projects. ARRA broadband projects had to certify their compliance with environmental regulations, at both the national and state levels, as well as historical preservation, zoning, and other state or local construction requirements. Of the 233 NTIA awards made by September 30, 2010, over 100 required environmental assessments before the projects could break ground; as of October 8, 2011, 31 draft assessments had been submitted, and 11 of these had been approved.[48] The Department of Commerce's OIG reported in November 2011 that environmental assessments often took six months or more to complete and that twelve award recipients still had not filed environmental assessments, for a total of about $500 million in funding.[49] RUS projects similarly experienced delays in environmental reviews, securing permits, and rights-of-way agreements; and because of weather and terrain challenges, RUS was required to extend completion deadlines.[50]

Given the importance of the ARRA broadband projects to the states' economic development goals, the governors' offices often tried to facilitate the completion of the permit and approval processes within the states. For example, in California the ARRA Task Force helped to expedite state review so that projects could begin by working directly with the relevant state agencies—for example, Transportation, Environment, Fish and Games, and Historic Preservation. As projects were approved and as needed, the task force and governor's office held meetings with all the state actors who were involved in the environmental approvals to determine how to get necessary approvals quickly. The new coordination required here was facilitated by the task force. Previously, the state PUC had tracked individual projects but had not done the trouble-shooting that the California Technology Agency and task force could do.

Meeting Broadband Deployment Goals

One of the initial and continuing concerns with the ARRA broadband program was that it would in the end not extend service to new, unserved, or underserved areas but would instead overbuild in areas that already had broadband. Both NTIA and RUS conducted studies to estimate jobs created, miles of broadband deployed, homes and schools connected, and so on. NTIA awarded a $5 million contract to ASR Analytics to measure the impact of BTOP grants on broadband deployment and adoption and to assess the economic and social conditions in the grantee areas.[51]

For the RUS BIP program, ARRA required that 75 percent of the service areas were to be "rural areas" without sufficient access to high-speed broadband and that RUS give priority to projects that would provide service to the highest proportion of rural residents without broadband access and projects that would provide end users with a choice of broadband service providers. Before ARRA, RUS did not fund projects in areas where there was an existing RUS loan or grant recipient. BIP did not have that restriction, and there was some concern, expressed by the Department of Agriculture's OIG, that an overlap with existing RUS recipients might result in overbuilding in some areas.[52] Additionally, the definition of "rural" was broad enough that it was sometimes difficult to distinguish rural and suburban communities.

A March 2013 US Department of Agriculture OIG audit reviewed 87 BIP projects and found that funded projects did sometimes overlap with preexisting RUS-subsidized providers; the auditors estimated from the audit sample that 10 projects overlapped. It concluded that BIP could have been focused more exclusively on rural residents without broadband access. Although the OIG's audit recognized that RUS did not have the maps needed to precisely determine areas covered by preexisting providers, the OIG noted that RUS could have done a better job at estimating overlap with the information it had.[53] A 2014 GAO report offered harsh criticism, noting that information on broadband subscribership maintained by RUS's BIP was unreliable.

In many cases, states had in place concepts that could be adopted as criteria for "unserved or underserved" areas, which avoided the problems of using the unclear NTIA and RUS criteria. California had already been using "unserved" and "underserved" in its California Advanced Services Fund program, with an "unserved area" defined as "an area that is not served by any form of facilities-based broadband, or where internet connectivity is available only through dial-up service or satellite," and "underserved" defined as "an area in which broadband is available but no facilities-based provider offers at speeds of at least 3 Mbps download and 1 Mbps upload."[54] Florida had long used the designation of RACEC to identify rural communities adversely affected by economic events or natural disasters, which permitted the governor to waive criteria for economic development incentives and give that area priority status for funding. The RACEC designation worked well for ARRA funding, especially RUS funding. Somewhat similarly to Florida, Virginia had a designation in place that had been used for those areas that were transitioning from tobacco farming and thus were eligible for special funding.

Private-sector firms were carefully watching the awards process with an eye on any ARRA competition with their projects. At a 2012 House Agriculture Rural Development Subcommittee hearing on the rural development programs, the National Cable and Telecommunications Association, in particular, was critical of RUS for not focusing on "unserved" areas and for instead overbuilding in areas where there were already projects funded by risk capital that had to compete with new ones funded by government subsidies.[55] A 2015 *Politico* report noted that "even RUS admits it's not going to provide better service to the 7 million residents it once touted; instead, the number is in the hundreds of thousands."[56] This is indeed the case, for RUS reported that as of March 2015, a total of 230,323 subscribers received new or improved broadband as a result of RUS/BIP projects.[57]

Conclusion

The ARRA broadband program was among the most challenging of the stimulus programs. It involved stringent statutory requirements in terms of timelines but unclear standards for key elements of program implementation—for example, the definitions of "unserved" and "underserved" and of "broadband" itself. It entailed a new role for the federal government and coordination among three federal agencies (NTIA, RUS, and FCC), with one of the main agencies (NTIA) having never played a role in grants before. At the state level, the ARRA broadband program required leadership from the governor's office in coordinating state agencies, nonprofits, and private companies—all with the possibility, if not the promise, of much-needed funding for a critical component of the infrastructure for economic development. At the same time, the success of the grants program hinged on the federal players being able to make clear decisions on grant requirements and funding quickly, on the state partners being able to marshal knowledgeable staff within state offices and well-qualified teams to submit grants, and on the nonprofit and for-profit sectors being willing to take risks and cooperate with each other and with governmental units in this new sandbox.

The success of the ARRA broadband programs was mixed. At the federal level, NTIA and RUS clearly learned from the round one funding experiences and were able to make needed adjustments to make round two go more smoothly. Although RUS was able to fairly effectively ramp up its grants and loan office to accommodate the demands of the BIP program and to make awards in a timely fashion, it was less effective in monitoring the implementation of those awards. RUS's previous problems in administering its smaller pre-ARRA broadband funding continued to trouble the agency as it ramped up for the more ambitious ARRA funding. Moreover, when ARRA funding was dispersed to agencies, RUS was without an administrator, and during the course of ARRA's implementation RUS changed administrators four times. The *Politico* investigation characterized RUS as "miserly and risk averse at times—and unfocused and overly generous at others—the rural regulator arrived at its monumental stimulus task with more questions than answers."[58] Although NTIA was faced with the larger initial administrative challenge, it was able to fill in the gaps in its own capacity by contracting with Booz Allen Hamilton and developing MOUs with NIST, NOAA, and the FCC for help with grant processing, management support, and technical assistance. At the same time, NTIA continued to face implementation delays for completed projects and suffered from a lack of clarity on state roles.

At the state level, experiences varied, with the most critical factor in successful implementation being whether there was an existing network of public and private actors that understood broadband, had worked together previously, and were energized by the possibilities offered by the ARRA grants. The governors' offices played pivotal roles in catalyzing networks within their states, fostering collaboration among various broadband actors, and facilitating ways to more quickly overcome seeming roadblocks. At the state level, existing personal and professional relationships appear to have been key to success. Nonprofits were willing partners in grant submissions but in general lacked expertise in the broadband area and depended on private-sector or governmental partners to help craft proposals. Small private companies understood that ARRA grants provided opportunities for them, but larger private companies were reluctant to get involved.

Throughout the implementation cycle, the ARRA broadband programs continued to face fairly significant challenges, which resulted in a mixture of successes, failures, and maybes. As noted above, a percentage of the grants fell behind schedule and several did not catch up in time to meet the completion dates. NTIA was more successful in the timely completion of projects than RUS. As numerous GAO and OIG reports pointed out, many grants had been faulted for administrative or financial problems—sometimes in time for the agency to correct problems and sometimes too late for that. And some grants appeared to be targeted to areas that may not have actually needed broadband or that were unlikely to be able to use the new broadband capacity effectively.

However, at the same time, there are indeed many successes among the ARRA broadband programs. Broadband infrastructure has clearly been enhanced, although not without significant slippages and cost-effectiveness issues. These implementation growing pains were not unprecedented but in fact were to be expected following the launch of such a daunting national initiative requiring collaboration among unfamiliar implementation partners. ARRA's high stakes and ambitious time frames placed stress on every network, regardless of how well established and accomplished it might have been. These difficulties were most pronounced with a program like broadband, where the implementation airplane had to be constructed during and after takeoff.

Notes

1. Most of the background information used here is derived from a number of Congressional Research Service reports, including those by Lennard G. Kruger, "Distribution of Broadband Stimulus Grants and Loans: Applications and Awards," Report R41164, September 9, 2010, and January 4, 2011; Lennard G. Kruger, "Broadband Infrastructure Programs in the American Recovery and Reinvestment Act," Report R40436, January 4, 2011; Lennard G. Kruger, "Broadband Loan and Grant Programs in the USDA's Rural Utilities Service," Report RL33816, January 4, 2011; and Lennard G. Kruger, "Background and Issues for Congressional Oversight of ARRA Broadband Awards," Report R41775, May 17, 2013, and August 4, 2015.

2. Mark L. Goldstein, "Recovery Act: Preliminary Observations on the Implementation of Broadband Programs," Testimony before the Committee on Commerce, Science and Transportation, US Senate, October 27, 2009, GAO-10-192T, 3, http://gao.gov/assets/130/123616.pdf.

3. Federal Communications Commission, "Policy Statement on Broadband Internet Access FCC 05-151," August 5, 2005, http://hraunfoss.fcc.gov/edocs_public/attachmatch/FCC-05-151A1.pdf.

4. Kruger, "Broadband Loan and Grant Programs."

5. Ibid.; US Government Accountability Office, *Broadband Deployment Is Extensive throughout the United States, but It Is Difficult to Assess the Extent of Deployment Gaps in Rural Areas*, GAO-06-426 (Washington, DC: US Government Accountability Office, 2006), www.gao.gov/new.items/d06426.pdf; US Department of Agriculture, Office of Inspector General, Southwest Region, "Audit Report: Rural Utilities Service Broadband Grant and Loan Programs," Audit Report 09601-4-Te, September 2005, www.usda.gov/oig/webdocs/09601-04-TE.pdf; Michael Martinez, "Broadband: Loan Fund's Strict Rules Foil Small Municipalities," *National Journal's Technology Daily*, August 23, 2005.

6. Goldstein, "Recovery Act," 3–4.

7. The original ARRA funding for BTOP was $4.7 million, including administration and oversight costs. In August 2010, there was a $302 million rescission. BTOP awarded $3.9 billion in grants in the second round. US Department of Commerce, Office of the Inspector General, "NTIA Has an Established Foundation to Oversee BTOP Awards, but Better Execution of Monitoring Is Needed," OIG-12-013-A, November 17, 2011, 1n1.

8. These data are from www.recovery.gov/Transparency/RecipientReportedData/Pages/JobSummary.aspx?qtr=2010Q1.

9. Testimony of the Honorable Lawrence E. Strickling, assistant secretary for communications and information, National Telecommunications and Information Administration, US Department of Commerce, before the Broadband Loans and Grants Hearing, Committee on Energy and Commerce, Subcommittee on Communications and Technology, US House of Representatives, May 16, 2012.

10. Statement of Jonathan Adelstein, administrator, Rural Utilities Service, US Department of Agriculture, House Energy and Commerce Subcommittee on Communications and Technology, May 16, 2012.

11. Council of Economic Advisers, *The Economic Impact of the American Recovery and Reinvestment Act Five Years Later: Final Report to Congress* (Washington, DC: Council of Economic Advisers, 2014), 41, www.whitehouse.gov/sites/default/files/docs/cea_arra_report.pdf.

12. Division B, Title VI; Kruger, "Broadband Infrastructure Programs."

13. Department of Commerce, Office of the Inspector General, "NTIA Must Continue to Improve Its Program Management and Pre-Award Process for Its Broadband Grants Program," ARR-19842-1, April 2010, 2. The Office of the Inspector General criticized NTIA for relying on a few key individuals and not establishing clear lines of authority and procedures (pp. 5–6) and for the application intake system during the first round (p. 9).

14. Ibid., 2. NTIA signed MOUs with two Commerce Department agencies and the FCC for help with grant processing, management support, and technical assistance. Ibid., 4.

15. US Government Accountability Office, *Recovery Act: Further Opportunities Exist to Strengthen Oversight of Broadband Stimulus Programs*, GAO-10-823 (Washington, DC: US Government Accountability Office, 2010), 5.

16. US Department of Agriculture, Rural Utilities Service and Department of Commerce, National Telecommunications and Information Administration, "Broadband Initiatives Program and Broadband Technology Opportunities Program," 74 *Federal Register* 58940–44, November 16, 2009.

17. Kruger, "Broadband Loan and Grant Programs."

18. Federal Communications Commission, *Connecting America: The National Broadband Plan* (Washington, DC: US Government Printing Office, 2010).

19. NTIA, "Fact Sheet: Broadband Technology Opportunities Program," November 10, 2010, www2.ntia.doc.gov/files/Interconnection_Nondiscrimination_11_10_10_FINAL.pdf.

20. Rachelle Chong (commissioner of California Public Utilities Commission), "Testimony before the Subcommittee on Communications, Technology, and the Internet re Broadband Programs Related to the American Recovery and Reinvestment Act," April 2, 2009.

21. In this effort, Virginia also leveraged $12.7 million from the US Department of Commerce's Economic Development Agency. See "Final Report of Commonwealth's Broadband Roundtable," presented to Governor Timothy Kaine, September 9, 2008, www.wired.virginia.gov/pdf/Governor_report.pdf.

22. Barry Ray, " "Florida State Helps Secure $30 Million to Increase Internet Access in Rural North Florida," Florida State News and Events, March 15, 2010, www.fsu.edu/news/2010/03/15/internet.access/.

23. Richard Anguiano, "Marion/Alachua Group to Seek Stimulus Millions for Broadband," *Ocala Business Journal*, June 26, 2009.

24. Kevin Taglang, "Carriers Big and Small Weigh In on Broadband and Universal Service Reform," December 8, 2009, http://benton.org/node/30362.

25. Kruger, "Background and Issues," March 14, 2012, 2–3.

26. Ibid.

27. Mark Muro and Sarah Rahman, "Design Snapshot: Cape Cod and Southeastern Massachusetts Modernize with New Broadband Infrastructure—Advancing Regional Connectivity," August 2009, www.brookings.edu/research/papers/2009/07/0826-arra-massachusetts.

28. US Government Accountability Office, *Recovery Act: USDA Should Include Broadband Program's Impact in Annual Performance Reports*, GAO-14-511 (Washington, DC: US Government Accountability Office, 2014), 10.

29. Kruger, "Background and Issues," (2012), 7–8.

30. Data from Office of the Inspector General, November 2010; US Government Accountability Office, *Recovery Act*, 31.

31. Data from Office of the Inspector General, November 2010.

32. US Government Accountability Office, *Recovery Act*, 9.

33. Todd J. Zinser (inspector general for the US Department of Commerce), "Testimony before the House Energy and Commerce Committee, Subcommittee on Communications and Technology," May 16, 2012, 2.

34. "Broadband Technology Opportunities Program (BTOP) Quarterly Program Status Report," submitted to the Senate Committees on Appropriations and Commerce, Science, and Transportation, and the House Committees on Appropriation, Energy, and Commerce, by NTIA, July 2015, 3, www.ntia.doc.gov/files/ntia/publications/ntia_btop_25th_qtrly_report.pdf.

35. US Government Accountability Office, *Recovery Act*, 11.

36. Kruger (August 2015), 5–6.

37. Tony Romm, "Wired to Fail: How a Little-Known Agency Mishandled Several Billion Dollars of Stimulus Money Trying to Expand Broadband Coverage to Rural Communities," *Politico*, July 28, 2015, www.politico.com/story/2015/07/broad band-coverage-rural-area-fund-mishandled-120601#ixzz3v9PcppPq.

38. Committee Memorandum, May 14, 2012.

39. Ibid., 2.

40. Ibid., 3–4.

41. Ibid., 11.

42. Jonathan Adelstein, RUS administrator, Statement to the House Energy and Commerce Subcommittee on Communications and Technology, May 16, 2012, 4.

43. Derek Gilliam and Kaitlin Mulhere, "Internet Stimulus Project Investigated," *The Ledger*, September 25, 2011, http://theledger.com/article/20110925/NEWS/1109 29554?template=printart.

44. "Broadband Stimulus Scandals: Missteps in the Buildout and What's at Stake," *FierceTelecom*, February 28, 2012, www.fiercetelecom.com/special-reports/broadband -stimulus-scandals-missteps-buildout-and-whats-stake. The article also notes that "Florida in general is a blooming garden of bad press around mismanaged stimulus funds."

45. Jeffrey Boatright, "High Speed Internet on the Way," *Suwannee Democrat*, March 26, 2012, http://suwanneedemocrat.com/suwannee/x1437239544/High-speed -Internet-on-the-way. Two local entities—Bradford County and Perry City—have since pulled out of the project, in part because broadband is already available in those areas. See Samantha Bookman, "Perry, Fla. Drops Out of North Broadband Authority," *FierceTelecom*, April 12, 2012, www.fiercetelecom.com/story/perry-fla-drops-out -north-florida-broadband-authority/2012-04-12.

46. US Department of Commerce, Office of Inspector General, "Misrepresentation Regarding Project Readiness, Governance Structure Put at Risk the Success of the San Francisco Bay Area Wireless Enhanced Broadband (BayWEB) Project," January 10, 2012, www.oig.doc.gov/Pages/Misrepresentations-Put-at-Risk-Success-of -San-Francisco-BayWEB-Project.aspx.

47. "Some Broadband Stimulus Recipients Return Funding," *ILEC Advisor*, March 25, 2011, www.jsicapitaladvisors.com/the-ilec-advisor/2011/3/25/some-broad band-stimulus-recipients-return-funding.html.

48. US Department of Commerce, Office of the Inspector General, "Broadband Program Faces Uncertain Funding, and NTIA Needs to Strengthen Its Post-Award Operations," OIG-11-005-A, November 4, 2010, 2.

49. US Department of Commerce, Office of the Inspector General, "NTIA Has an Established Foundation," 2.

50. US Government Accountability Office, *Recovery Act*, 8.

51. Kruger, "Background and Issues," (2012), 8.

52. David R. Gray (deputy inspector general of the US Department of Agriculture), "Statement before the Subcommittee on Communications and Technology, Committee on Energy and Commerce," May 16, 2012.

53. US Department of Agriculture, "American Recovery and Reinvestment Act of 2009: Broadband Initiatives Program—Pre-Approval Controls," Audit Report 09703-001-32, March 2013, www.usda.gov/oig/webdocs/09703-0001-32.pdf.

54. Rachelle Chong, "Testimony," 2–3.

55. John Eggerton, "NCTA: Things Have to Change with RUS Implementation of Broadband Programs," *Broadcasting & Cable*, April 25, 2012, www.broadcastingcable .com/article/483592-NCTA_Things_Have_to_Change_With_RUS_Implementation _of_Broadband_Programs.php.

56. Romm, "Wired to Fail."

57. US Department of Agriculture, Rural Utilities Service, "Broadband Initiatives Program Quarterly Report," March 31, 2015, 3, www.rd.usda.gov/files/reports/ utpBroadbandInitiativesProgramReportMarch2015.pdf.

58. Romm, "Wired to Fail."

6

Weathering Explosive Growth

WEATHERIZATION ASSISTANCE GRANTS UNDER ARRA

Alan J. Abramson

THE GOAL OF THE FEDERAL Weatherization Assistance Program (WAP) is to reduce the heating and cooling bills of low-income households. To do so, WAP provides funding for local weatherization workers to seal air leaks, add insulation to walls and attics, upgrade heating and air conditioning equipment, and implement other energy conservation measures. Special targets for assistance are the low-income elderly, disabled, and families with children.

Like many federal programs, WAP provides assistance indirectly to its target population. Under WAP, the federal Department of Energy (DOE) makes grants to state governments, which then pass funding to more than nine hundred local subgrantees that oversee the weatherization work. The vast majority of the local subgrantees are nonprofit and public community action agencies that were created in the 1960s War on Poverty and administer a variety of grants targeted at low-income individuals.[1] Local subgrantees either do the weatherization work themselves or contract the jobs out to local, for-profit building contractors.[2]

The Recovery Act provided WAP's state grantees and local subgrantees with huge funding increases for weatherization activities. In particular, the American Recovery and Reinvestment Act (the Recovery Act, or ARRA) allocated $5 billion in new funds for WAP, to be spent over three years, from April 1, 2009, through March 30, 2012.[3] With these funds, total annual funding for weatherization during the period of ARRA's spend-out was about four and one-half times previous levels.

Like the other case studies in this book, the main goal of this chapter is to consider the impact that new funding through ARRA—in this case massive new funding—had on program outcomes and on the network of organizations and individuals—federal, state, and local—involved in implementing the program, especially including federal managers. Of special interest in this particular case study is the role of private, nonprofit organizations. Federal and state governments rely heavily on nonprofits to deliver services in a broad range of health, human services, education, arts, housing, community development, and other programs. Rather than placing legions of federal and state employees in neighborhoods to provide services, government often funds nonprofit organizations to deliver these services. As we discuss here, the experience of WAP under ARRA demonstrates some of the benefits—and challenges—of involving nonprofits in government-funded programs.

To understand how WAP unfolded under the Recovery Act, the author reviewed relevant documents, reports, and articles, and interviewed twenty individuals involved in WAP at all levels.[4] To promote candor, interviewees were promised confidentiality, and are not cited by name in this report. Research on state and local experiences with WAP under ARRA focused on the WAP programs in New Mexico, New York, and Virginia. Virginia was a common state for all the chapters in this volume. New Mexico and New York were added so that this analysis could explore weatherization activities during ARRA in a variety of contexts that affect the kind of weatherization work that gets done (e.g., in warm states air conditioning systems are a major concern; urban states have more weatherization of multifamily dwellings). Thus, the three states examined for this case include states with different climates (New York—cold; Virginia and New Mexico—moderate); states with different urban/rural character (New York—more urban than average; New Mexico and Virginia—average urban/rural mix); states with different amounts of per capita spending on WAP (New York—high; New Mexico and Virginia—moderately low); states from different regions (New York—Northeast; Virginia—South; New Mexico—West); states of different population sizes (New York—very large; Virginia—large; New Mexico—small); states with different poverty rates (Virginia—low; New York—medium; New Mexico—high); and, since WAP was highly politicized, states with different political leanings (New York—solid Democratic; New Mexico—leaning Democratic; Virginia—competitive). This study also includes a state, Virginia, where program experts believed there were some early difficulties with implementing WAP under ARRA as well as other states, New Mexico and New York, that experts suggested were having a more positive experience.[5]

To preview the discussion that follows, what the reports and interviews indicate is that the huge infusion of funding under ARRA resulted in significant achievements, including the weatherization of 800,000 homes, which was significantly higher than the 635,000 target when ARRA was passed.[6] WAP was also consistently ranked among the top ten job-creating programs under ARRA.[7]

However, though WAP had important accomplishments under ARRA, it also experienced significant challenges, and WAP was among the most highly criticized of all Recovery Act initiatives. In particular, the program was faulted for being very slow to get started and for the poor quality of some of the weatherization work that was done. Although production started off slowly, it did pick up and, as noted above, eventually exceeded—by a large margin—initial ARRA targets. In contrast, criticism about the poor quality of some ARRA-funded weatherization projects lingered and proved harder for program supporters to overcome.

The Evolution of WAP

The seeds of WAP were planted during the oil crisis of 1973, when oil prices rose sharply with the Arab oil embargo. The sudden rise in oil prices posed a particular challenge for low-income households, which were hard-pressed to pay their home energy bills. According to a longtime program observer, in the fall of 1973 community action agency staff in Maine teamed up with Richard Saul and other staff at the federal Office of Economic Opportunity in Washington to make funds available to help meet the energy needs of the poor. In 1975, the Community Services Administration (CSA), which was the successor to the Office of Economic Opportunity, received its first appropriation of $16.5 million for energy programming. CSA's on-the-ground implementers were the nation's nine hundred community action agencies, most of which had been established in the mid-1960s federal War on Poverty effort to coordinate programs for the poor in communities around the country.[8] Thus, the important role of local community action agencies in the federal weatherization program was established from the start.

The Weatherization Assistance Program was formally created by Title IV of the Energy Conservation and Production Act of 1976, and by 1979 the new federal Department of Energy had taken over the administration of the weatherization program from CSA.[9] In its earliest years, WAP relied on volunteers and low-cost labor to cover windows with plastic sheets and caulk and weatherstrip windows and doors as temporary emergency measures.[10] As several interviewees commented, with its mission of serving the poor, WAP was an awkward fit in DOE, which otherwise had an engineering culture that emphasized research and weapons building. Perhaps not surprisingly, with its move to DOE's more technically oriented culture, WAP also became more sophisticated and put a greater emphasis on implementing cost-effective and permanent measures. In the 1990s the development and use of advanced home energy audits enabled weatherization workers to carefully evaluate homes so

Table 6.1. DOE Appropriations for WAP (millions of dollars)

Fiscal Year or ARRA	Appropriation
1999	133.0
2000	135.0
2001	153.0
2002	230.0
2003	223.5
2004	227.2
2005	228.2
2006	242.6
2007	204.6
2008	227.2
2009	441.0[a]
ARRA	5,000.0
2010	180.0[b]
2011	174.3
2012	68.0
2013	131.7
2014	173.9
2015	193.0
Mean, 1999–2008	200.4
Mean, 2009–11[c]	1,931.8
Mean, 2012–15	141.7

[a] Excludes $9 million for Sustainable Energy Resources for Consumers (SERC) grants.
[b] Excludes $30 million for the Weatherization Innovation Pilot Program (WIPP).
[c] Includes ARRA.
Sources: Fred Sissine, "DOE Weatherization Program: A Review of Funding, Performance, and Cost-Effectiveness Studies," Congressional Research Service, January 11, 2012, 44–45; Kelsi Bracmort and Fred Sissine, "Energy Efficiency and Renewable Energy (EERE): Appropriations and the FY2016 Budget Request," Congressional Research Service, November 4, 2015, 5–6.

that the most cost-effective weatherization measures could be implemented.[11] In 1994 WAP also began to promote efficiency in cooling as well as heating. By the late 2000s just before the Recovery Act, more than 6 million homes had been weatherized through WAP.[12]

Core funding for WAP came through an annual appropriation for DOE's weatherization program. In federal fiscal years (FYs) 1999–2008, the decade before the passage of the Recovery Act, WAP received an average of $200 million per year in its DOE appropriation, as shown in table 6.1.

In addition to the WAP appropriation, significant funding for state-run weatherization activities also came from the Low-Income Home Energy Assistance Program (LIHEAP). LIHEAP, which is administered by the federal Department of Health and Human Services, is a grant to states to help low-income households pay their home energy bills. States are allowed to use up to 15 percent of their LIHEAP grants to fund WAP-related activities. With overall LIHEAP funding at approximately $2 billion per year in the decade before ARRA, LIHEAP support for weatherization activities was typically equal to or even greater than the WAP appropriation, as shown in table 6.2.

Besides WAP and LIHEAP, important additional funding for state-administered weatherization activities came from utility companies, the Regional Greenhouse Gas Initiative, state general funds, and other sources. Total funding for weatherization activities from all sources averaged $615 million per year in the ten years, program years (PYs) 1999–2008, before the Recovery Act was passed.[13]

Before ARRA, WAP was "one of America's best kept secrets," according to one longtime program insider. The program was of moderate size and stable. An operation that generally "flew under the radar" is how another interviewee described WAP. This all changed with the huge allocation of ARRA funds that WAP received.

Overview of WAP under ARRA

As noted above, the 2009 Recovery Act provided a massive $5 billion in new funding for WAP. In addition to this extraordinary influx of ARRA funds, WAP continued to receive regular appropriations during the period of the spending out of the Recovery Act funds. Thus, including both ARRA and non-ARRA funding, the DOE average annual appropriation for weatherization was $1.9 billion during FYs 2009–11, or almost ten times previous levels, as shown in table 6.1. Total annual funding for weatherization from all sources was $2.7 billion, or about four and one-half times previous levels, during PYs 2009–11, as shown in table 6.2. After ARRA, WAP appropriations have fallen back to—or even below—pre-ARRA levels, averaging $141.7 million in FYs 2012–15.

The Obama administration transition team who put the recovery bill together had a variety of reasons for giving WAP a significant boost in funding: It was help for low-income households; it was a down payment on a Green Jobs initiative that would create new work in the energy field; and it saved energy. Moreover, the program looked like it could spend money fast and thereby create new jobs and stimulate the economy quickly. According to one journalist's account of the Recovery Act, "Weatherization was the low hanging

Table 6.2. Funding and Production for WAP from All Sources
(millions of dollars or percent)

Program Year	DOE Amount	DOE Percent	LIHEAP Amount	LIHEAP Percent	Other Amount	Other Percent	Total Amount	Units Produced
1999	134.3	35	168.9	44	84.8	22	388.0	
2000	136.8	31	193.1	44	109.0	25	438.9	
2001	158.7	31	230.8	45	125.3	24	514.8	
2002	223.1	39	211.8	38	130.8	23	565.7	
2003	223.8	37	219.5	37	156.9	26	600.2	
2004	224.1	37	225.7	38	152.9	25	602.7	158,751
2005	228.9	36	247.4	39	163.9	26	640.2	171,233
2006	238.3	33	312.7	43	180.6	25	731.5	163,205
2007	206.4	30	260.1	38	216.6	32	683.1	139,679
2008	237.5	24	332.8	34	409.7	42	980.0	231,375
2009	413.3	35	601.3	51	174.7	15	1,189.3	171,386
ARRA	4,746.0	100	0.0	0	0.0	0	4,746.0	794,424
2010	204.7	20	604.1	59	210.2	21	1,019.0	143,192
2011	243.3	26	452.1	49	237.8	22	1,088.2	175,722
2012	206.6	23	436.4	49	249.3	28	892.3	129,015
2013	146.9	16	408.9	45	358.6	39	914.4	129,495
2014	196.5	23	397.7	46	278.4	32	872.5	141,125
Mean, 1999–2008	201.2	33	240.3	39	173.1	28	614.5	172,849[a]
Mean, 2009–11[b]	1,872.1	70	601.1	22	207.6	8	2,680.8	428,241
Mean, 2009–11[b] vs. mean, 1999–2008	9.3		2.5		1.2		4.4	2.5[a]

[a] Covers the period 2004–8.
[b] Includes ARRA.

Source: National Association for State Community Services Programs, "Weatherization Assistance Program Funding Survey," various years.

fruit of Obama's green jobs plan, or as Energy Secretary Steven Chu liked to say, it was 'fruit on the ground.' It didn't require a college degree or any advanced technology training. It didn't require a new building or breakthrough technology. It simply required a caulking gun."[14] Thus, the conventional wisdom was that WAP was as "shovel ready" as almost any federal program, and especially any program within DOE.[15]

Adding money to WAP was so appealing, in fact, that the Obama team allocated more funding to WAP in the Recovery bill than even many program supporters wanted, according to several interviewees. The fear of some program insiders, who preferred perhaps an additional $2 billion rather than $5 billion from ARRA, was that too large of a funding increase would "put a bull's eye on the back of the program," which it did.

Overall, ARRA appropriated $5 billion to WAP, which was allocated as follows:

- $4.75 billion to state grantees for program operations and materials, training and technical assistance, and administration;
- $0.14 billion for DOE training and technical assistance;
- $0.09 billion for new Sustainable Energy Resources for Consumers grants, which funded local agencies to install solar and other technologies that are not normally supported under WAP; and
- $0.03 billion for DOE management and oversight.[16]

WAP grant monies are distributed to states according to a complicated calculation that includes a "base allocation" and a "formula allocation," which takes into account states' low-income population, climatic conditions, and residential energy expenditures by low-income households. The base allocation, which favors cold-weather states, counts for more when total funding for states is in the range of $170 million or less. The formula allocation, which favors warm-weather states, takes effect when total funding is above $170 million.[17] Because of the way the allocation formula works, warm-weather states, which had relatively smaller WAPs before ARRA, received proportionally greater increases in funding under ARRA than cold-weather states, as shown in table 6.3. For example, when ARRA funding is spread out over three years, annual ARRA funding for Texas was almost twenty times greater than 2008 levels, whereas funding for North Dakota was only two times greater. New York State received the largest allocation of DOE WAP funds in 2008, just before ARRA, and also received the largest allocation under ARRA, almost $400 million to be spent over three years.

In addition to providing WAP with an enormous boost in funding, the Recovery Act also changed several important features of the program. ARRA

Table 6.3. State Allocations from DOE WAP, ARRA versus 2008
(thousands of dollars)

State	2008	ARRA	ARRA vs. 2008	Annualized ARRA vs.2008
Other	410.4	80,439.4	196.0	65.3
Texas	5,549.4	326,975.7	58.9	19.6
Arizona	1,128.8	57,023.3	50.5	16.8
Nevada	831.7	37,281.9	44.8	14.9
Georgia	2,914.6	124,756.3	42.8	14.3
Florida	4,669.4	175,984.5	37.7	12.6
South Carolina	1,780.9	58,892.8	33.1	11.0
North Carolina	4,139.2	131,954.5	31.9	10.6
California	5,870.6	185,811.1	31.7	10.6
Mississippi	1,640.9	49,421.2	30.1	10.0
Alabama	2,396.4	71,800.6	30.0	10.0
Connecticut	2,495.3	64,310.5	25.8	8.6
Virginia	3,998.0	94,134.3	23.5	7.8
New Jersey	5,079.0	118,821.3	23.4	7.8
Arkansas	2,061.0	48,114.4	23.3	7.8
Kansas	2,518.8	56,441.8	22.4	7.5
Missouri	5,975.4	128,148.0	21.4	7.1
Maryland	2,904.4	61,441.7	21.2	7.1
Indiana	6,710.9	131,847.4	19.6	6.5
New York	20,100.0	394,686.5	19.6	6.5
Delaware	731.4	13,733.7	18.8	6.3
Louisiana	2,735.7	50,657.5	18.5	6.2
Massachusetts	6,615.1	122,077.5	18.5	6.2
Utah	2,067.6	37,897.2	18.3	6.1
Ohio	14,626.9	266,781.4	18.2	6.1
Oklahoma	3,399.6	60,903.2	17.9	6.0
Illinois	13,784.5	242,526.6	17.6	5.9
Rhode Island	1,151.0	20,073.6	17.4	5.8
Pennsylvania	14,638.2	252,793.1	17.3	5.8
Nebraska	2,482.4	41,644.5	16.8	5.6
Wisconsin	8,608.5	141,502.1	16.4	5.5
Iowa	4,966.1	80,834.4	16.3	5.4
Michigan	15,118.8	243,399.0	16.1	5.4
New Mexico	1,714.5	26,855.6	15.7	5.2
Kentucky	4,550.3	70,913.8	15.6	5.2
New Hampshire	1,501.8	23,218.6	15.5	5.2
Idaho	1,964.4	30,341.9	15.4	5.1
Colorado	5,454.3	79,531.2	14.6	4.9
Hawaii	282.3	4,041.5	14.3	4.8

Table 6.3. (*cont.*)

State	2008	ARRA	ARRA vs. 2008	Annualized ARRA vs.2008
Oregon	2,808.4	38,512.2	13.7	4.6
Vermont	1,272.1	16,842.6	13.2	4.4
Minnesota	9,989.1	131,937.4	13.2	4.4
Maine	3,235.7	41,935.0	13.0	4.3
Washington	5,033.9	59,545.1	11.8	3.9
Alaska	1,540.1	18,142.6	11.8	3.9
West Virginia	3,196.9	37,583.9	11.8	3.9
Tennessee	8,868.5	99,112.1	11.2	3.7
Montana	2,507.8	26,543.8	10.6	3.5
District of Columbia	836.7	8,089.0	9.7	3.2
Wyoming	1,128.9	10,239.3	9.1	3.0
South Dakota	3,020.1	24,487.3	8.1	2.7
North Dakota	4,500.0	25,266.3	5.6	1.9
Total	237,506.7	4,746,250.2	20.0	6.7

Source: National Association for State Community Services Programs, "Weatherization Assistance Program: Funding Survey PY 2011," 11, 17.

applied the Davis-Bacon Act to weatherization workers for the first time, which meant that these workers had to receive prevailing, county-specific wages and had to be paid weekly, and that local agencies had to submit certified payrolls weekly. There were also new requirements for historic preservation clearance for weatherization projects. Other significant, permanent program changes enacted in ARRA included

- Raising the average maximum amount of WAP funds that could be spent on each weatherized home from $2,966 in 2008 to $6,500 in 2009, with a continuing annual adjustment for inflation;
- Increasing the threshold for income eligibility from 150 percent to 200 percent of the poverty level; and
- Increasing the proportion of program funds that could be spent for national, state, and local training and technical assistance from 10 percent to 20 percent.

In FY 2010 another program, the Weatherization Innovation Pilot Program, which was authorized by the Energy Policy Act of 2005, was funded for the first time by ARRA with an appropriation of $30 million. This pilot program's grantees, which include organizations like Habitat for Humanity and YouthBuild, were using new materials, technologies, and financing mechanisms and were not among the traditional WAP grantees.

Program Effects

The massive new Recovery Act funding for WAP and the programmatic changes that were enacted in ARRA had important effects on the WAP program and the network of organizations that implement WAP. As noted above, the $5 billion in new funding resulted in the weatherization of 800,000 units, which was significantly above the 635,000 target figure for the program. Thus, as shown in table 6.2, production increased by 250 percent, from about 175,000 units weatherized annually before ARRA to 430,000 units annually with ARRA and regular funding.[18]

The weatherization work that was done helped reduce long-term home energy bills and health and safety costs for low-income households. According to studies by DOE's Oak Ridge National Laboratory (ORNL) of WAP's pre-ARRA program, every $1 invested in WAP yielded savings of $4.10 in energy, health, and safety costs. In its evaluation of WAP during ARRA, ORNL found that savings from weatherization were reduced somewhat during ARRA because of higher administrative and program costs stemming from the implementation of Davis-Bacon and other new requirements. However, these savings were still substantial, especially with health and safety benefits taken in account.[19]

One of the major purposes of the Recovery Act was job creation or job protection to maximize employment during the Great Recession. In fact, WAP produced significant numbers of jobs, especially after the program took off after its slow start. WAP was consistently among the top ten federal programs in terms of job production under ARRA, and, in fact, it was ranked the second-highest job producer in the first quarter of 2012, with more than 10,000 new jobs produced.[20]

Network Effects

Beyond these programmatic effects, ARRA also had an important impact on the organizations and individuals involved in implementing WAP. By the late 2000s, a relatively stable network of federal, state, and local organizations had evolved that was engaged in the implementation of WAP. Federal staff members in DOE's Office of Weatherization and Intergovernmental Programs write program rules and regulations, review and approve state program plans, make grant awards, provide training and technical assistance to state and local agencies, monitor state performance, and periodically undertake more comprehensive program evaluations through the ORNL, another agency within DOE.

For their part, state weatherization offices—which are in state housing, community services, human services, or other departments—develop their own program plans, receive federal funding, and in turn award funding to community action and other local agencies, monitor the local providers, and provide training and technical assistance to local agencies and their weatherization workers. Community action and other local agencies on the ground receive funding from the state, hire weatherization workers in house or through subcontracting, buy weatherization materials, recruit households to apply for the program, review and approve applications, conduct pre-audits on homes to determine what weatherization measures to implement, complete the weatherization work, and conduct inspections after the work is finished. Businesses that provide goods and services to support weatherization are also loose members of the WAP network.

In addition to DOE staff members, state administrators, and local agency workers, several Washington-based organizations also play important roles in the WAP network. The National Association of State Community Service Programs (NASCSP), a membership association of state administrators involved with the community services and weatherization programs, educates state officials about WAP and convenes federal, state, and local WAP officials to exchange information. NASCSP also hosts an online reference library of program rules, regulations, policies, and procedures.[21] The National Community Action Foundation is a major Washington lobbyist for programs like WAP that are operated by community action agencies for the benefit of low-income families and individuals. Economic Opportunity Studies is a Washington-based research and training organization that supports the work of community action agencies and the people they serve. With respect to WAP, Economic Opportunity Studies provides technical assistance to local agencies to develop private partnerships, especially utility partnerships, and hosts the WeatherizationPLUS online reference library of "tools." The Community Action Partnership, a membership association of 1,100 community action agencies across the United States, has a limited role vis-à-vis WAP.

Networkwide Effects

ARRA had some across-the-board effects on the WAP network. In the first place, with pressure to produce hundreds of thousands of new weatherized units in a relatively short amount of time and with heightened oversight from skeptical politicians and journalists, ARRA put significant stress on all the organizations and individuals in the WAP network.[22] The DOE inspector general (IG) concluded that "the federal, state, and local government infrastructures were, simply put, overwhelmed" and that, "pushing this much money through the weatherization program [was] akin to hooking up a garden hose to a fire hydrant."[23] In fact, one interviewee suggested that the added stress resulted in an increased number of government staff retiring on disability during the period of ARRA.

Some of the pressure was eventually relieved by the hiring of new staff at all levels, especially by local agencies. But the new hiring itself had consequences. With the acquisition of new staff and the promotion of old staff to new positions, previous working relationships were disrupted, which slowed program operations. Moreover, many new staff did not know WAP very well, although ARRA-supported training helped them learn what they needed to know. ARRA also required that individuals at different levels interact more frequently in monitoring and other activities, and this helped to tighten the network and overcome some of the problems resulting from the newness of many network members.

Increased requirements for monitoring—including greater federal oversight of state grantees and greater state oversight of local agencies—were an important feature of ARRA. The expanded oversight activity elicited many comments from case study interviewees and is the focus of the discussion of network effects that follows.

FEDERAL STAFF

At the federal level, federal project and contract officers in the WAP office in DOE significantly increased their monitoring of state activities through desk reviews of reports, phone calls, and in-person visits. Each federal program officer had responsibility for overseeing one to three states. The WAP office also hired a contractor to conduct independent inspections of weatherized homes, an activity previously left to state and local agencies. Although some state officials appreciated the need for increased federal oversight, others grumbled that federal staff were "intrusive" and "micromanaging," and that it was very time consuming for states to meet the needs of federal monitors. "If they would only leave us alone, we could actually get some work done," was one overburdened state official's suggestion.

In addition to DOE program staff undertaking increased oversight under ARRA, the DOE IG and the Government Accountability Office (GAO) were also much more active monitors under ARRA, with the IG especially issuing several harsh critiques of the WAP program. Even with the increased federal monitoring under ARRA, there was still a widely shared feeling among program observers that this oversight was inadequate and needed to be improved. According to at least some of these observers, federal staff paid more attention to getting production numbers up than to ensuring that the work was of high quality.

STATE AGENCIES

States also had to ramp up their staff to manage the much-expanded WAP program. New staff had to be hired, and new procedures had to be put in place. Important among state achievements was the establishment of more state-based training centers (although a couple of interviewees wondered whether too many training centers had been created with ARRA funding). States also increased their monitoring of local agencies. States expanded their program, financial, and production reviews through more document analyses, phone calls, and visits with local agency staff. States had already been required to independently inspect 5 percent of weatherized units, and many increased their inspections under ARRA.

Much as state officials complained about federal oversight, local staff resented some of the state monitoring.[24] In fact, some state staff who had experience with other types of government programs besides WAP expressed a feeling that the monitoring of local agencies in WAP was much more intrusive and paternalistic than monitoring of locals in many other programs. Overall, state officials reported experiencing many more challenges earlier in ARRA than later. According to a GAO survey, a majority of state recipients indicated that in the first year of ARRA, they were strongly or somewhat challenged in twenty-six of twenty-nine program implementation areas that the GAO survey asked about. By the third year of ARRA, a majority of state recipients reported being strongly or somewhat challenged in only thirteen of twenty-nine areas. "Implementing Davis-Bacon requirements" was among the challenges that declined the most for state officials during ARRA.[25]

However, some challenges persisted throughout ARRA. Even in the third year of ARRA, 75 percent of state recipients reported that they were still strongly or somewhat challenged by "having additional federal reporting requirements." Also in the third year, 48 percent of state respondents indicated that "adjusting to changes in existing reporting requirements for monitoring" remained a challenge. And finally, 63 percent of recipients reported that "balancing training and technical assistance requirements with production targets" was a challenge, even at the end of ARRA.[26]

LOCAL AGENCIES

More than nine hundred nonprofit and public agencies are involved in implementing WAP at the local level. Most of the local agencies are community action agencies, including both nonprofit and public entities, whereas others are local units of government or other kinds of nonprofits. They vary in size and scope of activities, with many local agencies overseeing a wide range of programs, while some focus exclusively on WAP.

States relied on existing local agencies to implement ARRA, and these agencies—like their federal and state network colleagues—faced significant pressure to ramp up their operations quickly to meet production targets. To do the weatherization and inspection, local agencies either hired new staff in house or subcontracted with outside contractors. Although there are no hard data, interviewees suggested that local agencies turned more to outside hires during ARRA because they knew the new positions would be temporary and by subcontracting they could avoid having to lay off in-house staff when ARRA monies ran out.

With the high number of unemployed workers around the country, identifying new hires was not difficult for many local agencies, although, as one interviewee noted, it was easier to find a carpenter than a skilled technician who would be able to do the more sophisticated pre- and post-weatherization inspections. In any case, once hired, new weatherization workers went through expanded and improved training programs to ensure they had the necessary skills. However, as one local agency director emphasized, "Workers could not be in two places at once," and so striking a balance between time for training and time for production was a challenge for local agencies.

Implementing Davis-Bacon rules for paying workers was another challenge for many local agencies, especially small ones. Because different rules applied to ARRA-funded and non-ARRA-funded weatherization activities, local agencies had to maintain separate processes for two programs, which was an added burden that imposed increased costs on the agencies.

Challenges for WAP under ARRA

The written record about WAP under ARRA as well as the interviews for this chapter point to two major problems that afflicted the program: the slowness with which production activity began and concerns about the quality of the weatherization work that was done.

Slow Takeoff

The DOE inspector general has noted that when the 2009 Recovery Act was being formulated, the conventional wisdom was that WAP was "about as close to meeting the definition of 'shovel ready' as virtually any program in the Department's portfolio." WAP boasted an existing programmatic infrastructure; relied on well-known and relatively uncomplicated technologies to do its work; had established, relatively easy-to-use performance metrics; and had clear benefits for low-income individuals and energy usage. There seemed to be a high probability that the $5 billion allocated to WAP would have a quick, positive—if somewhat modest—impact on job creation and the economy.[27]

However, as the DOE IG went on to report, the hoped-for results proved much more difficult to achieve than originally envisioned:

> The results of our review confirmed that as straightforward as the program may have seemed, and despite the best efforts of the Department, any program with so many moving parts was extraordinarily difficult to synchronize. In this case, program execution depended on the ability of the Federal government (multiple agencies, in fact), state government, grant subrecipients and weatherization contractors, working within the existing Federal and state regulatory guidelines, to respond to a rapid and overwhelming increase in funding. Further, the anticipated stimulus impact was affected by certain events and conditions clearly outside of Departmental control including state budget difficulties; availability of trained and experienced program staff; and, meaningful changes in regulatory requirements.[28]

In congressional testimony regarding DOE's experience with the Recovery Act generally, the IG concluded, "In reality, few actual 'shovel ready' projects existed. The department programs which benefited from the huge influx of Recovery Act funds, as it turned out, required extensive advance planning, organizational enhancements, and additional staffing and training."[29]

Two major causes of the slow program takeoff were the new imposition of the Davis-Bacon rules and the budget difficulties of many states. As described above, Davis-Bacon required, for the first time, the payment of prevailing, county-specific wages to weatherization workers. The hitch was that the necessary wage guidelines did not exist at the time the Recovery Act was passed, and the program had to wait from the February 2009 passage of ARRA until September 2009 for the US Department of Labor to issue the necessary guidance. On the positive side, even though the WAP wage-determination process took six to seven months, this was actually about half the time it normally took. However, perhaps because the process was rushed, the Department of Labor had to issue corrected guidance in December 2009.

Table 6.4. Number of Units Weatherized as of February 6, 2010, as a Percentage of Total Units Planned for Weatherization under ARRA

State	Percent Weatherized
Delaware	34.01
Mississippi	26.92
Ohio	21.17
West Virginia	18.47
Idaho	17.70
Vermont	17.37
Utah	16.09
Virginia	14.77
Washington	14.04
Tennessee	13.59
New Hampshire	13.38
Colorado	13.07
Maine	12.65
North Dakota	12.30
Arkansas	11.20
Montana	9.85
Minnesota	8.44
Massachusetts	7.74
Oklahoma	7.37
Alabama	7.17
Arizona	5.60
New Mexico	5.56
Iowa	5.14
Missouri	5.06
Indiana	4.94
Kentucky	4.75
Nebraska	4.75
Kansas	4.59
Georgia	4.56
South Carolina	4.40
Oregon	4.12
Maryland	4.07
Wisconsin	3.73
South Dakota	2.28
Louisiana	2.02
Florida	1.63
Nevada	1.52
Pennsylvania	1.28
Illinois	1.23

Table 6.4. (*cont.*)

State	Percent Weatherized
Michigan	1.15
North Carolina	0.89
New York	0.62
New Jersey	0.41
Connecticut	0.31
California	0.03
Alaska	0.00
District of Columbia	0.00
Hawaii	0.00
Rhode Island	0.00
Texas	0.00
Wyoming	0.00
Other	0.00
Total	5.17

Source: Office of the Inspector General, US Department of Energy, "Special Report: Progress in Implementing the Department of Energy's Weatherization Assistance Program under the American Recovery and Reinvestment Act," February 2010, appendix II.

In any case, until the Davis-Bacon guidance was in place, little ARRA-funded weatherization work was done. It was not until fall 2009, six months after the passage of the Recovery Act's supposed quick jolt of job creation, that weatherization work began in earnest.

An additional reason for the slowness in implementation was the lack of staff capacity, especially at the state level. Because of their recession-related loss of revenues, many states—including, for example, California, Illinois, New York, and Pennsylvania—were trying to keep spending down through furloughs and/or hiring freezes. Finding a way around these constraints to hire new state staff to manage WAP took time, and this slowed the program down in many states. Nationally, one year after the passage of ARRA only 5 percent of the ARRA target of 600,000 units had been weatherized, as shown in table 6.4.[30]

Quality Concerns

Although program production did eventually pick up, the other major challenge for WAP under ARRA—dealing with charges of poor quality work—proved more difficult to address. To be sure, there were undoubtedly some instances of inferior work being done, as is the case with any major undertaking, whether organized by the government, business, or nonprofit sector. Perhaps not surprisingly, the multitude of program inspectors and auditors at the local, state, and federal levels who were tasked with reviewing the work that was done by WAP under ARRA were able to identify numerous deficiencies. As one state weatherization official put it, "I've had several of our state monitors tell me that if they want to find something wrong at a job site, they always can. Always—every unit completed. That doesn't mean those units aren't safe and aren't saving energy."

In any case, reports about program problems were eagerly picked up by the army of journalists writing about the rollout of the Recovery Act who seemed especially interested, as journalists typically are, in focusing on what was not working.[31] For example, reports by the DOE IG that poor-quality weatherization work in Illinois had resulted in gas and carbon monoxide leaks received extensive coverage, although several interviewees suggested that the IG's criticisms were overblown.[32] Even television's generally progressive *Daily Show with Jon Stewart* poked fun at WAP and its problems.[33]

Stories about poor-quality work were also fodder for Republican opponents of the Obama administration ready to find fault with a major presidential initiative. A strongly worded report from the House Committee on Oversight and Government Reform, chaired by California Republican Darrell Issa, recited many of the most worrisome claims about low-quality work. For example, the House report observed that "with some states exhibiting a failure rate [of] 80 percent (12 out of every 15 homes fail inspection) due to substandard workmanship, this program is far from being a shining example of what the government can do for its citizens."[34]

On the other side, program supporters tried to counter the negative publicity with more positive information about program performance. For example, while the House Oversight Committee report and the DOE IG highlighted program deficiencies, DOE secretary Chu testified that there were problems in only 3 or 4 percent of weatherization projects.[35] Along the same lines, NASCSP claimed that only 3,500 of 400,000—or less than 1 percent of projects—had significant problems.

With so much money at stake, some disagreement about program quality between program supporters and program skeptics may be inevitable. However, also underlying the difference in opinions about the quality of work done under WAP is the lack of accepted standards for the program. The numerous inspectors and auditors reviewing program performance—who come from both within and outside WAP—use different evaluation approaches and benchmarks. Unfortunately, it is not clear from their reports whether problems are major and commonplace, major and rare, minor and commonplace, or minor and rare. Improving the quality assessment system would seem to be a good first step in getting more accurate information about program quality, which program managers could then draw on to improve program performance where it is subpar.

As for the faulty work that was sometimes done, program experts and stakeholders suggested a variety of explanations for the problems. Some of the weatherization work was technical and complicated and required appropriate training and/or experience to be completed properly. Unfortunately, not all the weatherization workers were well qualified or trained. There was a big push for increased training under ARRA, but with the strong push for increased production that was also being made there was a trade-off in taking time to put workers through training. Finally, with many local agencies looking to employ the hard-to-employ and having the capacity to pay only modest wages, WAP did not always have the highest-skilled workers in weatherization jobs, although agencies did pay higher, Davis-Bacon wages with ARRA funds.

An additional reason for some of the quality problems is that the local agencies doing the weatherization work are the ones that have the main responsibility for inspecting the units after the work is completed. A critical question is whether inspectors working for or hired by local agencies have the necessary independence to conduct high-quality inspections. Of course, weatherizing should be done right the first time. But perhaps the next best option is to have local inspectors catch—and fix—problems before jobs are reported as complete to the state and federal government.

Conclusion: WAP after ARRA

The Weatherization Assistance Program engages a far-flung network of organizations and individuals from the federal government through state governments to local agencies on the ground in communities around the country. Under ARRA, WAP had some significant successes, weatherizing 800,000 homes, saving millions in energy costs, and putting thousands to work. However, the program's important accomplishments were unfortunately diminished by concerns about the slowness of production and the quality of the work that was done. Justified or not, WAP faced withering criticism through much of the ARRA period.

In the face of the wilting disparagement of WAP, at least one interviewee suggested that the program needed something "bold and dramatic," "a game changer," and that program supporters needed to "rethink everything" in order to change perceptions of the program. Whether the WAP network can find a game changer remains to be seen. However, program supporters have already had some successes, with program funding rebounding from a low of $68 million in FY 2012 to $132 million in FY 2013, $174 million in FY 2014, and $193 million in FY 2015. Moreover, the program's supporters are pursuing several strategies to improve its quality.

Addressing Quality Concerns

For WAP, a critical question is how federal staff in Washington can "change the story about quality," as one interviewee put it, and ensure that local weatherization agencies around the country are delivering high-quality services. A good early step would be to get a better-quality assessment system in place for WAP.

Currently in the WAP program, initial inspections are completed by local agencies using in-house or outside inspectors. Some argue that inspectors are not sufficiently independent in the current system, especially when in-house local agency inspectors review work done by in-house local agency work crews. One possible fix is to require local agencies to hire more independent inspectors or increase the role of federal and state officials in the inspection process, although new costs would be an issue under the latter option.

Besides getting better information about program quality, program managers will, of course, want to improve program quality where they can. ARRA provided for increased and improved training for local weatherization workers, and this seemed to help performance quality to some degree. Another approach to improving program outcomes is to inject more competition into WAP's delivery system. Thus, instead of routinely funding the same local subgrantees year after year, federal and state agencies could require that local organizations compete for WAP funding. In fact, some states have already moved down this path.

Although moving to a competitive process should be considered and might bring some benefits, it could also be disruptive to the program, especially in the short term. If WAP funding is channeled to a new local agency, it is not clear whether and how quickly other weatherization funding streams, such as funding from utility companies, will follow.[36] Moreover, even with a more competitive selection process for local subgrantees, federal and state agencies would likely still have to increase their inspection and monitoring activities to ensure that subgrantees are doing high-quality work. Finally, a selection process that emphasizes subgrantees' efficiency may fail to appreciate other values, such as the ability of subgrantees to employ hard-to-employ workers, serve hard-to-serve clients, or help to develop new community leaders, which have been some of the strengths of the community action agencies that now make up by far the largest number of subgrantees.

Taking into Account the Paradox of Nonprofit Performance

More generally, as program managers and policymakers push for higher-quality performance, they should guard against having too narrow a definition of "performance" that focuses too heavily on the quality of the weatherization work that is done and fails to take sufficiently into account other important aspects of performance, such as reaching particular target client populations and employing certain kinds of workers to do the weatherization work.

Ideally perhaps, local program providers will be able to do high-quality weatherization work for needy, hard-to-reach clients by employing hard-to-employ workers. In reality, however, legitimate trade-offs may need to be made among these values. Although moving to raise performance in WAP may make great sense and local agencies certainly want to avoid doing shoddy work that puts clients at significant risk, federal officials and other stakeholders should be mindful about the costs of pushing too hard on narrow measures of performance.

Tapping New Sources of Funding

An additional strategy for federal officials and others in the WAP network in the post-ARRA period is to look for ways to expand support for the program and find new sources of government funding. A 2012 White House conference on WAP highlighted how the program energizes a whole "supply chain" that goes beyond the federal, state, and local agencies in the current WAP network to also include businesses that supply equipment and material to weatherization activities.[37] Thus far, representatives from the supply chain have not been very active in advocating for the program, and program supporters believe their more active involvement might help secure more funding for WAP.

Program supporters are also looking to leverage new and different sources of funding besides WAP, LIHEAP, and funding from utilities. A growing number of federal and state Healthy Homes Initiatives—which provide support for lead abatement, asthma prevention, pest control, and similar measures—are one possible new funding source for weatherization programs.[38] Many would also like to increase utility funding for weatherization. Another option is to provide loans for weatherization that could be repaid from energy bill savings.

Serving New Markets

Federal and other network members also talk about the possibility that local nonprofit agencies could serve a middle-income weatherization market, perhaps by setting up for-profit subsidiaries that would rely on fees for service rather than federal funding. Although there is hope for a broader market for weatherization, it is not clear how much demand currently exists for weatherization. When the economy was down, households did not have significant financial resources to spend on optional home improvements like weatherization, even if the energy conservation measures would save them money in the longer run. The price of home fuel will help to determine the size of the market for weatherization. If prices rise significantly, then more demand may materialize. Tax breaks for improving household energy efficiency also help to expand interest in weatherization. However, it is not clear that community action agencies, which are experienced at working with low-income clients, are well suited to serve a middle-class market. Another possible source of earned revenue is state-run training centers, which could provide more fee-based training for weatherization workers not involved in WAP.[39]

Program supporters will employ these and other strategies in the years ahead as they seek to improve WAP and develop a more compelling case for the program. WAP's prospects may be enhanced because of the contribution it can make to reducing energy consumption in a time of concern about global warming. However, the program will also likely face continuing challenges because of broad constraints on government funding, the modest political strength of its supporters, and lingering concerns about the quality of the weatherization work completed with WAP funding.

Notes

1. One program expert estimated that about 75 percent of the community action agencies involved in WAP are private, nonprofit organizations and about 25 percent are public agencies. See also National Association for State Community Services Programs (NASCSP), *Community Services Block Grant: Annual Report 2010* (Washington, DC: NASCSP, 2011), 6.

2. Program experts estimate that roughly half the weatherization work is done by local agencies with in-house crews and half with outside contractors, although more work was contracted out under the 2009 Recovery Act.

3. DOE eventually permitted states, on a case-by-case basis, to extend their ARRA spending for up to eighteen months beyond March 30, 2012, to September 30, 2103.

4. Several interviewees also provided very helpful, detailed comments on a draft of this chapter.

5. On state climate zones, see Bruce Tonn, Erin Rose, and Beth Hawkins, "National Weatherization Assistance Program Characterization Describing the Recovery Act Period," Oak Ridge National Laboratory, ORNL/TM-2015/195, 2015, 6. On state urban/rural populations, see US Bureau of the Census, *2010 Census of the Population*, "Urban and Rural Population by State, 2010," www.census.gov/geo/www/ua /2010urbanruralclass.html. On state per capita spending on WAP, see Richard W.

Caperton, Adam Jones, and Matt Kasper, "Federal Weatherization Program a Winner on All Counts," Center for American Progress, September 28, 2012. On state regions, see US Bureau of the Census, "Census Regions and Divisions of the United States." On state populations, see US Bureau of the Census, *2014 Population Estimates*, "American FactFinder: Annual Estimates of the Resident Population, April 1, 2010, to July 1, 2014," http://factfinder.census.gov/faces/tableservices/jsf/pages/productview.xhtml ?src=bkmk. On state poverty rates, see Thomas Gabe, "Poverty in the United States: 2013," Congressional Research Service, January 2015, 17. On state political leanings, see Jeffrey M. Jones. "Massachusetts, Maryland Most Democratic States," Gallup, February 4, 2015.

6. National Association for State Community Services Programs, "Weatherization Assistance Program: Funding Survey PY 2014," 3, www.nascsp.org/data/files /weatherization/publications/nascsp2014_wap_funding_survey_final062015 _print508.pdf.

7. Recovery.gov, "Jobs Summary: National," www.recovery.gov/Pages/TextView .aspx?data=jobSummaryProgram&topnumber=200&qtr=2012Q1.

8. Richard Saul, "The Beginnings of Weatherization," n.d., 5–6, Richard Saul Papers, Edmund Muskie Archives, Bates College.

9. Ibid., 10.

10. DOE, "History of the Weatherization Program," www1.eere.energy.gov/wip /wap_history.html.

11. Ibid.

12. Ibid.

13. The Regional Greenhouse Gas Initiative is a program of nine Northeast states to reduce greenhouse gas emissions in the United States. As part of the initiative, carbon dioxide (CO_2) emission allowances are auctioned off, with some of the proceeds devoted to weatherization activities. See RGGI Inc., "Investment of Proceeds from RGGI CO_2 Allowances," February 2011, www.rggi.org/docs/Investment_of _RGGI_Allowance_Proceeds.pdf. Information on funding for weatherization activities is available from National Association for State Community Services Programs, "Weatherization Assistance Program: Funding Survey," various years, http://waptac .org/WAP-Basics/Funding-Survey.aspx. While federal budget figures are generally presented on a federal fiscal year (FY) basis, NASCSP collects WAP spending data on a program year (PY) basis. The federal FY runs from October 1 through September 30 and takes the name of the year in which it ends. Thus, FY 2015 ran from October 1, 2014, to September 30, 2015. The PY for most state WAP programs runs from April 1 through March 31 and takes the name of the year in which it begins. Thus, PY 2015 ran from April 1, 2015, to March 31, 2016.

14. Michael Grabell, *Money Well Spent? The Truth Behind the Trillion-Dollar Stimulus, the Biggest Economic Recovery Plan in History* (New York: PublicAffairs, 2012), 122.

15. Fred Sissine, "DOE Weatherization Program: A Review of Funding, Performance, and Cost-Effectiveness Studies," Congressional Research Service, January 11, 2012, 9.

16. US Government Accountability Office, *Recovery Act: Progress and Challenges in Spending Weatherization Funds* (Washington, DC: Government Accountability Office, 2011), 9.

17. DOE, "Weatherization Assistance Program Allocation Formula," http:// energy.gov/eere/wipo/weatherization-assistance-program-allocation-formula.

18. National Association for State Community Services Programs, "Weatherization Assistance Program: Funding Survey," various years.

19. US Department of Energy, Energy Efficiency and Renewable Energy, Office of Weatherization and Intergovernmental Programs, "Weatherization Assistance Program: National Evaluations—Summary of Results," http://weatherization.ornl .gov/WAP_NationalEvaluation_WxWorks_v14_blue_8%205%2015.pdf. A 2015 study by economists at the University of California, Berkeley, and the University of Chicago found significantly lower savings than ORNL from weatherization through WAP. See Meredith Fowlie, Michael Greenstone, and Catherine Wolfram, "Do Energy Efficiency Investments Deliver? Evidence from the Weatherization Assistance Program," E2e Working Paper 020, June 2015, http://e2e.haas.berkeley.edu/pdf /workingpapers/WP020.pdf#page=1. However, while the study by Fowlie et al. received significant media coverage, critics of the study, including many WAP program supporters, downplay its differences with the ORNL estimates because of the former study's limited sampling frame, its exclusion of health and safety benefits, and several other factors. See Kathleen Hogan, "Getting It Right: Weatherization and Energy Efficiency Are Good Investments," US Department of Energy, Office of Energy Efficiency and Renewable Energy, August 2015, www.energy.gov/eere/articles /getting-it-right-weatherization-and-energy-efficiency-are-good-investments.

20. Recovery.gov, "Jobs Summary—National, Top Programs as Reported by Recipients," www.recovery.gov/Transparency/RecipientReportedData/Pages/Job Summary.aspx.

21. See the website of the Weatherization Assistance Program's Technical Assistance Center, www.waptac.org.

22. Bruce Tonn, Erin Rose, and Beth Hawkins, "National Weatherization Assistance Program Characterization Describing the Recovery Act Period," Oak Ridge National Laboratory, ORNL/TM-2015/195, March 2015, 7.

23. Gregory H. Friedman (DOE inspector general), "Testimony before the US House of Representatives, Committee on Oversight and Government Reform, Subcommittee on Regulatory Affairs, Stimulus Oversight, and Government Spending," November 2, 2011, 6; US House of Representatives, Committee on Oversight and Government Reform, "The Department of Energy's Weatherization Program: Taxpayer Money Spent, Taxpayer Money Lost," staff report, March 20, 2012, 3.

24. Tonn, Rose, and Hawkins, "National Weatherization Assistance Program," 7.

25. US Government Accountability Office, "Recovery Act," 19–22.

26. Ibid., 22–24.

27. DOE IG, "Progress in Implementing the Department of Energy's Weatherization Assistance Program under the American Recovery and Reinvestment Act," February 2010, 4–5.

28. Ibid., 5.

29. Friedman, "Testimony," 2.

30. DOE IG, "Progress," appendix II.

31. For a sample of newspaper articles about WAP under ARRA, see James Drew, "State Slow to Spend Stimulus Funds to Weatherize Homes," *Dallas News*, December 20, 2009; Tom Infield, "Stimulus Funds Finally Flowing to Weatherization," *Philadelphia Inquirer*, November 22, 2009; Kate Linthicum, "State's Slow Start Puts Federal Stimulus Funds at Risk, Audit Finds," *Los Angeles Times*, July 12, 2011; Mark Lisheron, "Shoddy Workmanship Found in $22 Million Federal Stimulus Contract to Improve

the Homes of the Poor," *Texas Watchdog*, May 31, 2010; Carolyn Lochhead, "Energy Stimulus Program Plagued by Problems," *SFGate*, November 3, 2011; Louis Radnofsky, "Audit Faults Stimulus-Funded Weatherization Program in West Virginia," *Wall Street Journal*, June 16, 2011; Saqib Rahim, "Beseiged DOE Weatherization Program Faces Republican Attack," *New York Times*, September 9, 2011; Christine Vestal, "Weatherization Program Ramps Up after Slow Start," *Stateline*, June 8, 2010; Matthew L. Wald and Leslie Kaufman, "Hiring Freezes Hamper Weatherization Plan," *New York Times*, February 24, 2010

32. DOE IG, "Audit Report: Management Alert on the Department's Monitoring of the Weatherization Assistance Program in the State of Illinois," December 2009; DOE IG, "Audit Report: The State of Illinois Weatherization Assistance Program," October 2010.

33. *Daily Show with Jon Stewart*, October 24, 2011, www.thedailyshow.com/watch/mon-october-24-2011/weather-blunderground. One interviewee suggested that the show had mistakenly identified a program in Seattle as a WAP project even though it was not.

34. US House of Representatives, Committee on Oversight and Government Reform, "Department of Energy's Weatherization Program," 3.

35. US House of Representatives, Committee on Oversight and Government Reform, "Oversight of the Department of Energy's Stimulus Spending," Hearing, serial no. 112-136, March 20, 2012, 18–19, http://oversight.house.gov/wp-content/uploads/2012/09/2012-03-20-Ser.-No.-112-136-FC-Oversight-of-the-Department-of-Energys-Stimuls-Spending.pdf.

36. The ORNL's recent evaluation of WAP during ARRA makes the point that much of the non-WAP funding that is leveraged for weatherization flows directly to local subgrantees. See Tonn, Rose, and Hawkins, "National Weatherization Assistance Program," 15. Changing subgrantees might disrupt this flow.

37. On the June 15, 2012, White House discussion on the weatherization supply chain, see www.youtube.com/watch?v=GU_FZc-lMow and www.youtube.com/watch?v=8CP0iftuJ6M.

38. See the NASCSP's resources on Healthy Homes Initiatives, www.nascsp.org/Healthy-Homes.aspx.

39. Unfortunately, a recent study reported that many training centers are experiencing financial difficulty and believe it will be difficult to recruit new trainees. See Bruce Tonn, David Carroll, Erin Rose, Beth Hawkins, Scott Pigg, Daniel Bausch, Greg Dalhoff, Michael Blasnik, Joel Eisenberg, Claire Cowan, and Brian Conlon, "Weatherization Works II: Summary of Findings from the ARRA Period Evaluation of the US Department of Energy's Weatherization Assistance Program," Oak Ridge National Laboratory, ORNL/TM-2015/139, 44. As noted above in the text, several interviewees suggested that ARRA's funding may have created a surplus of training centers, so a thinning of these centers may have been preordained.

7

A Bump in the Road

THE BENEFITS OF ESTABLISHED NETWORKS FOR IMPLEMENTING ARRA UNDER THE NEW MARKETS TAX CREDIT PROGRAM

Lehn M. Benjamin

IN 2009 the New Markets Tax Credit (NMTC) Program, housed within the Department of the Treasury's Community Development Financial Institutions (CDFI) Fund, received $3 billion in additional tax credit authority as a part of the American Recovery and Reinvestment Act (the Recovery Act, or ARRA). By all accounts, ARRA's implementation by the CDFI Fund was uneventful. Federal managers worked diligently to allocate the additional tax credit authority to the community development entities (CDEs) eligible to receive tax credit allocations under the program, and these CDEs in turn worked to secure investments and finance a range of infrastructure projects. An additional fifty-six CDEs received an allocation, and though the exact job figures are unknown, for the reasons discussed below, some estimates suggest the ARRA funds helped support the creation of 500,000 jobs through the NMTC Program.[1] The question explored in this chapter is, Why? Why did the NMTC Program not experience any hiccups as federal managers implemented one of the largest federal policy initiatives under a tight timeline and intense scrutiny?

In contrast to the preceding chapters, the ARRA program examined here employed tax credits rather than grants. It is thus helpful in this chapter to provide more background on how tax credits work, as this is a policy tool that is less familiar to many readers. The chapter's focus remains the same as that of the earlier chapters, however; it examines ARRA's impact on the CDFI Fund's NMTC Program and the network of for-profit and nonprofit organizations on which the CDFI Fund relied to realize the program's policy objectives. While not downplaying the effectiveness of federal managers in allocating the additional tax credits, the case shows how diverse and established networks, along with minimal accountability requirements for tax tools under

ARRA, eased the implementation of ARRA under the NMTC Program. As will be seen below, the NMTC Program is a particularly useful case for understanding the differences between policy tools because many of the staff members who ran the NMTC Program also administered the grant programs managed by the CDFI Fund. The grant program had a similar purpose and involved some of the same third parties, so both the federal managers and the third parties could observe the differences between implementing the tax program and the grant program.

The findings presented here rely on organizational documents, research reports, and more than thirty interviews. The interviews were conducted with federal managers, NMTC investors, and staff members of CDEs who received the tax credit allocations and were located in one of three states: California, Minnesota, or Virginia. These states were selected to mirror to some extent the state selection in other cases for this project, with the intent of identifying any significant state patterns across cases.[2] There was no compelling reason to choose one state over another for the NMTC program because the states were not involved in administering the credit and many of the CDEs that received the credit operate in a multistate or national service area. CDEs within these states were selected to ensure that they included different markets—local, state, regional, and national—and were the subsidiaries of nonprofit, for-profit, and public agencies. These distinctions proved meaningful for understanding the program but will not be discussed here, given space constraints.

The chapter proceeds by giving an overview of the NMTC Program, how it is administered, how the credit works and how the program has evolved over time. As noted above, the credit is complex and this background is necessary to understand the impact of ARRA on the NMTC Program in the following section. After describing this impact, the next two sections examine the primary reasons the implementation of ARRA by the NMTC Program proved to be a bump in the road for federal managers rather than a major challenge: differential accountability requirements for the tax tool and established third-party networks. The chapter concludes by considering the implications for federal officials of using the tax tool, as well as the networks this tool assumes, to achieve policy objectives.

Background and Evolution of the New Markets Tax Credit Program

When the NMTC Program was enacted, as a part of the Community Renewal Tax Relief Act, then president Bill Clinton and the National Economic Council wanted to ensure that all Americans benefited from the booming economy. They wanted to bring private equity into economically distressed communities and level the playing field for investors between investing in high-income and low-income census tracks. The latter were often viewed as more costly because of zoning regulations, fewer business partnerships, the need to assemble parcels, and less-established hiring networks for employees. At the same time, as one former federal official explained, the administration wanted to create a tax credit that did not distort the market, subsidize uncompetitive business ideas, or undermine charitable giving but was significant enough for investors to sit up and take notice.

The NMTC Program was designed as a flexible program that has enjoyed bipartisan support, and in 2008 and again in 2011 the program was named one of the top twenty-five programs for the "Innovations in American Government Award" from the John F. Kennedy School of Government at Harvard University. To achieve the goal of encouraging private equity investment in low-income communities, the NMTC provides a 39 percent credit against federal tax liability for investors who make equity investments in certified CDEs.[3] These CDEs in turn provide favorable financing for projects located in low-income areas. Projects supported by the NMTC have included charter schools, health care facilities, grocery stores, historic theaters, manufacturing facilities, and training centers.[4] Demand for the credit has exceeded availability by 7 to 1 on average since the start of the program, and as of June 2015, $43.6 billion in tax credits have been allocated.[5]

The NMTC Program is jointly administered by the CDFI Fund and the Internal Revenue Service (IRS). The CDFI Fund is responsible for implementing the program, and the IRS is responsible for writing the rules for eligible uses of funds and ensuring compliance for the use of those funds.[6] The CDFI Fund awards the tax credit allocations on a competitive basis to CDEs. A CDE is a domestic corporation or partnership that is an intermediary vehicle for the provision of loans, investments, or technical assistance in low-income communities.[7] CDEs may be nonprofit or for-profit organizations, but they must have a primary mission of community development and be accountable to their target service area. Once organizations are certified as a CDE by the CDFI Fund, they submit an application to the CDFI Fund for a tax credit allocation. CDEs selected to receive an allocation of tax credits, "allocatees," must sign an allocation agreement with the CDFI Fund.

Once the CDE is awarded a tax credit allocation—typical allocation awards range between $20 and $80 million—the CDE has five years to issue the tax credits (i.e., qualified equity investments, QEIs) to investors and one year from the date of QEI issue to use substantially all the investor proceeds to make qualified low-income community investments (QLICIs). QLICIs include (1) making a loan or investment in a qualified active low-income business

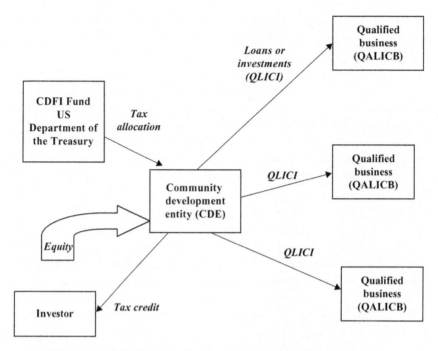

Figure 7.1. The Basic Structure of the NMTC Program
Source: Office of the Comptroller of the Currency, "Community Development Insights," February 2007.

(QALICB), which is a business that primarily operates in a census tract with at least a 20 percent poverty rate or 80 percent median family income or primarily serves targeted populations; (2) providing technical assistance to the QALICB; (3) investing in other CDEs; and (4) purchasing qualified loans from other CDEs.

To receive the equity investment, nonprofit CDEs must set up a for-profit sub-CDE, and typically all CDE allocatees set up several sub-CDEs for each project to manage risk.[8] Figure 7.1 shows how the program works.

Investors purchasing the credit receive 39 percent over seven years—5 percent of the total amount of QEI in each of the first three years and 6 percent in each of the final four years. Investors receive 39 cents of credit per $1 of investment. Investors risk recapture of the tax credit by the IRS if:

1. The CDE fails to deploy substantially all (85 percent) of its investment and fails to have this invested over the course of the seven years (e.g., if the business repays some of the QLICI and the CDE fails to redeploy these funds to another QALICB within one year);

2. The CDE fails to remain a CDE (in other words, it no longer has a primary mission of community development or is no longer accountable to its target service area); or

3. The qualified, active low-income business fails to remain a qualified, active low-income business.

Several early developments shaped the implementation of the NMTC Program.[9] Federal managers at the CDFI Fund took steps in the program's first couple of years to maximize the impact of the credit by using evaluation criteria that gave points to applicants that committed to investing in more severely distressed communities and to providing more favorable terms and rates on their business investments. Both these program changes went above and beyond what was required in the regulations. But one of the most significant developments was the IRS ruling that cleared the way for CDEs to use what became known as the "leveraged structure." In 2003, responding to questions from third parties trying to use the credit, the IRS issued a ruling that provided guidance on how an intermediary structure could be set up to receive equity from investors as well as debt from other sources and then the entire pool could be invested in a CDE.[10] This leveraged structure allowed the tax credits on the entire pool to flow to the equity investors, while the debt investors in the pool received their negotiated interest payments and return of principal from their loan. For example, an equity investor could put in $3 and a lender could put in $7 into the same investment fund but the equity investor would get $10 * 39 percent (or $3.90) worth of credits instead of $3 * 39 percent ($1.17) worth of credits (see figure 7.2).

The leveraged structure bifurcated the credit; instead of the investors receiving the credit and a return on the deal from owning and managing the CDE, which was the original intent of the credit, the investors would receive all their financial return from the higher amount of credits available from the larger investment pool, and the leveraged lenders would receive their capital with interest. This improved the appeal of the credit for investors because it increased the value of the credit and separated the debt and equity, making it easier to compare projects. Investors argued that they could not easily evaluate transactions that included a blend of tax credits and the financial return from the CDE itself. Without the leveraged structure, it is uncertain whether investors would have participated in the program at all or to the extent that they have.

Yet, the leveraged structure may have indirectly increased the transaction costs associated with using the NMTC because the deal structures were more complicated.[11] Now CDEs had to find debt capital in addition to investors, but the recession meant that many banks were reticent to put debt capital into the

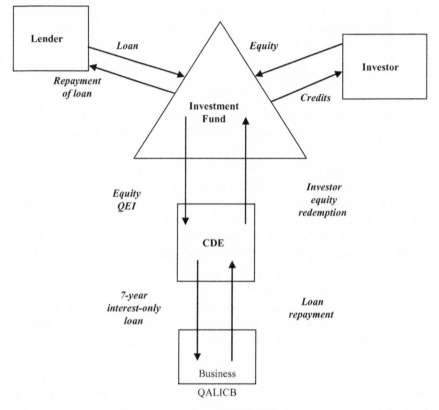

Figure 7.2. Leveraged Structure
Source: Lehn M. Benjamin.

leveraged structure.[12] Consequently, CDEs turned to smaller banks, charitable sources, bonds, and public subsidies from other programs to find leveraged debt. With all these sources of funding going into one deal to increase the yield for the investor—what some referred to as a "capital stack"—the deals became more complex. Lawyers needed to make a determination about whether these alternative sources of funds were "true debt," and they had to work out the terms for all these parties contributing to the leveraged structure. Interviewees talked about sitting on calls with fifteen attorneys trying to work out the details of the deal, about multiple 5-inch binders with legal documents, and about spending years with potential borrowers to help them get comfortable with the structure.[13] One former federal manager commented, "I don't think people envisioned all the ancillary players getting involved—the accountants, the lawyers, the auditors, and the consultants— all taking a bite out of the apple." In a 2014 report, the Government Accountability Office (GAO) noted that this complexity created transparency problems, masking the rates of return for investors and distorting a true measure of the public benefit of the credit.[14]

High transaction costs have steered CDEs away from smaller deals, as it has become hard to justify the expense of undertaking deals below $2 million.[15] Interviewees even suggested that doing deals under $5 million was increasingly rare. These larger deals have had positive impacts, but the high transaction costs have resulted in less money flowing down to the low-income qualified business for project costs. The GAO issued a report in 2010 suggesting ways to simplify the NMTC transaction structures and increase the equity available to low-income businesses through the NMTC. This included "replacing the tax credit with a grant," in part because the fees associated with legal opinions and accounting issues reduce the overall capital invested in the qualified low-income businesses.[16]

However, it is important to note that the transaction costs are not solely the result of the leveraged structure. The diversity of projects that can be financed with the NMTC—everything from a historic arts theater to a grocery store to a job-training center—not only makes the credit incredibly appealing and adaptable to local community needs but also prevents standardization of the transactions and keeps costs high. At the same time, the increasing competition for the credit and the size of the deals mean that multiple CDEs are participating in a project. CDEs do not want to spend all their allocation on one deal; they want to spread their allocation around to demonstrate more impact and to be more competitive if they apply to the NMTC Program again. But multiple CDEs also increase the transaction costs because they each have their own attorneys. It is worth noting, however, that transaction costs for the NMTC Program may not be higher than for other complex tax credit programs, like the Low-Income Housing Tax Credit or the Historic Preservation Tax Credit.

The American Recovery and Reinvestment Act

The American Recovery and Reinvestment Act included fifty-four specific provisions to reduce tax liability and spur economic recovery. These tax provisions represent more than a third of the total estimated cost, or approximately $288 billion, of $787 billion for the Recovery Act.[17] Most of the recovery tax credits are targeted to individuals and administered by the IRS.[18] However, the IRS was not responsible for implementing all provisions, including in the tax section of the Recovery Act. The CDFI Fund was responsible for implementing the provisions for the NMTC and allocating the $3

billion in additional tax credit authority. The Recovery Act split this $3 billion
in tax credit authority into two calendar years: $1.5 billion allocated for 2008
and $1.5 billion allocated for 2009. This brought the total tax credit authority
for each year to $5 billion.[19]

In December 2008 the CDFI Fund was notified that it would be receiving this additional tax credit allocation authority through the Recovery Act.
The fund, under the direction of the chief accountability officer, put together
a working group and developed a plan on how to best deploy the additional
funds for both the NMTC Program as well as the additional $100 million in
funding that the CDFI Fund received for its grant programs. As required by
the Office of Management and Budget (OMB), staff were assigned to focus
exclusively on ARRA, although none of these staff were dedicated to the
NMTC Program. With little excess capacity the NMTC Program staff
worked nonstop to award the allocations.

The Recovery Act included a special rule for the $1.5 billion allocation
authority that was to be disbursed retroactively for the 2008 funding round.
The fund could either increase the size of the awards already made to CDEs
or they could make an allocation to CDEs that had not received an award in
2008.[20] To disburse the funds, federal managers went back to the applications submitted by CDEs in the 2008 allocation round and made awards to
the next highest-scoring applicants. In total the CDFI Fund made $1.5 bil-
lion in what they called "look back awards."[21] The second $1.5 billion of the
remaining tax credits were awarded in the next competitive round in 2009.
Here the CDFI Fund made the decision to give the stimulus credits to the
highest-scoring organizations, with the rationale that the top scoring organizations would be better able to handle the added scrutiny of receiving ARRA
credits.

At the time the credits were allocated, the staff still had not been in-
formed about the accountability requirements for ARRA. Federal managers
included a contingency clause in the allocation agreements signed for each
stimulus award stating that they would be expected to provide data to the
federal government on a quarterly basis reporting how award dollars were
spent and the effects (e.g., job creation). But agencies administering tax provisions and the recipients of the tax benefits were not required to report data to
the Recovery Act website. Although the exact reasons for this were not clear at
the time, it may be because of the IRS's desire to adhere to its mission—to
administer the tax code—not administer the increasing number of social
policies using the tax code.[22] In the end, NMTC allocatees had to report on
only ten additional data points quarterly and did not report or upload this to
the central Recovery.gov site but rather to the CDFI Fund directly.

In addition to limited accountability requirements, the Recovery Act did not introduce any major regulatory changes that affected the implementation of the NMTC Program. This was in contrast to programs like Weatherization Assistance, which were required to follow Davis-Bacon rules. Regulatory changes made to some other tax credit programs also proved challenging.[23] These regulatory changes, coupled with the push to get the money out the door, proved challenging for many agencies implementing the Recovery Act. The absence of these types of regulatory changes for the NMTC program undoubtedly eased implementation of the Recovery Act.[24]

Overall, the CDEs did not report any significant difference between receiving stimulus funds and a regular allocation. CDEs did have to submit additional data quarterly on ten measures. None of the CDEs interviewed reported that the ten data points posed a significant burden, particularly because the 10 data points represented a small fraction of what CDEs were required to report to the CDFI Fund on an annual basis. Conversely, some CDEs reported challenges raising the equity and leveraged debt to allocate the credits quickly because of the credit market freeze. The credit market freeze meant that the big banks pulled away from investing in more risky deals, some banks merged, and others were not profitable. At the same time, there was a major reduction in the upper tier debt.

Consequently, CDEs had to spend more time cultivating relationships with different kinds of lenders, and credit was more difficult to price. One CDE reported that it still had not utilized the tax credits that had been awarded as a part of ARRA, and another discussed the challenges posed by having defined a small local service area. However, the difficulty in utilizing the credits was not necessarily unique to the stimulus funds, as allocatees receiving a regular allocation during this time also faced similar problems. The credit crunch, coupled with the definition of the allocatees' service area (local, state, multistate, or national) and the types of deals they were trying to do presented some obstacles for quickly disbursing the tax credit allocations they received.[25]

But this was not true for all the CDEs interviewed for this study; some CDEs had enough "deal flow"—that is, enough projects in the pipeline—so they were able to select projects with their stimulus allocation that were likely to generate more jobs. At the same time, CDEs have five years from the time their allocation agreement is executed with the CDFI Fund to issue the tax credits to investors, and one year from the date the QEIs are issued to use substantially all the investor proceeds to make QLICIs.[26] This means that the window they have to utilize the allocations is longer than for many grant programs, likely relieving some pressure.

Overall, in comparison with the other cases in this volume, ARRA's implementation by the NMTC Program was just a bump in the implementation road for federal managers. Federal managers at the CDFI Fund allocated the credits quickly, reporting requirements were minimal, and there were no implementation issues identified by the inspector general.[27] It was the CDEs that faced the challenge of utilizing the credit. Although some reported no issues with using the credit, others reported challenges, but these challenges were less related to ARRA and more related to the slowdown in the economy.[28]

Differential Accountability Requirements for the Tax Tool

Shortly after the Recovery Act was passed, the OMB issued a sixty-two-page memorandum detailing the new accountability and transparency requirements for federal agencies.[29] This memo outlined requirements for administering grant, contract, loan, and loan guarantee programs. There was no mention of tax credit programs. As noted above, agencies administering tax provisions and the recipients of the tax benefits were not required to report data to the Recovery Act website. Although recovery.gov included a chart on the estimated dollars distributed through the tax provisions, this estimate was not based on actual provision use but instead is based on estimates created by the Treasury's Office of Tax Analysis before the act was implemented.[30] And even though federal managers in both the IRS and the CDFI Fund did collect additional data to improve transparency under the Recovery Act, including jobs numbers for the NMTC Program, very few of these data were publicly available.[31] The Treasury inspector general did issue more than twenty reports citing problems with the implementation of tax provisions under the Recovery Act, but none were related to the NMTC Program. Overall, though, the GAO reported, "While the Recovery Act calls for unprecedented levels of transparency and accountability in how Recovery Act dollars are being spent, information on the tax provisions is generally not included in mandatory Recovery Act reporting."[32]

This differential treatment of tax credits under the Recovery Act reflects a distinct orientation to tax credits more generally. For the federal managers administering the NMTC Program, the accountability requirements of tax credits stood in stark contrast to their experience administering grants for the other CDFI Fund programs. As one federal manager stated, "The big difference is that at the end of the day, this is not federal dollars, this is not a grant going out [the] door; even though the size of the [award] is huge, there is not a single federal dollar going out the door, so A-133 requirements, OMB requirements . . . there is less of a burden of reporting."

Yet it would be a mischaracterization to suggest that there is less oversight of tax credits. The CDFI Fund requires that CDEs report detailed transaction and institutional-level data annually to help monitor CDEs' compliance with their allocation agreement. At the same time, New Markets investors also play a significant role in ensuring compliance to avoid the harsh recapture penalty. This penalty requires that investors pay back the credits with interest for all seven years—even if, for example, a business fails to remain a qualified low-income business during the sixth year. To avoid recapture, investors have put in place a number of systems to ensure that CDEs are in compliance. One investor explained: "As an investor, we are very concerned with the recapture. That is our focus. So in their [CDE] operating agreement, we put in place provisions that we think that will prevent a recapture. We have removal rights if they stop doing their responsibilities. We have reporting requirements, and deadlines for those reporting requirements, we have guarantees that say if there is a recapture they will be responsible for repaying us the loss."

With investors ensuring compliance, the federal managers at the CDFI Fund do not have to monitor NMTC transactions the way they would if investors were not playing this oversight role. However, relying on third parties to ensure oversight also has had consequences. In this case, investors' focus on recapture has also increased transaction costs as they have put in place a substantial back office structure to ensure compliance. Higher transaction costs ultimately result in less subsidy flowing down to the ultimate beneficiary, the qualified business.

Like other tools of government, tax expenditures are intended to achieve specific policy objectives, in this case by reducing or eliminating tax liability. But the differential accountability requirements for the NMTC Program under ARRA raise a larger question for federal officials about how to best ensure accountability for tax programs more broadly. Comments by federal managers suggest some ambiguity about how to manage this tool.[33] With the increasing use of tax expenditures to achieve public policy objectives, more support is needed for federal managers to manage third parties using this policy tool.[34]

Diverse and Established Networks

Governance networks include nonprofit, for-profit, and public organizations that are interdependent, working on a common problem and involving relationships that are structured by neither hierarchy nor contract. Federal managers are dependent on these networks to achieve public policy objectives.[35]

Although third parties offer expertise and extend the federal government's capacity, they also have their own interests and agendas that can make it difficult for federal managers to ensure results.

Other chapters in this volume illustrate some of the challenges that federal managers faced as they worked to disburse a sudden infusion of funds from the Recovery Act through implementation networks. As discussed above, for the CDFI Fund's NMTC Program, the infusion of $3 billion in tax credit authority did not pose significant challenges for federal managers and their relationships with the CDE allocatees. This section considers whether there was something about the third-party network involved in the NMTC Program that may have eased the implementation of the Recovery Act. It describes the various parties involved in the NMTC Program, the relationships among these parties, and the federal government's role in this network. The section concludes by offering some observations on the NMTC network and the implementation of the Recovery Act.

To better understand whether there might be something distinctive about the NMTC network, this analysis makes some limited comparisons to the CDFI Program, a grant program also administered by the CDFI Fund. Both programs involve a competitive award process, where the awards are made directly to third parties rather than passing through the states; and the broader purpose of both programs is the same, to spur economic revitalization in low-income areas by bringing in private capital to support development. Some of the same third parties (certified community development financial institutions) are eligible to apply under both programs, and federal managers worked on both programs.

Network Actors

The third parties involved in the NMTC Program are extremely diverse. They also have highly sophisticated financial and accounting expertise.[36] One federal manager characterized the difference between the grant program and the tax credit program in the following way: "It is like playing in the local park versus in the stadium." Another federal manager working on the NMTC Program explained, "The people on my team are experts in putting together programs and making funding decisions. It is [a] . . . completely different expertise to become the guy that is going to underwrite deals, involving multiple sources of financing, pairing historic credits with NMT credits. It's a lot of brainwork and people build expertise over the years. They are probably making $200,000 to $300,000 a year doing this, and it is hard to recruit this kind of person to your team."

Five types of third parties are involved in the NMTC Program. First, there are the CDEs, which raise the equity and invest in the businesses. Other than being a domestic corporation, having a primary mission of community development and demonstrating accountability to their target service area, there are no other requirements. CDEs can be nonprofits or for-profits to receive an allocation from the CDFI Fund, but to receive an equity investment from an investor a CDE has to be organized as a for-profit. Nonprofits create for-profit sub-CDEs—limited liability companies or limited partnerships—for this purpose, although for-profit CDEs also create sub-CDEs for each transaction in an effort to manage risk. Consequently, one CDE can have several sub-CDEs. For example, Midwest Minnesota Community Development Corporation, a CDFI that was one of the original Community Action Programs started in the early 1970s, has twenty-seven sub-CDEs, while US Bank CDE has almost a hundred sub-CDEs.

There are almost six thousand CDEs representing about nine hundred organizations. The parent organizations include banks (e.g., US Bank, Bank of America); nonprofits (e.g., Midwest Minnesota Community Development Corporation, Local Initiative Support Corporation); government agencies (e.g., Saint Paul Port Authority; Norfolk Redevelopment & Housing Authority), and other for-profit firms (e.g., real estate development companies like 123 Capital Impact; subsidiaries of corporations like Chevron NMTC Fund LLC). Comparing the roughly nine hundred organizations that have CDEs with the nine hundred community development financial institutions certified by the CDFI Fund, the diversity of implementation partners is much greater for the NMTC Program. The bar is much higher for receiving certification as a CDFI, and they have much more in common than the CDEs.[37]

The second set of organizations involved in the NMTC network is made up of the investors. Regulated depository institutions represent the largest proportion of investors (86 percent of NMTC investors).[38] Four big banks—US Bank, JPMorgan Chase, PNC, and Bank of America—along with other national, regional, and local banks, have invested in the credit. US Bank has been the biggest investor.[39] Other investors include corporations, unregulated financial service firms, insurance companies, and individuals. The investors play a significant role in shaping the implementation of the NMTC Program. As noted above, they ensure compliance and require CDEs to follow certain procedures, like using specific accounting firms to model transactions.[40] One investor explained that they play several different roles, including lender, compliance monitor, fund manager, marketer of successful deals, and convener, bringing together CDEs to share lessons learned and to solve problems.

The third group of actors is made up of the leveraged lenders who provide the debt in the leveraged structure. Leveraged lenders include the banks that are providing the equity to the leveraged structure; other banks; public funding sources; charitable donors, like private foundations; and project sponsors. As noted above, there can be many debt sources in one leveraged structure, creating what some have referred to as a capital stack.

The fourth group of actors involved in the NMTC Program is made up of the accountants and lawyers. An entire ancillary structure of accountants and lawyers has developed around the NMTC Program, many of whom worked on the Low-Income Housing Tax Credit and the Historic Preservation Tax Credit. Two accounting firms dominate the market: CohnReznik and Novogradac & Company. The law firms include Nixon Peabody, Bryan Cave, Leverage Law Group, Husch Blackwell, Grant Thorton, and Armstrong Teasdale, among others. The accountants and lawyers also play important roles in implementing the NMTC Program. For example, the accounting firms hold semiannual conferences and working groups on the NMTC.

Finally, the fifth set of actors is made up of the Qualified Active Low-Income Community Businesses, the actual recipients of the favorable financing, which can include nonprofits, small businesses, and developers as well as educational and government-controlled entities.

Network Relationships

The networks in the NMTC Program were described by many interviewees as transactional, and some suggested temporary. The five sets of actors described above come together to finance a project in a low-income area and are organized around an investment fund—a legal structure, the CDE—that defines their relationship and responsibilities for seven years. One former federal manager explained the difference between CDFIs, which receive grant awards, and CDEs: "A CDE is a structure for a transaction. Not brick-and-mortar entities—they don't have a front door." One interviewee commented, "We have to be realistic about the partnerships that have been created and whether they will last. It may have been a one-time thing for Morgan or NY Community Bank to invest in non–metropolitan areas that they have never heard of in the mountains, where you have 2,000 inhabitants. Maybe those are just once [one-off transactions], but they have done it, and it changed the lives of the people in that community."

However, the data collected for this case suggest that the picture of these networks as temporary, structured by contracts, and motivated by fee income, may be too simplistic. Trust, or "getting comfortable," was frequently discussed as interviewees described their project partners and their effort to use the NMTC Program. One investor discussed the reticence of a CDE to work with them initially, but slowly, over time, the CDE developed a level of comfort with the investor. A CDE talked about trusting another CDE enough so that they could share legal counsel and reduce the transaction costs of a deal involving multiple CDEs. Another CDE explained how one investor agreed to a blind pool, where they did not have "authority or influence" in how the funds were invested. Banks and equity investors also had to learn how to work together to understand each other's risks. At the same time, many of the individual interviewees had a history of working on community development finance and leveraged some of these relationships in the NMTC Program, suggesting that the relationships were not all short term: "All of these relationships in [the] New Markets space are relationships we already had in the housing and health care finance."

Although the network of third parties involved in implementing New Markets rested to some extent on previous relationships, almost all the CDEs interviewed for this project reported that the NMTC spurred new relationships with investors with whom they had never worked before. Data collected by the CDFI Fund between 2002 and 2007 show that more than 76 percent of NMTC investors were not affiliated with the CDEs in which they made an investment, and more than 61 percent of the dollars invested came from entities that had never before made an investment in the CDE.[41] Similarly, a GAO report found that 69 percent of investors were new in 2006, making their first investment in a particular CDE.[42] One investor noted that 95 percent of the entities with which they work on these transactions were not in their Low-Income Housing Tax Credit portfolio and were very diverse, including for-profits, nonprofits, venture capitalists, and other corporate entities. Moreover, interviewees—specifically, the CDFIs that were also CDEs—reported that the NMTC Program had increased their bargaining position relative to these banks; it leveled the playing field because the nonprofit CDEs now had something that investors wanted: the credits.

In some ways the NMTC network is similar to how others have described the emergency response networks: They remain somewhat dormant until there is an emergency, and then the relationships are very structured in the execution.[43] However, unlike emergency response networks, the actors are constantly changing, new third parties are coming in all the time, and though the relationships are highly structured in some respect, they are not standardized and trust is a key determinant in whether third parties participate in a transaction at all.

The Federal Government's Role in Implementation Networks

The federal government's role in third-party networks has not received much attention in the literature. One description suggests that the federal government plays three roles: (1) activating networks, whereby it encourages third parties to participate in public problem solving; (2) orchestrating networks, so that individual actors contribute to problem solving in productive ways; and (3) modulating networks, whereby the federal government uses rewards and penalties to elicit desired behavior.[44]

The findings from this study support this characterization but also suggest other possible roles. Comparing the CDFI Fund's role in a tax credit network to its role in a grant network shows that in the case of New Markets, the federal government plays more of a steering-and-meditating role versus a building-and-legitimating role. In the NMTC Program the fund's role is one of steering third parties into new areas, and to a lesser extent one of mediating relationships between large for-profit firms and smaller nonprofit organizations. In contrast, through the grant program the CDFI Fund has built and legitimated a network of third parties to provide capital for underserved populations.

The CDFI Fund's role in these networks—steering a network versus building and solidifying a network—partly reflects the purpose of the programs; but these roles were also evident in how the two programs were implemented and in their impact on the third parties mobilized by each tool. The purpose of the NMTC Program is to bring private investors into low-income areas by changing the incentive structure and lowering the real and perceived risk of investing in businesses within these areas. The purpose of the CDFI Program is to build the capacity of local organizations that already lend and invest in these distressed communities. On the NMTC side, the fund used the competitive application to reward third parties for going beyond the minimum requirements set by the IRS in the regulations to, as one interviewee put it, "steer these [investments] to the best communities."[45] As already noted above, the CDFI Fund put in place criteria that rewarded CDEs for committing to invest in more severely distressed communities than was required by the regulations. Similarly, federal managers evaluated third parties based on the favorable terms and rates of their investment in or loans to businesses, something not specified in the regulations but that federal managers felt was important to ensure that CDEs passed on the benefits of the credit to the businesses.

Steering these various nongovernmental parties to achieve public objectives was more necessary with the NMTC Program because the program set out to engage a wide range of third parties, many of which did not have a mission that naturally aligned with the program's intent.[46] Although federal managers used the competitive application to steer third parties toward delivering higher impact, staff were challenged by the level of sophistication of the groups they sought to direct toward low-income areas. As one federal manager put it, "There is a level of sophistication. They are constantly wanting affirmation from the fund [about whether] they're thinking outside the box, doing new wrinkles, whether it conforms to IRS rules. So it is hard to stay one step ahead of that kind of industry when they have people who are single-mindedly focused on that activity and have so much more knowledge of IRS rules than we do. So much more finance ability than anyone on my team has." Another former federal manager commented, "The need for checks and balances become much, much higher, . . . and the fund has no ability [to evaluate this]. . . . These guys are very good at marketing."

On the grant side, federal managers were not trying to steer third parties into low-income communities, because these organizations were already working in these communities. Here the focus was on building the capacity of these organizations to deliver results. Toward this end, grants were made to support a business plan. The grant increased the equity position of the organization, allowing CDFIs to leverage greater debt and increase their capacity to invest in their communities. The CDFI Fund also provided funds to support technical assistance for CDFIs. One federal manager explained, "CDFIs are long-term entities in communities for generations and generations. The CDFI Program is all about giving those groups the capacity to grow. That is why specifically under the CDFI Program our funds are not tied to a specific activity. [On the tax credit side] we are not trying to build up a network of CDEs at all; we are just trying to build up a bunch of funds for seven years, and then everyone walks away. [If] you have a project in a low-income community, it's a good outcome."

Aside from its steering role, the CDFI Fund also found itself mediating third-party relationships in the NMTC Program. For example, a few interviewees mentioned that early in the program, a big investment bank tried to use nonprofits as a shell or pass-through for the credit, insisting on tight control over the nonprofit CDEs. Later guidance addressed the issue of control. Managers also made other adjustments. Federal managers also changed the weight of the four components of the application so that it elevated community impact and business strategy over capitalization strategy and management capacity. This change was intended to level the playing field among CDEs affiliated with big Wall Street banks and those affiliated with mission-driven nonprofits.

The NMTC includes a diverse and sophisticated set of third parties. The relationships among the actors are short term and highly structured to execute each deal, but these formal network structures depended on a store of existing social capital. The federal government's role in the NMTC network is more reactive than proactive. It involves steering these diverse sets of actors toward projects in low-income communities that will have the greatest economic benefit, and to a lesser extent it involves mediating relationships among third parties. The analysis suggests that three features of this tax credit network may have eased the implementation of the Recovery Act for federal managers at the CDFI Fund. First, the wide pool of possible implementation partners meant that when some parties backed away from participating in the network, others stepped forward. Second, the CDFI Fund was not in the position of creating a new network under the intense pressure of ARRA, as was true for the network in the broadband case. The NMTC Program had been operating for five years when the Recovery Act passed. The CDFI Fund managers and IRS staff had worked out their respective roles in administering the credit; and the third parties engaged in New Markets had learned how to use this tool to support diverse development deals. Finally, in addition to fewer accountability requirements under ARRA, the NMTC Program itself, with its harsh recapture penalties, meant that the third parties themselves, specifically the investors, took responsibility for ensuring that CDEs were compliant and accountable for program objectives. This relieved some of the accountability burden of federal managers.

Conclusion

For the CDFI Fund's NMTC Program, the infusion of $3 billion in tax credit authority brought intense pressure, but federal managers were able to disburse the additional authority quickly and without complications. Initial results of this analysis suggest several reasons for this. First, the tax provisions under ARRA did not have the same accountability and transparency requirement as grants, contracts, loans, and loan guarantees. Without pressure to report job numbers on a regular basis, or the need to adhere to extra accountability requirements, federal managers were not put in a position of transferring this pressure to the CDEs. Also, ARRA did not introduce any significant changes in the regulations for allocating the tax credits, which undoubtedly made allocating the additional authority easier. This was not true for other programs and other tax provisions, which posed challenges for administering ARRA funds. Second, the diverse and established network of third parties under the New Markets program eased implementation. When some outside parties pulled back from participating in the program because of the credit crunch, other external parties came to the table.

The case of the NMTC Program raises larger questions about how to best prepare federal policymakers and managers for shared governance. For example, the case sheds light on how different tools create different accountability systems and recast the federal role in those accountability systems. What are the implications of having third parties—like the major investors in the NMTC program—in the role of ensuring compliance? While reducing the burden on federal managers, does this lead to higher transaction costs as these parties put in place provisions to reduce the risk associated with noncompliance, reducing the overall efficiency of the tool? Or does it make the credit more effective as their expertise is leveraged for public purposes? Similarly, the case shows how the composition and the form of the tax credit network requires a different level of financial knowledge and skill on the part of federal managers in order to effectively steer diverse for-profit entities to serve public purposes. How can we best support and train public managers for working with these financially sophisticated partners? What level of expertise is necessary? Many questions remain in our efforts to prepare federal managers for shared governance.

Notes

1. New Markets Tax Credit Coalition, *The New Markets Tax Credit 10th Anniversary Report* (Washington, DC: New Markets Tax Credit Coalition, 2010), http://nmtccoalition.org/wp-content/uploads/NMTCC-10th-Anniversary-Report.pdf.

2. E.g., all the case studies examine the experiences of Virginia; the case studies of broadband and accountability examine the experience in California; and the case study of education examines the experience in Minnesota.

3. US Department of the Treasury, Community Development Financial Institutions Fund, "About Us," www.cdfifund.gov/about/Pages/default.aspx.

4. Martin D. Abravanel, Nancy M. Pindus, Brett Theodos, Kassie Bertumen, Rachel Brash, and Zach McDade, *New Markets Tax Credit (NMTC) Program Evaluation: Final Report*, Prepared for US Department of the Treasury, Community Development Financial Institutions Fund (Washington, DC: Urban Institute, 2013), www.cdfifund.gov/Documents/NMTC%20Program%20Evaluation%20Final%20Report.pdf#search=analysis%20of%20selected%20NMTC%20projects.

5. US Department of the Treasury, Community Development Financial Institutions Fund, "A Year of Engagement And Action for the Future: 2015 Year in Review," www.cdfifund.gov/Documents/FY2015%20Year%20in%20Review_web.pdf#search=2015%20nmtc%20program%20awards.

6. The CDFI Fund is a government corporation established in 1994 and is housed within the US Department of the Treasury. The CDFI Fund also oversees several grant programs, including a grant program that supports community development financial institutions (CDFIs) that automatically qualify as CDEs. The IRS is also housed within the Department of Treasury, and the NMTC is one of the many tax credit programs that it regulates.

7. Donald J. Marples, "The New Markets Tax Credit: An Introduction," Congressional Research Service, Report RS22680, June 19, 2007.

8. Ibid.

9. Other early decisions that shaped the implementation of the program included (1) the decision by the IRS to require that investments in other CDEs needed to be traced ultimately to a qualified low-income business to prevent a situation where investments are sitting in the CDE and (2) the decision by the CDFI Fund to weigh the four components of the application so that it elevated community impact and business strategy over capitalization strategy and management capacity. This change was intended to level the playing field among CDEs affiliated with big Wall Street banks and those affiliated with small mission-driven nonprofits, as management capacity and capitalization strategy favored the former CDEs.

10. The ruling was in response to what one interviewee called "code hackers," individuals who know how to work the tax code. In this case, someone realized that the statute did not require equity. I was unable to confirm the source of this idea. Some suggested that it came from Novogradac & Company, one of two main accounting firms in New Markets industry; others suggested that nonprofit CDFIs came up with the idea in an effort to make the program work for noncorporate investors and then was picked up by accounting firms and morphed into something else. However, interviewees explained that the credit was so shallow that there was no other way to make it work.

11. However, another interviewee questioned whether the transaction costs were higher for the leveraged structure versus the simple structure. At the time of this writing, I was not able to answer this question. So few deals were done with the simple structure that it is a difficult comparison.

12. Banks' reticence was partly the result of the credit crunch after the collapse of the economy but also a concern over how regulators would view nonrecourse loans. In order to secure interests of the investors in a leveraged structure, lenders had to agree to making a nonrecourse loan and consequently did not have recourse in the normal sense. Lenders are assigned the A and B note as collateral and could replace the ownership of the leveraged structure if the investor or the CDE failed to meet their obligation. However, other terms of the structure—like investors' right to redeploy capital in the event of a business failure or repayment to avoid recapture of the credit—is not something lenders felt comfortable with, according to one interviewee. This is why the debt often times comes from the equity investor themselves or from public sources or private philanthropy. However, over time even investors have been less likely to put in the debt, in part because they have so many worthy borrowers looking for debt and New Markets lending is complicated.

13. One interviewee explained, "You have a health care provider that is building a building. You come to them with a new markets tax credit allocation and say 'we believe [this] is a better financial solution for you than borrowing 5 million dollar at a market rate. You can't afford a market rate because you are a service-oriented nonprofit living on donations and government income; let me sit down and explain what a leveraged loan transaction model looks like. It is hugely complex; . . . it is going to cost you about $150,000 in transaction fees. You are going to need a lawyer, and we are going to need a lawyer, and the investor is going to need a lawyer. There will be a lot of legal meetings. And you are going to have to hire an accounting firm to come in and model the transaction, and that is going to be another $30,000. But trust me; this is a better option for you.' These are the conversations we are having."

14. GAO, "Oil And Gas Resources: Actions Needed for Interior to Better Ensure a Fair Return," GAO-14-50, December 6, 2013, www.gao.gov/products/GAO-14-50.

15. According to one interviewee, the leveraged structure may have steered CDEs toward low-risk and more conservative deals, such as real estate deals, because the lender was not getting any tax benefit and therefore wants to be sure that its loan is repaid with interest. Other interviewees raised similar concerns about the low-risk nature of the deals. One interviewee suggested that early on CDEs were going for more conservative low-risk deals as they tried to figure out the program, but this was not the result of the leveraged structure.

16. See GAO, "New Markets Tax Credit: The Credit Helps Fund a Variety of Projects in Low-Income Communities, but Could Be Simplified," GAO-10-334, 28, www.gao.gov/products/GAO-10-334. Novogradac & Company issued a response to this report suggesting that the analysis ignored elements of the NMTC, including the time value of money as well as additional costs of the cash grant program. See Novogradac & Company "NMTC Program Outperforms Comparable Cash Grant Program," Special Report, October 11, 2011.

17. GAO, *Recovery Act: IRS Quickly Implemented Tax Provisions, but Reporting and Enforcement Improvements Are Needed*, GAO-10-349 (Washington, DC: GAO, 2010), www.gao.gov/assets/310/300837.pdf. There are different estimates of the costs of the tax provisions associated with the Recovery Act. The Joint Center on Taxation estimates the costs to be $325 billion, the Congressional Budget Office estimates the costs at $212 billion, and the administration estimates $297 billion on recovery.gov.

18. For a review of the IRS's implementation of ARRA, see GAO, "IRS Quickly Implemented Tax Provisions."

19. Text of ARRA, www.gpo.gov/fdsys/pkg/BILLS-111hr1enr/pdf/BILLS-111hr1enr.pdf.

20. Ibid.

21. The CDFI Fund's staff took a similar approach for the additional ARRA funds they received for their grant programs.

22. "In the past, IRS officials said that IRS's role is to collect data only to the extent that the data help it to administer the tax code. However, for the Recovery Act, the IRS went beyond its typical efforts in order to provide transparency over the use of the tax provisions and to collect more reportable data on the tax provisions." GAO, "IRS Quickly Implemented Tax Provisions," 13. Also see Christopher Howard, "Tax Expenditures," in *The Tools of Government: A Guide to the New Governance*, ed. Lester M. Salamon (New York: Oxford University Press, 2002).

23. GAO, "IRS Quickly Implemented Tax Provisions."

24. Text of ARRA. For the related IRS Code, see www.gpo.gov/fdsys/pkg/USCODE-2010-title26/pdf/USCODE-2010-title26-subtitleA-chap1-subchapA-partIV-subpartD-sec45D.pdf.

25. E.g., interviewees indicated that CDEs that had a national service market could more easily locate deals and redeploy investments if a deal went under, which was appealing to both investors and lenders. This was true regardless of whether a CDE had a regular allocation or a stimulus allocation.

26. This is the requirement of the statute. The Allocation Agreement actually requires CDEs to raise 60 percent of the qualified equity investment by the third year to remain in compliance.

27. The inspector general has identified issues with other tax credits. E.g., the inspector general cited that millions of individuals may have erroneously received plug-in electric and alternative motor vehicle credits. See Treasury Inspector General for Tax Administration, "Recovery Act," www.treasury.gov/tigta/auditreports /2011reports/201141011fr.html.

28. One interviewee suggested that those CDEs without a prior allocation would find it more difficult to raise the qualified equity investment because it takes time for investors to feel confident that the CDE has the ability to remain in compliance and not risk recapture of the credit.

29. Office of Management and Budget, "Initial Recovery Act Implementing Guidance," February 18, 2009.

30. GAO, "IRS Quickly Implemented Tax Provisions." The IRS has noted that its role is to collect data only to the extent necessary to administer the tax code. See ibid. Also see Howard, "Tax Expenditures."

31. GAO, "IRS Quickly Implemented Tax Provisions"; interviewees. Consequently, obtaining job data for ARRA's allocations for the New Markets Tax Credit required submitting a Freedom of Information Act request. One notable exception is the role of the inspectors general in overseeing the management of the Recovery Act funds.

32. GAO, "IRS Quickly Implemented Tax Provisions." The administration of the tax provisions under the Recovery Act was still subject to oversight by the Treasury's inspector general for tax administration.

33. E.g., the IRS has noted that its role is to collect data only to the extent necessary to administer the tax code. See GAO, "IRS Quickly Implemented Tax Provisions"; and Howard, "Tax Expenditures." Similarly federal managers at the CDFI Fund struggled with how to best administer this tax credit, with some suggesting that the staff was trying to administer the credit in the same way it would a grant program.

34. See *Tools of Government*, ed. Salamon.

35. "Contracts may be a way in which two or more organizations are linked, but a set of contractual relationships is not the same as a network." Jocelyn M. Johnston and Barbara S. Romzek, *Implementing State Contracts for Social Services: An Assessment of the Kansas Experience* (Washington, DC: IBM Center for the Business of Government, 2000), cited by H. Brinton Milward and Keith G. Provan, *A Manager's Guide to Choosing and Using Collaborative Networks* (Washington, DC: IBM Center for the Business of Government, 2006).

36. According to one interviewee, "It is a completely different level of expertise to be a person who is going to underwrite deals involving multiple sources of financing and pairing historic credits with NMTCs. It is a lot of brainwork, and people build expertise over the years."

37. CDFIs include both nonprofits and for-profits that are certified by the CDFI Fund as having met seven criteria: (1) primary mission of community development, (2) accountable to its target market, (3) primary activity is financing, (4) serve an eligible target market (certain distress criteria), (5) be a nongovernmental entity, (6) provide development services in conjunction with its financing activities, and (7) be a legal entity at the time of application.

38. New Markets Tax Credit Coalition, "Progress Report," 2012.

39. In addition to receiving the tax credit, banks can also get CRA credit.

40. One interviewee explained, "This industry only has a handful of accounting firms considered experienced. Investors are driving all business to those accounting firms, which is leaving transaction costs very high because they have a captured market. . . . We have new relationships with Novagradac and CohnReznik—we have to—we have to use them to model the transactions—otherwise no one will touch it—no one will come in."

41. CDFI Fund, "Promoting Investment in Distressed Communities: New Markets Tax Credit Program," October 2008.

42. GEO, "New Markets Tax Credit Appears to Increase Investment by Investors in Low-Income Communities, but Opportunities Exist to Better Monitor Compliance," GAO 07-296, January 2007, www.gao.gov/new.items/d07296.pdf.

43. See Donald P. Moynihan, *From Forest Fires to Hurricane Katrina: Case Studies of Incident Command Systems* (Washington, DC: IBM Center for the Business of Government, 2007).

44. *Tools of Government*, ed. Salamon, 16–17.

45. E.g., the statute defines a qualified low-income community as any census tract that has a 20 percent poverty rate or above or median family income as at or below 80 percent of area median income. A total of 39 percent of the census tracts meet that criteria, and "it is not that rigorous of a screen." The CDFI Fund inserted a question that asks whether the tax credit applicant will make a majority of their investments (75 percent) in "severely" distressed communities; if the applicant checked yes and received an allocation, they will be required to meet that standard as specified in their allocation agreement. Most deals have been done in these more distressed communities.

46. One interviewee suggested that the whole issue of who qualified as a CDE ended up being pretty open-ended: "As long as you could say that the majority of the organization's activities were going toward low-income community and as long as you have some nominal representation on the board or advisory board, you qualified. Ostensibly people had to have a mission of community development, but as long as you had the right words in your by-laws or articles of incorporation. That has become a real issue. You have a number of folks playing in this game who are no more community development oriented than the man on the moon."

8

Governing without Networks?

IMPLEMENTING THE ADVANCED ENERGY TAX CREDIT PROGRAM

Stefan Toepler and Matthew Sommerfeld

THE ADVANCED ENERGY MANUFACTURING TAX CREDIT, also known as the 48C tax credit after the section of the Internal Revenue Code that authorizes it (herein referred to as 48C tax credit or 48C program), was a new tool created under the American Recovery and Reinvestment Act of 2009 (the Recovery Act, or ARRA), and one without any direct precedents in federal energy policy. The credit provided a total of $2.3 billion for investments in "qualifying advanced energy projects" to support the reequipment or expansion of existing, or the establishment of new, manufacturing facilities for various types of clean energy products. The 48C program was added as an additional tax incentive for clean energy technology, with the express objective to stimulate domestic *manufacturing* (as opposed to generation and transmission) capacity.

However, various other forms of tax credits and incentives did exist to support federal clean energy objectives. Some of these other tax incentives were also extended, expanded, or modified through ARRA and were available to eligible producers as an alternative or a supplement to the 48C credit, such as the Production Tax Credit (PTC) and the Investment Tax Credit (ITC). The PTC, which was introduced in 1992, is targeted at certain renewable energy technologies—including wind, biomass, geothermal, landfill gas / solid waste, or hydropower—and allows producers to take an inflation-adjusted credit against corporate income tax for ten years. The ITC, which was introduced in 2005, is available for a range of commercial renewable energy projects, including solar, photovoltaic, wind, geothermal, and biomass.

The ITC provides a credit of either 30 percent (for solar, fuel cell, and small wind projects) or 10 percent of qualifying project costs.

These subsidies were meant to address issues resulting from the dwindling investment funds available to clean energy projects as a result of the financial crisis, which imperiled parts of the industry. As one author described the situation,

> Until the Recovery Act, the government's main instrument for subsidizing renewable energy development came in the form of tax credits. But many renewable firms couldn't use them because, like most startups, they struggled to turn a large enough profit. The solution was to partner with investment banks, such as Lehman Brothers, which would provide financing in exchange for the tax credit, which they could use to offset other earnings. Wind farms were tethered like a power line to the titans of Wall Street. So when the banking system collapsed and credit froze, the clean energy industry came crashing down with it.[1]

To address the lack of investment partners that could utilize the benefits of tax credits, ARRA allowed eligible renewable energy companies to elect cash grants in lieu of the tax credits (known as Section 1603 cash grants) for a limited time, thus providing a more direct subsidy. This chapter examines the implementation of an ARRA program that used tax credits rather than contracts and grants as its primary tools; was a new tax program, unlike the New Markets Tax Credit; and was in the energy field, which constituted an important component of the overall stimulus strategy. The analysis explores whether the dynamics of the Advanced Energy Manufacturing Tax Credit, or 48C program, are similar to those programs relying on grants or contracts, particularly in view of the federal government's ability to mobilize and steer vast networks of public and private actors. The experience of the 48C program suggests that the answer is "no." Private actors were involved in the 48C implementation process, but it did not require the activation of newly formed networks or actors. As is the case with tax credits in general, the implementation was largely noncoercive, as the goals and incentives of the private actors largely aligned with those of the program. However, unlike most tax expenditures, 48C required more direct involvement by the government in the form of ex ante evaluations (by the Department of Energy, DOE) and acceptance and ex post compliance checks (by the Internal Revenue Service, IRS). Additionally, there was no particular role for states in the process; thus, unlike the other program chapters, this chapter does not focus on implementation in three states. Accountability, oversight, and timeliness were the primary considerations for public officials throughout the duration of the process for implementing 48C.

This chapter begins with a brief overview of the 48C program—the goals of the program and the criteria for awarding funds. It then describes the implementation process and timeline, oversight issues, and the program's reception and impact on renewable energy production and job creation. Finally, we discuss the impact (or lack thereof) of networks.

Overview of the Advanced Energy Manufacturing Tax Credit

ARRA's Section 1302 amended Section 48C of the Internal Revenue Code to specify that projects qualifying for the Advanced Energy Manufacturing Tax Credit included

- Solar, wind, geothermal, and other renewable energy equipment;
- Energy storage for electric or hybrid vehicles;
- Transmission and storage of renewable energy sources;
- Energy storage systems;
- Equipment for capturing and sequestering carbon dioxide;
- Technology for renewable fuel refining or energy conservation;
- Plug-in electric vehicles or component parts; or
- Other advanced energy projects for reducing greenhouse gas emissions.

The tax credits awarded under 48C-supported manufacturing projects received a 30 percent tax credit in the year in which the qualifying project was put in service. Covered were investments that were made after February 17, 2009, the day President Barack Obama signed ARRA into law.

As a collaborative effort between the Treasury Department and DOE, the 48C program was intended to simultaneously address several different objectives in both energy policy and economic development. Both departments supported the program from both an environmental and an economic perspective. Secretary of the Treasury Tim Geithner was quoted as saying, "This program will help encourage innovation in design of clean energy technologies [and add] an important new dimension to the incentives created in the Recovery Act to improve energy efficiency, and develop alternative sources of energy." Energy secretary Steven Chu at the same time focused on the economic aspects by noting that the 48C credits "will help create thousands of high-quality manufacturing jobs in some of the highest-growth segments of the economy, [providing] an opportunity to develop our global leadership in clean energy manufacturing and build a secure, sustained base of jobs for America's workers."[2]

Apart from the economic development and job creation objectives of ARRA, the larger energy policy concern underlying the 48C program was that the United States was standing to lose out in the increasingly globalized clean energy manufacturing industry. In addition to those countries taking a leadership role in clean energy technology in Western Europe (e.g., Denmark, Spain, and Germany) and in Asia (e.g., Japan and South Korea), China in particular has been emerging as a growing manufacturer as well as consumer of clean energy products.[3] The clean energy market worldwide is predicted to grow substantially during the next decade, with global investments expected to reach $600 billion by 2020. At the same time, the renewable energy products trade deficit has increased in recent years, export market shares are declining, and the United States has become the largest clean energy technology import market. As most jobs are in manufacturing, rather than installation and maintenance of, clean energy products, the growth of overseas manufacturing at the expense of US production capacity poses a serious policy challenge.[4]

Implementation Process and Timeline

Although the introduction of the 48C program should be seen as part of the larger US energy policy, as a tax credit, the authority for it rested with the Department of the Treasury; however, Section 48C stipulated that the secretary of the Treasury would work in consultation with the secretary of energy in developing the program. The tax credits, totaling $2.3 billion, were awarded on a competitive basis. The selection criteria were statutorily prescribed and included likely commercial viability, as well as the

- Greatest direct and indirect impact on domestic job creation,
- Greatest net impact on air pollutants and greenhouse gas reductions,
- Greatest technological innovation and commercial deployment potential, and
- Shortest time frame for project completion.

Additional program policy factors were also considered, such as diversity of geography, technology, project size, and regional economic development (table 8.1).

Projects that received the highest ranking based on these criteria were to be awarded the full amount of credits requested before funds were allocated to the next-ranked project, and so forth. The DOE and the IRS had some discretion to exercise their best judgment as to how to make their evaluations, as long as the criteria outlined here were the primary basis for the decision.

**Table 8.1. Notice 2009-7 48C Program Project Eligibility
and Evaluation Criteria**

Evaluation criterion 1: provides the greatest domestic job creation (both direct and indirect) during the credit period (February 17, 2009, through February 2013).

Evaluation criterion 2: provides the greatest net impact in avoiding or reducing air pollutants or anthropogenic emissions of greenhouse gases.

Evaluation criterion 3: has the greatest potential for technological innovation and commercial deployment as indicated by (i) the production of new or significantly improved technologies, (ii) improvements in levelized costs and performance, and (iii) manufacturing significance and value.

Evaluation criterion 4: has shortest project time from certification to completion.

Program policy factors:
  ✓ Geographic diversity
  ✓ Technological diversity
  ✓ Project size
  ✓ Regional economic development

Source: US House of Representatives, Committee on Science, Space, and Technology, Subcommittee on Investigations and Oversight and the Subcommittee on Energy and Environment, "Hearing Charter: Impact of Tax Policies on the Commercial Application of Renewable Energy Technology, Thursday April 19, 2012," 13, https://science.house.gov/sites/republicans.science.house.gov/files/documents/hearings/HHRG-112-SY21-20120419-SD001.pdf.

The IRS specifically cited rule-making authority and the general language of the law as the basis for its decision to use the additional criteria.[5]

In the development of the program, the IRS, as the responsible service within the Treasury Department, coordinated the overall program parameters with DOE and then essentially "contracted" DOE to evaluate and rank applications. There were no formal mechanisms for external input, but the IRS and DOE provided opportunities to meet with interested parties, such as various manufacturers and industry groups, and received comments to help inform the development of the application process. The release in August 2009 of *Internal Revenue Bulletin 2009-37*, containing the program description and application guidelines, was accompanied by a conference call, which made officials from both the Treasury Department and DOE available to answer questions raised by interested parties, including manufacturer representatives, industry groups, and tax law and consulting firms (see below).

The 48C tax credits were awarded through a two-stage application process.[6] The first stage required preliminary and final applications for a recommendation by DOE. This required a uniform application format that allowed for a standardized review of highly technical information pertaining to the evaluation criteria. The DOE provided recommendations for projects that met eligibility (as an advanced energy project) and economic viability requirements as well as a ranking of projects to the IRS based on the criteria listed above. The DOE undertook a five-step evaluation process before sending recommendations to the IRS. First, applications were grouped by similar technologies (e.g., wind, solar, or geothermal), which resulted in 594 project applications categorized into nineteen groups. Second, applications were given an eligibility and technical merit score according to their technology group. Technical experts within DOE based the scoring on the criteria given above, resulting in 418 of the 594 projects being qualified to receive a tax credit. Third, applicants were evaluated using the Program Policy Factors (see table 8.1), which were assessed by a cross-functional team within DOE. Separate analyses were performed for each Program Policy Factor, and they compared them across technology groups for each factor. Fourth, projects were ranked based on the results of the Program Policy Factor analyses. The highest-ranked projects received consistently high scores across the various Program Policy Factors, in addition to their technical merit analyses. The remaining projects were compiled and put aside for future consideration, if future funds were to be available (but were not formally ranked). Fifth and finally, DOE made its recommendations to the IRS as to which programs were worthy of funding for 48C tax credits.[7] In a second stage, applicants that received DOE's recommendations needed to apply for certification to the IRS. Starting with the highest-ranked DOE recommendation, the IRS allotted the full amount of the requested credit until the total available credit amounts were exhausted.

The implementation of the tax credit proceeded on a fixed and fairly tight time schedule. Preliminary applications for DOE's recommendations were due on September 16, 2009, just seven months after ARRA was signed into law, with final applications due to DOE on October 16, 2009. The second-round applications for certification were due to the IRS by December 16, 2009, and the IRS was then scheduled to accept or reject applications by January 15, 2010. There were also provisions for a second allocation round for the following year in case the available $2.3 billion in tax credits was not fully allocated during the initial allocation round.[8]

Slightly ahead of schedule, the White House announced the allocation of the 48C tax credits in a press release on January 8, 2010.[9] With more than 500 applications requesting a total of $8 billion in tax credits, the Recovery Act authorized $2.3 billion in credits to 183 manufacturing projects in 43 states (table 8.2), obliterating the need for a second allocation round. Based on employment effects estimated in awardee applications, approximately 17,000 new jobs would be created directly within the four-year span, until all projects

Table 8.2. 48C Allocations by State

State	Number of Projects	Amount of Funding
Michigan	11	$237,405,791
California	9	$235,500,989
Tennessee	4	$200,390,169
Ohio	7	$124,981,680
Connecticut	5	$120,911,520
Oregon	3	$87,243,801
Colorado	8	$75,239,310
Texas	9	$68,616,631
South Carolina	5	$55,428,300
Kentucky	4	$53,364,900
Illinois	4	$46,762,479
North Carolina	1	$39,087,000
Indiana	6	$35,417,042
Arizona	4	$33,787,596
Nebraska	2	$33,536,241
New York	5	$33,252,411
Arizona	6	$29,793,373
Florida	1	$20,400,000
Wisconsin	7	$19,279,336
Pennsylvania	7	$17,626,013
Oklahoma	4	$14,198,526
Iowa	4	$13,601,285
Louisiana	2	$12,060,000
Vermont	1	$11,860,058
Georgia	2	$7,911,000
North Dakota	1	$7,073,316
Alabama	1	$6,491,180
Nevada	1	$5,889,149
Massachusetts	4	$5,113,370
New Mexico	2	$5,059,730
Idaho	1	$3,000,000
New Hampshire	1	$2,044,500
Minnesota	1	$1,374,300
New Jersey	1	$1,068,986
Maine	1	$903,480
Maryland	2	$814,350
Virginia	1	$774,937
Missouri	1	$570,000
Kansas	1	$157,500
Subtotal	140	$1,667,990,249
Not specified by IRS	43	$632,009,772
Total	183	$2,300,000,021

Source: IRS data, available through White House, "Fact Sheet: $2.3 Billion in New Clean Energy Manufacturing Tax Credits," January 8, 2010, www.whitehouse.gov/the-press-office /fact-sheet-23-billion-new-clean-energy-manufacturing-tax-credits.

Table 8.3. Types of Projects Supported through 48C Tax Credits

Technology Area	Amount	Percent
Solar		
Solar components and materials	$357,367,730	15.54
Solar (California Solar Initiative)	$75,661,231	3.29
Solar (Concentrating Solar Power)	$48,959,978	2.13
Solar hot water	$214,500	0.01
Solar hot water	$592,401	0.03
Solar photovoltaic	$358,116,359	15.57
	$840,912,199	36.56
Wind		
Wind blades	$50,798,372	2.21
Wind towers	$95,158,791	4.14
Wind turbines	$112,562,818	4.89
	$258,519,981	11.24
Industrial	$166,503,955	7.24
Buildings	$146,647,642	6.38
Nuclear	$73,800,000	3.21
Vehicles	$46,790,145	2.03
Smart grid	$35,652,663	1.55
Other		
Carbon capture and storage	$4,842,438	0.21
Fuel cell	$5,510,100	0.24
Geo/buildings	$8,941,626	0.39
Battery	$29,360,400	1.28
Biomass	$29,304,480	1.27
	$77,959,044	3.39
Subtotal	$1,646,785,629	71.60
Not specified by the IRS	$653,117,943	28.40
Total	$2,299,903,572	100.00

Source: IRS data, available through White House, "Fact Sheet: $2.3 Billion in New Clean Energy Manufacturing Tax Credits," January 8, 2010, www.whitehouse.gov/the-press-office/fact-sheet-23-billion-new-clean-energy-manufacturing-tax-credits.

must be in service; corresponding private-sector investment in these projects would amount to about $5.5 billion; and ripple effects of the spending might support as many as 41,000 additional jobs indirectly.[10]

Based on the information submitted by companies to DOE, solar energy projects received the largest portion of tax credits, both in terms of the proportion of funding ($840.9 million, or 36.56 percent) and in the number of projects (forty-seven), followed by wind energy projects ($258.5 million, or 11.24 percent), as shown in table 8.3.[11] The size and scope of the individual projects that received tax credits varied dramatically. For instance, Hemlock Semiconductor Group, one of twelve companies in Michigan to receive 48C tax credits, was awarded $141.8 million to support a $1 billion expansion of its polysilicon production (an essential raw material for the solar industry).[12] Unlike many renewable energy ventures, the production of polysilicon is one of the solar manufacturing sectors in which the United States had produced a significant proportion (40 percent) of the global market share *before* the passage of ARRA. Construction on their site was expected to temporarily support approximately eight hundred workers, in addition to three hundred to five hundred new and permanent jobs in various fields, ranging from mechanical engineers to pipefitters to chemical operators.

Many of the projects funded by the 48C program were more modest in size, however. McQuay International, for example, was awarded $2 million to expand its line of energy-efficient heating, ventilating, and air-conditioning products at two of its plants, located in Minnesota and Virginia.[13] This enabled it to bring back previously furloughed workers who had been let go during the recession. The tax credits facilitated the investment of $7 million in McQuay's Staunton, Virginia, plant, which expanded operations to manufacture a new line of air-cooled chillers, which achieve 50 percent greater efficiency than its old models. The increased efficiency produced by these technological advances has had rippling effects on the economy, saving companies in California as much as $50,000 in rebates from the Sacramento Municipal Utility District. On a smaller scale, companies such as Enertech, Inc., were also able to expand renewable energy production efforts as a result of the tax incentives. Located in Newton, Kansas, Enertech received $157,500 in tax credits to accommodate the development, fabrication, and assembly of two new small-scale wind turbine models that utilize innovative blade designs and fabrication processes.[14]

However, not all the companies receiving tax credits have experienced long-term success in renewable energy production. For instance, both Stirling Energy Systems, Inc. (Scottsdale, Arizona) and United Solar Ovonic, LLC (Auburn Hills, Michigan) have declared bankruptcy since receiving 48C tax credits.[15] As part of their Imperial Valley Solar Project, Stirling made large 38-foot reflective dishes, which concentrate sunlight onto an engine to generate electricity. Notwithstanding its $10.4 million tax credit, it filed for bankruptcy in September 2011 due to falling costs of solar photovoltaics, caused by Chinese manipulation of the industry via subsidies. Similarly, United Solar, which received $13.2 million to build rooftop thin-film solar laminates that convert sunlight to energy, filed for voluntary Chapter 11 bankruptcy in February 2012 due to an influx of below-market, imported Chinese-manufactured solar panels.[16] Despite these setbacks and the negative media attention that typically followed a plant closing, most independent reviews failed to find unacceptable risk in the loan or tax incentive programs as a whole. In fact, the number of bankrupt companies has actually been smaller than initially anticipated when the program was designed, indicating that the population of companies receiving credits has largely been successful as a whole.[17]

Pre- and Post-Award Oversight

Unlike most tax expenditures, 48C recipients *were* subject to both ex ante and ex post accountability mechanisms, which aligns with the administration's general emphasis on oversight and accountability for ARRA as a whole.[18] For most tax expenditures, taxpayers can claim tax credits without any prior administrative review or approval. As discussed above, rather than simply claiming tax breaks, eligible firms in the 48C case were required to apply for a finite amount of credits on a competitive basis *before* receiving the credits. Post-award oversight procedures were also spelled out at the beginning of the program and involved information that the tax credit recipients must report to the IRS. Specifically, recipients—within one year of the acceptance date—had to provide documentation that all requisite construction permits had been secured and that the project had sufficiently progressed to ensure that it would be placed in service within the following three years. All projects supported by the initial 48C tax credits had to be in service no later than January 2014.

Recipients that successfully complied with these requirements were able to claim the tax credit in the year of the project's completion. However, and in contrast to other tools, particularly grants and contracts, there was no room for negotiation. Failure to provide the requisite documentation within the first year of acceptance or failure to bring the project in service within three years thereafter would result in a forfeiting of the credit. Likewise, significant changes to the project would also result in a forfeit if, in the eyes of the IRS, the changes were of a nature that might have led to a lower ranking or even a nonrecommendation in the initial DOE review. The post-award oversight of the program was therefore fairly straightforward, as it involved only compliance checks by the IRS.

In some ways, the 48C tax credit was intended to steer and help accelerate manufacturing investment decisions that eligible companies might have made anyway in some shape or form.[19] As such, the investment decision is subject to the accountability demands of the recipient company's regular stakeholders—such as owners, shareholders, and investors—whose interests are here largely aligned with the government's interests and thus reduce the need for anything more elaborate than standard compliance checks.

Despite these oversight mechanisms, a report filed in 2014 by the Treasury inspector general for tax administration indicated that there were some issues with monitoring location changes or other alterations to the project plans. However, the IRS's monitoring processes identified noncompliance and issued forfeit letters to 32 projects (of the initial 183) that were canceled due to market conditions (see the examples above), failed to provide sufficient documentation after certification, or had been moved abroad. The recaptured credits amounted to $150 million.[20]

Program Reception and Impact

With roughly only one-third of applications and a little more than one-quarter of the applied-for credit amounts awarded, the 48C program can be considered an instant success from a demand point of view. The availability of a sufficient number of eligible projects that did not get funded led the administration to call on Congress to allocate an additional $5 billion in credits to expand the program. In February 2013, a second phase was in fact launched, but it was limited to the $150 million in forfeits from first-phase allocations.

Despite its apparent initial success, the 48C program was limited by its relatively small size. The total ARRA spending for clean energy-related issues is estimated at some $90 billion, of which the 48C credits account for just about 2.5 percent.[21] Likewise, the 48C program was overall among the smaller tax expenditures for the energy industry at large. As shown in table 8.4, the Congressional Research Service estimates the total energy-related tax incentives at around $70 billion for 2011 to 2015. Renewable energy projects claim $43 billion, or nearly three-quarters of the total. Accounting for credits already claimed for projects that went into service in 2009 and 2010, the remaining 48C allocation of $1.4 billion was dwarfed by spending on the ARRA-created option on cash grants in lieu of production or investment tax credits of $16 billion, alternative fuel credits of $12 billion, PTCs of $9 billion, and ITCs of $2.5 billion.

Still, in a global clean energy economy that is currently estimated at $260 billion, the 48C program was a significant policy marker for the United States. Industry analysts are ready to credit the 48C program with encouraging foreign renewable energy companies to enter the US market and establish production facilities here.[22] Although a variety of other policy programs and incentives, both in and outside ARRA, also play important roles,[23] the 48C program did play a significant part in generating investments that, overall, in

Table 8.4. Energy-Related Tax Incentives (in billions of dollars)

Tax Incentives for	2011–15 Costs
Fossil fuels	12.50
Renewable energy, therein:	43.10
Production tax credit	9.10
Investment tax credit	2.50
Cash grants in lieu of tax credits (1603 grants)	15.90
Alternative fuel credits	11.80
48C tax credits[a]	1.40
Other renewables	2.40
Energy efficiency and conservation	4.50
Alternative vehicle technology	2.50
Other	7.60
Total	70.20

[a] The difference to the overall $2.3 billion appropriation for the program reflects tax credits claimed for projects that were put into service in 2009 and 2010.
Source: Based on Molly Sherlock and Margot Crandall-Hollick, "Energy Tax Policy: Issues in the 112th Congress," Congressional Research Service, March 28, 2012, table 1.

2011 started to outpace China's clean energy investments again for the first time in three years.[24] In particular, both solar and wind capacities increased dramatically after ARRA was enacted. For instance, the number of wind turbine manufacturing facilities increased more than tenfold from 2004 to 2011, which resulted in a sharp increase in domestic production of turbine components from 2008 to 2012. From 2006 to 2007, only 25 percent of wind turbine equipment was manufactured domestically, yet by 2012 that number had grown to 72 percent.[25] Moreover, the number of renewable energy patents rose significantly from 2009 to 2012, as did manufacturing jobs involving the production of solar components. These results have been echoed by officials from the Obama administration, who claim that energy generation from wind and solar sources have nearly doubled since 2009.[26]

Implementation Concerns

Overall, the 48C program was implemented quickly and efficiently and avoided the problems and delays that plagued many other aspects of ARRA—including, for example, the weatherization effort in the energy arena (see chapter 6 in this volume). In most ways, the 48C program remained below the radar screen, which focused attention on other issues related to clean energy or on broader ARRA programs, such as loan guarantees in the Solyndra case. The tax credits drew neither much public attention nor any significant academic or industry analysis outside political contexts.[27] In his review of AR-RA's clean energy provisions, for example, Joseph Aldy, who served as special assistant to the president for energy and the environment in 2009 and 2010, referred to the 48C program only in passing.[28] Although the reasons behind this relative disinterest are subject to speculation, contributing factors may be the generally noncontroversial nature of the program's objectives (i.e., establishing a domestic manufacturing presence, and manufacturing jobs, in a global growth industry) as well as different priorities within the broader clean energy policy debate.

Despite the positive reception of the program, a few concerns have nevertheless been noted. A persistent issue in the renewable energy field has been that the majority of component parts of clean energy projects (e.g., wind towers and turbines or solar photovoltaic cells and panels) have been imported from overseas. Although the 48C program and the advanced battery manufacturing grants constituted the primary ARRA programs to focus on capacity building for domestic clean energy manufacturing, some questions were raised about the significant shares of 48C credits that were awarded to foreign-based companies to establish or improve manufacturing facilities in the United States, thereby crowding out smaller and younger US firms rather than granting them a much-needed competitive edge.

Various conservative publications and Republican political candidates criticized tax credits, and even the 48C program directly, on the grounds that it outsourced jobs with stimulus-funded projects. During the 2012 presidential campaign, Republican candidate Mitt Romney, for example, charged that 65 percent of wind turbines in stimulus-funded projects came from foreign manufacturers.[29] However, about one-third of 48C credits ($761.5 million) received by the top twenty-five projects went to the US operations of foreign-based entities (table 8.5), moving manufacturing capacities to the United States.[30] Thus, many renewable energy industry leaders in the United States have been quick to praise the tax credits as a "net job creator."[31]

Although this may or may not be a significant issue in the future, a number of adjustments to the 48C program have been suggested if the program were to be extended into the post–Recovery Act era.[32] Specifically, some of the evaluation criteria of the initial allocation were designed to support ARRA's immediate goals rather than serving longer-range industrial development objectives. This includes the criterion of "shortest timeframe to project completion," which favored projects already under way, which were also projects that would likely have gone forward even without the tax credit's subsidy.

**Table 8.5. 48C Tax Credits to the Top 25 Recipients
(by location of parent companies)**

Country	Credits Requested	Percent of Total
United States	$1,820,541,087	39
Germany	$429,793,266	19
Norway	$154,896,429	7
Other	$176,843,182	8

Source: Clearview Energy Partners LLC, using data from the US Department of Energy and corporate sources.

The "greatest domestic job creation" criterion similarly provides a bias, as it may discourage innovative and promising projects that happen to be more capital than labor intensive. Rather, as some observers argued, technological innovation and commercialization should be weighed more heavily, and manufacturing projects should be emphasized that aim to capture economies of scale, develop production know-how, expose domestic manufacturers to international competition, and focus on domestic component production.[33]

Network Effects

As a new policy instrument that was developed and implemented fairly rapidly (e.g., it had a seven-month time span from ARRA becoming law to the due date for preliminary applications), there were no 48C-specific networks to be mobilized. Interested parties had opportunities to contact the federal agencies to provide informal comments and input in the development of the application process and guidelines. After the announcement of the application procedures, interest groups and industry associations in the clean energy arena geared toward monitoring federal developments picked up information about the 48C eligibility criteria and application requirements from DOE and IRS announcements, and published or republished the pertinent information for further distribution to their own membership and client bases. As pictured in figure 8.1, whereas large manufacturers were likely to pick up this information on their own, smaller manufacturers were able to receive information through their industry and umbrella groups or form the law, accounting, and consulting firms with which they were in contact. For instance, Ernst & Young, a company that provides advisory services in tax and transaction services, disseminated a press release to potentially interested firms that outlined 48C criteria

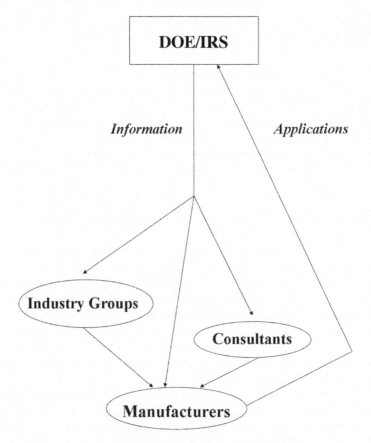

Figure 8.1. 48C Relationships

and what they can do to help with the process. The consultancy offered to help qualified firms determine whether they were eligible as well as sort through the application process. It secured awards for 60 percent of its clients in the first round, with projects primarily involved in chemical, steel, vehicle, aircraft and solar manufacturing, and engine assembly.[34]

Redistributing pertinent federal information is a basic member service of industry groups and trade associations. For consultants—such as law, accounting, tax, government relations, and general management consulting firms—it is a form of business development. Smaller and newer manufacturers lacking sufficient in-house capacity, or foreign companies unfamiliar with the US tax programs, may turn to consulting firms to help with feasibility studies as well as proposal development and preparation. As an example, one

such firm included information about the tax credits in a newsletter shortly
after ARRA was signed, noting

> We will continue to monitor and await guidance from the Treasury De-
> partment on this program, but in the meantime, taxpayers with potentially
> eligible projects, should prepare to reserve a place in line (and apply) for
> these credits. With a limited allocation of $2.3 billion nationwide, it will be
> important to act swiftly once details of the program are announced.
> [Consulting firm's tax group] can assist taxpayers with this process, includ-
> ing analysis of qualifying projects as well as application for the credits with
> the Treasury Department.

A different firm described the process of working with its client in retrospect:

> The firm was notified approximately 10 days before the application dead-
> line that [a client] was interested in pursuing a 48C Tax Credit applica-
> tion . . . Our first step was an exhaustive information gathering exercise . . .
> Simultaneously, [the firm] put together a detailed proposal outline, which
> highlighted all of the needed components for a successful proposal.
>
> Once the [firm's] information gathering process was complete, most of
> our team spent 5 days on-site with [the client]. In this time, we completed a
> first draft of the proposal. Being on-site allowed us to easily access needed
> team members when questions arose . . .
>
> At the end of the 5 days on-site with [the client], [the firm] had com-
> piled all of the necessary client input for a successful application. From
> there, the team refined the narrative and supplemented it with appropriate
> market data to strengthen the client's argument for funding. A complete
> draft was reviewed internally and by [the client]. Upon completion of final
> edits and review, the application was submitted to the Department of Energy
> in the format requested in the RFP.[35]

Regardless of whether or not clean energy manufacturers utilized consultants
to help with the preparation, the process ended with manufacturers' submis-
sion of the recommendation application to DOE and later on the certification application to the IRS.

Overall, the 48C tax credit thus did not require a mobilization of the
usual networks in the clean energy community. Existing relationships among
energy manufacturing firms, consultants, and industry groups were able to
absorb the necessary information and respond in a timely fashion. Although
manufacturers may have tapped their own business networks (i.e., consulting
firms) to aid in the application preparation, the administration of the 48C tax
credit therefore did not involve the kind of public networks that require the
kind of steering and coordinating that are otherwise often needed by federal

managers to ensure that nonfederal institutions and organizations involved in these networks remain focused on the program's federal objectives. Arguably, a variety of different reasons help account for this.

First, network-steering issues typically arise where a range of horizontal relationships are involved. In the 48C tax credit case, notwithstanding the role of industry groups and consulting firms in information distribution and proposal preparation, the relationship between the IRS (as the credit-awarding authority) and the individual applying manufacturer is vertical and direct.

Second, networking in general increases uncertainty about the ability to deliver specified public objectives because network participants' objectives may not always be fully aligned with public ones. In the case of the 48C program, however, the reward is more or less made available after the fact (rather than before delivery of the required good or service), which makes it very difficult for recipients to redirect or misappropriate public resources or to engage in outright fraud. In general, manufacturers can apply the tax credits only after they have notified the IRS in writing that the supported project has been placed into service. Alternatively, credit may be claimed earlier for so-called qualified progress expenditures, which in turn require proof that such expenditures have been incurred. Moreover, if manufacturers violate conditions of the agreement (e.g., significant changes, time overruns, failure to keep the project in service for five years after completion), any unused parts of the tax credit are forfeited and the already-used credits are subject to re-capture.[36] This places a verification burden on the IRS (e.g., ensuring that projects actually went into service and stayed in service for five years), but this does not appear to be too overly complex, because specific manufacturing facilities are the subject.[37]

Third, the 48C program was conceived as a one-time commitment that would come to an end after the distribution of the initial $2.3 billion appropriation. As such, it did not lend itself to the creation of an institutionalized network structure whose own vested interests over time might countermand the initial program objectives. If the credit had been structured as a multi-year allocation, the beginnings of a specialized network might conceivably have emerged. As noted above, however, as the program unfolded, it did not even require a second allocation round. Multiyear allocations were, of course, not a design factor; to the contrary, ARRA's intention was to push the money out as soon as possible.[38]

Fourth, and in a similar vein, the 48C tax credit was introduced into the equivalent of a "seller's market," where the "demand" for such tax credits far outstripped the available "supply" of the initial $2.3 billion allocation by a factor of three or so. For clean energy manufacturers that had facility investments under way or under near-term consideration, the tax credit offer was a low-hanging fruit. It was a desirable subsidy option that furthered their own business interests without requiring changes in business strategy (presumably, manufacturers did fall back on already-planned projects rather than developing new ones from scratch in the short time frame) while requiring only a limited investment of time and resources for the application process.

Arguably, the need to employ, and perhaps even help build, new networks would have been much greater if the supply of suitable, technically sufficient eligible projects had been more constrained. If future 48C program extensions are more targeted and selective along the lines discussed above, for example, federal managers might need to rely more heavily on third parties to help find and develop eligible manufacturing capability to support through the program.

Fifth and finally, it bears noting that the experience of the 48C program does not necessarily present a representative case study of the use (or nonuse) of network relationships in the larger arena of the use of tax credit as a tool of government action more generally. Instead, to the contrary, the structure of the PTC and the ITC in the clean energy arena suggest a more complex set of network relationships between clean energy producers and investment banks and other types of financiers. Because they are highly capital intensive in their initial phases, clean energy technologies tend to be dependent on the availability of financing, most of which comes from investment banks and other "tax equity" investors.[39] These investors are primarily interested in gaining access to tax deductions, credits, and other incentives available to clean energy projects. This takes place through the formation of complex financial partnerships with clean energy firms, which might otherwise have little use for an incentive such as the PTC, because initial operations remain unprofitable for long periods of time after start-up. This appears to be quite similar to the complex networks deployed with the New Markets Tax Credit, as amply demonstrated in the respective case study (see chapter 7 above).

In the 48C case, the economic benefits of the credit accrue directly to the recipient, which keeps the underlying economic rationales relatively straightforward. Although this can also be the case with other kinds of tax credits, the complication of networks arises where the economic benefits provided by the tool are either shared among different third parties (producers and investors) or where the public objective is split from the economic interest (as may be the case in nonprofit/for-profit network collaborations). In the case of the 48C tax credit, by contrast, the public objective and the economic interests of the applicants are closely aligned.

Conclusion

Following in a long-standing tradition of using tax incentives to pursue energy policy objectives, the Advanced Energy Manufacturing Tax Credit program utilized $2.3 billion of the Recovery Act's total stimulus package to subsidize the creation, expansion, or retrofitting of clean energy manufacturing facilities in the United States. Greeted with a strong response from clean energy manufacturers, the program was expected to create about 17,000 new jobs directly and another 41,000 indirectly in addition to stimulating $5.5 billion in private investments. As a relatively small part of the stimulus package, the specific job impact of the 48C program is difficult to ascertain. Yet apart from some minor concerns and despite Congress's failure to extend the program, 48C was widely considered a successful contribution to firm up the domestic supply side of the clean energy policy equation.

In terms of network impact, the 48C tax credit turns out to be a tool of government action that does not require intense oversight with respect to agent–principal relationships. For the most part, the objectives of the administration (manufacturing job creation, renewable energy development) align with the interests of the private actors who benefited from the tax credits (profitable renewable energy production). Despite these aligned incentives, compliance checks were in place to deal with the aforementioned issues regarding changes in project locations and designs. Moreover, ex ante oversight in the form of competitive allocations ensured that a high proportion of the projects awarded credits were of high quality, because one of the top criteria for evaluation was commercial viability.

What is more, the design of the 48C program also counters one of the significant general shortcomings of tax credits as policy tools, which is exposing the government to risk in the form of noncompliance and a general lack of control regarding how the subsidy is spent.[40] Indeed, this particular tax credit was designed to resemble a grant, with a closed-ended fund allocated by government officials based on competition judged by governmental criteria. Moreover, unlike even most grants, the taxpayer may take the credit only after proof has been provided of performance to the IRS. As has been discussed, firms were awarded tax credits from a finite fund on a competitive basis in which they were required to fulfill specific criteria. This design of the program served as an accountability mechanism of sorts in that only the highest-quality programs received funding due to the fact that demand for the credits outpaced supply by a wide margin ($8 billion compared to $2.3 billion). Moreover, by requiring manufacturers to spend the subsidy in a very specific manner (renewable energy manufacturing), 48C was able to target the benefits of the program in a way more akin to a direct policy tool, in which the federal government had more control than most tax expenditures, which enhanced its ability to achieve specific policy goals. When utilized as part of an overall renewable energy development strategy, 48C was generally effective at accomplishing policy goals while simultaneously avoiding highly visible political liabilities.

Finally, contrasting the experience of the Advanced Energy Manufacturing Tax Credit with those of other kinds of tax credits suggests that it would be inadvisable to generalize about network uses, effects, and implications for federal managers for the tax credit tool at large. Although network issues were not apparent in the 48C program, a case could be made that networks play more of a role in the PTC, whereby various third parties (clean energy producers and investors) aim to untangle the more complex underlying economic incentives more similar to the New Markets Tax Credit (see chapter 7).

At a minimum, this suggests that the importance of networks should not be taken for granted, either across the broad spectrum of tools available for government action or necessarily across the different variations that may be inherent within any given type of tool. Considerably more work is needed to understand the variables and conditions that trigger network activity in order to provide federal managers with better guidance on how and when to anticipate that network issues may arise.

Notes

1. Michael Grabell, *Money Well Spent? The Truth behind the Trillion-Dollar Stimulus, the Biggest Economic Recovery Plan in History* (New York: PublicAffairs, 2012).

2. Department of the Treasury, "Treasury, Energy Announce More Than $2 Billion in Recovery Act Tax Credits for Energy Manufacturers," August 13, 2009, www.treasury.gov/press-center/press-releases/Pages/tg262.aspx. See also "Re-establishing US Leadership in Clean Energy, High-Technology Manufacturing, Statement of Henry Kelly, Principal Deputy Assistant Secretary, Office of Energy Efficiency and Renewable Energy, DOE, before the Subcommittee on Energy, Natural Resources, and Infrastructure," May 20, 2010.

3. R. Atkinson, "Clean Technology Manufacturing Competitiveness: The Role of Tax Incentives," Testimony before the Senate Finance Committee, Subcommittee on Energy, Natural Resources, and Infrastructure, May 20, 2010.

4. R. Atkinson, D. Hackler, J. Jenkins, D. Swezey, and M. Murd, "Strengthening Clean Energy Competitiveness," Information Technology and Innovation Foundation, Breakthrough Institute and Brookings Metropolitan Policy Program, June 2010.

5. Treasury Inspector General for Tax Administration, "Assessment of the Internal Revenue Service's Interpretation of Section 1302 of the Recovery Act: Qualifying Advanced Energy Project Credit," March 21, 2013, www.treasury.gov/tigta/auditreports/2013reports/201340029fr.html.

6. See IRS, "Notice 2009-72: Qualifying Advanced Energy Project Credit," *Internal Revenue Bulletin 2009-37*, September 14, 2009, www.irs.gov/irb/2009-37_IRB/ar06.html.

7. Treasury Inspector General for Tax Administration, "Assessment."

8. IRS, "Qualifying Advanced Energy Project Credit."

9. White House, "President Obama Awards $2.3 Billion for New Clean-Tech Manufacturing Jobs: Recovery Act Tax Credits to Enable More Than $7 Billion in New Manufacturing Projects and Create Tens of Thousands of Jobs," January 8, 2010, www.whitehouse.gov/the-press-office/president-obama-awards-23-billion-new-clean-tech-manufacturing-jobs.

10. White House, "Fact Sheet: $2.3 Billion in New Clean Energy Manufacturing Tax Credits," January 8, 2010, www.whitehouse.gov/the-press-office/fact-sheet-23-billion-new-clean-energy-manufacturing-tax-credits.

11. Ibid.

12. BlueGreen Alliance, "Advanced Energy Project Credit (Section 48C)," 2011.

13. DOE, Recovery Act Memos, "Virginia," 2010.

14. Eileen Horn, 2010, "Enertech of Newton, KS among Companies Receiving Tax Credits for Clean Technology Development," Climate+Energy Project, http://climateandenergy.org/news.1049195.enertech-of-newton-ks-among-companies-receiving-tax-credits-for-clean-technology-development.

15. Katie Fehrenbacher, "Solar Struggles: Stirling Energy Systems Files for Bankruptcy," Gigaom Research, 2011, https://gigaom.com/2011/09/29/solar-struggles-stirling-energy-systems-files-for-bankruptcy; Chris Gentilviso, "Fred Upton–Backed United Solar Ovonic Files for Bankruptcy," *Huffington Post*, February 15, 2012, www.huffingtonpost.com/2012/02/15/fred-upton-united-solar-ovonic-energy-loans_n_1279986.html.

16. S. Mufson, "Chinese Tariffs May Hurt US Makers of Solar Cells' Raw Material," *Washington Post*, July 23, 2013, www.washingtonpost.com/business/economy/chinese-tariffs-may-hurt-us-makers-of-solar-cells-raw-material/2013/07/23/01ac60a4-f3d9-11e2-aa2e-4088616498b4_story.html.

17. B. Boroughs, S. Deitz, D. Waggoner, and T. Williams, "Assessing the Value of Loan Guarantees as an Instrument for Supporting the Deployment of New Clean Energy Technology," Center for International Science and Technology Policy, George Washington University, 2012.

18. Christopher Howard, "Tax Expenditures," in *The Tools of Government: A Guide to the New Governance*, ed. Lester M. Salamon (New York: Oxford University Press, 2002).

19. Moreover, the report found that 1,149 individual taxpayers had erroneously filed for more than $3 million in tax credits from 48C. In response to these concerns, officials at the IRS agreed to develop processes that ensure adequate monitoring of projects in progress and compliance with individual tax returns.

20. US Department of the Treasury Inspector General for Tax Administration, *Processes for Ensuring Compliance with Qualifying Advanced Energy Project Credit Requirements Can Be Strengthened*, Report 2014-40-011 (Washington, DC: US Government Printing Office, 2014).

21. Joseph Aldy, "A Preliminary Assessment of the American Recovery and Reinvestment Act's Clean Energy Package," *Review of Environmental Economics* 7, no. 1 (2013): 136–55.

22. Felicity Carus, "Wind Rush: Europeans Take the Credit," *Breaking Energy*, November 17, 2011, http://breakingenergy.com/2011/11/17/wind-rush-europeans-take -the-credit/.

23. Not counting tax incentives administered through the Treasury Department, DOE's recovery funds allocation amounted to $35 billion, and many programs helped spur additional private investments. As an example, the Advanced Battery Manufacturing grants program supported the production of vehicle batteries and electric drive components, and the purchase and testing of electric vehicles, with $2.4 billion in recovery funds, but requiring a cost share. A non-ARRA incentive is the Production Tax Credit, an income tax credit for utility-scale electricity generated through turbines, that was introduced in 1992 with a ten-year life span. This tax credit is seen as crucial for sustaining investments particularly for the wind power industry and the Obama administration was seeking an extension of the Production Tax Credit along with the 48C program.

24. DOE, "Secretary Chu's Remarks at the World Renewable Energy Forum Press Availability—as Prepared for Delivery," May 16, 2012, http://energy.gov/articles /secretary-chus-remarks-world-renewable-energy-forum-press-availability-prepared -delivery; see also Atkinson, "Clean Technology Manufacturing Competitiveness."

25. Luis Mundaca and Jessika Luth Richter, "Assessing 'Green Energy Economy' Stimulus Packages: Evidence from the US Programs Targeting Renewable Energy," International Institute for Industrial Environmental Economics, Lund University, 2014.

26. White House, "President Obama Calls on Congress to Act on Clean Energy Tax Credits in 'To Do List,'" Office of the Press Secretary, 2012, www.whitehouse .gov/the-press-office/2012/05/22/president-obama-calls-congress-act-clean-energy -tax-credits-do-list.

27. Jon Greenberg, "Romney Says Stimulus Money for Solar and Energy Was 'Outsourced' to Overseas Companies," *Politifact*, 2012, www.politifact.com/truth-o -meter/statements/2012/jul/20/mitt-romney/romney-says-stimulus-money-solar-and -energy-was-ou/.

28. Joseph Aldy, "A Preliminary Assessment of the American Recovery and Reinvestment Act's Clean Energy Package," *Review of Environmental Economics* 7, no. 1 (2013): 136–55.

29. See Greenberg, "Romney Says."

30. Ibid.; US Senate Committee on Finance, Subcommittee on Energy, Natural Resources, and Infrastructure, "Testimony of Kevin Book, Managing Director, Research, Clearview Energy Partners, LLC," 2010.

31. Greenberg, "Romney Says"; US Senate Committee on Finance, Subcommittee on Energy, Natural Resources, and Infrastructure, "Testimony of Kevin Book."

32. The second-phase reallocation of the $150 million in forfeited first-phase credits cannot be considered an extension.

33. Atkinson, "Clean Technology Manufacturing Competitiveness."

34. Ernst & Young, "Advanced Energy Manufacturing Credit: IRC Section 48C Offers an Important Opportunity for Qualified Manufacturers of Advanced Energy Assets," 2012.

35. "LNE Group Helps Flabeg Win a $10.2 Million 48C Tax Credit," www .lnegroup.com/Clients/CaseStudies/CaseStudyDisplay?id=31.

36. IRS, "Qualifying Advanced Energy Project Credit," www.irs.gov/pub/irs
-drop/n-13-12.pdf.

37. An early 2014 report of the Treasury IG for tax administration found some
weaknesses in the IRS's evaluation of location changes as affecting eligibility and a
lack of clarity about whether projects only partially placed in service would require
forfeiture of the full credit; but the report essentially attested to the IRS's ability to
properly monitor and enforce the tax credit. See Treasury Inspector General for Tax
Administration, "Processes for Ensuring Compliance."

38. White House, "Fact Sheet."

39. Mark Bolinger, Ryan Wiser, Karlynn Cory, and Ted James, "PTC, ITC, or
Cash Grant? An Analysis of the Choice Facing Renewable Power Projects in the
United States," Berkeley National Laboratory, March 2009.

40. Howard, "Tax Expenditures," 410–44.

9

Accountability under Stress

THE AMERICAN RECOVERY AND REINVESTMENT ACT OF 2009

Paul L. Posner

ACCOUNTABILITY HAS BECOME an iconic concept in public management—and never more so than in the implementation of the American Recovery and Reinvestment Act (the Recovery Act, or ARRA). With more than $800 billion and economic growth at risk, the Obama administration placed its fiscal and political fortunes on the line with this high-stakes economic stimulus package. The ARRA called for an ambitious strategy of expedited spending and error-free administration in more than 250 programs, using far-flung intergovernmental, nonprofit, and private contracting networks. Faced with this daunting political and administrative challenge, the administration placed accountability institutions—audits, transparency reporting, and centralized administrative controls—at the center of its implementation strategy.

A principal impetus for this emphasis on accountability was the offer of symbolic reassurance by an administration seeking near-record amounts of federal funds for domestic programs. A key question is whether this substantial investment in accountability actually paid dividends for promoting the Recovery Act's goals and enhancing the president's own political prospects. Given the political and economic risks and the major investment in accountability, the Recovery Act provides an ideal case to explore what roles we can expect accountability institutions to play in resolving both the political and management challenges associated with high-stakes policy interventions for the future.

To provide an understanding of the accountability networks and strategies used under ARRA, the author reviewed a wide range of documents, research reports, and media stories covering implementation at the levels of federal, state, and local government. Although the chapter focuses on the entire range of ARRA programs, particular attention is devoted to the

management of intergovernmental grants because the reporting and accountability aspects of these programs were the focus of disproportionate attention in the law and by the administration. Interviews were conducted using
standard protocols with government-wide leaders of ARRA and of the accountability institutions at the federal level. These included senior staff in the
vice president's office, the Office of Management and Budget, the chairman of
the Recovery and Accountability Board, several inspectors general (IGs), leaders of the Government Accountability Office (GAO), congressional staff, and
federal agency managers responsible for ARRA leadership for their respective
agencies. The author's research also concentrated on the roles of state and local
governments, with fieldwork and interviews with state leaders in three states—
Virginia, California, and Florida. This diverse range of states had governors
from differing political parties and also had differing accountability institutions. The author met with staff in the governors' offices, budget offices, key
agency offices, audit offices, and selected local government offices. In addition,
he met with leaders of national associations of state and local officials in Washington. Finally, he met with researchers and thought leaders at think tanks in
Washington, at selected universities, and at the offices of international bodies
(including the Organization for Economic Cooperation and Development)
who were studying economic stimulus initiatives throughout the world. All
told, more than sixty people were interviewed for this chapter.

The Recovery Act as an Accountability Stress Test

Accountability provisions and institutions are vital mechanisms to demonstrate to the public that government programs are operating as expected in
meeting their goals, in expending taxpayers' dollars in a responsible fashion,
and in being administered in a fair and consistent manner. The high political
and economic stakes inherent in the Recovery Program prompted the administration and Congress to place an extraordinary emphasis on accountability
up front in the statute's design.

ARRA was created to solve an urgent national recession, and it gave rise
to major national policy expectations that were reinforced by strong federal
accountability provisions designed to institutionalize these national goals and
expectations throughout the thousands of providers and actors deployed to
implement these initiatives. Given the extraordinarily high level of monitoring by the media, congressional watchdogs, interest groups, and others with
a stake in the stimulus program, designing oversight strategies at the front
end of the legislation itself promised to be more effective than operating in a
firefighting mode once trouble surfaced.[1]

Relying as it did on extensive networks of state, local, and private actors, ARRA would confront many of the accountability challenges involved with third-party government.[2] These challenges had become familiar to observers and clients of national programs, as studies showed that large majorities of these programs required actions spanning two or more organizations.[3] The distinct challenge for ARRA stemmed from the federal government's reliance on independent actors to implement national goals and programs: state and local governments, nonprofit organizations and private businesses, and leaders of various other agencies with their own priorities. Classic early research by Pressman and Wildavsky on implementation pointed to the complexity of joint action and the obstacles to federal policy success posed by numerous nonfederal actors with their own agendas and authority to reshape federal programs.[4]

Classic Accountability Challenges for Third-Party Governance

Although classic principal–agent theory focuses on the different interests of federal agencies and independent implementation entities, the reality is that, typically, multiple principals and agents play a role in the delivery of complex national initiatives such as the programs that fall under ARRA.[5] In contrast to principal–agent theory, third-party government multiplies the range of principals as stakeholders with a legitimate voice in determining program goals at the outset. As Lester Salamon notes, what is involved here is not simply the delegation of clearly defined ministerial duties to the state's closely regulated agents but also the sharing with third-party actors of a far more basic governmental function: *the exercise of discretion over the use of public authority and the spending of public funds.*[6]

Not only are there multiple principals but, in most federal programs, there are also multiple agents because the delivery of programs takes place through long and complex implementation chains that work through numerous counties, cities, nonprofits, and private for-profit entities before reaching the ultimate client. These practices prompt some to argue that only a bottom-up view of implementation can provide a valid picture of program delivery.[7]

The effectiveness of federal programs is, therefore, a function of managing through increasingly interdependent and intertwined networks of federal, state, local, nonprofit, and private for-profit officials. Implementation research has shown that collaborative networks can deliver significant performance advantages by enhancing capacity, resources, and coproduction to achieve collective action.[8] As Robert Stoker suggests, the federal government's engagement of networks of nonfederal officials expands its effective role by giving it access to authorities, resources, and political consent that it would never have been able to reach on its own.[9] For instance, in our system it is difficult to imagine the federal government playing an important role in education or transportation infrastructure without working through networks involving states and local governments.

The fact that these networks also pose critical challenges for national officials is particularly important. Such network actors have their own independent values and priorities and answer to their own legislative bodies and boards of directors, which do not necessarily coincide with those of their federal partners. Some actors in these networks have little or no experience working across boundaries with federal or other nonfederal actors, and therefore significant learning is required to realize partnerships' potential for national goals.

It is no wonder that studies of federal domestic programs have long observed that the relationships between the federal government and nonfederal implementation partners can best be characterized as a bargaining, rather than a hierarchical, process.[10] Complicating matters is the fact that these partners often have monopolies over the means of program production and beneficiaries, which gives them further leverage when bargaining with the federal government about program formulation and implementation. For example, state and local governments are in many cases the only viable vehicles to implement a federal program such as education. This makes it hard for federal officials to invoke the ultimate weapon in their accountability arsenal to penalize noncompliance—the cutoff of federal aid—because such an action would ultimately hurt the beneficiaries themselves.[11]

Federal agencies that deliver services directly with their own employees have certain accountability advantages in that their transactions are internalized within hierarchies that are more cohesive and responsive to central leadership.[12] But obvious challenges arise when the federal government must use independent actors that it does not fully control to achieve its goals—especially because, as Don Kettl has noted, transferring who does the work does not relieve the federal government of responsibility for the performance.[13] With a Congress and other publics rightfully demanding answers to questions about implementation, it is far more difficult for federal officials to provide standardized nationwide information for third-party programs where the implementation responsibilities are so diffused across the wide range of third-party providers. Not only is information localized but there are also incentives for nonfederal partners to shirk their responsibilities and, at times, distort their reporting of results. In short, managing in collaborative, networked environments is no easy task and entails possessing unique skills in communications, engagement, and shared learning.[14]

ARRA's Unique Accountability Issues

The foregoing suggests how demanding third-party government can be for legislators, program managers, and affected publics alike. Moreover, ARRA ushered in additional challenges that proved vexing to managers at all levels and across a diverse range of programs: a greater focus on national accountability by top elected officials, program complexity, and conflicting goals and purposes.

ARRA built on existing accountability frameworks to establish a more centralized and prescriptive framework by adding a plethora of new accountability provisions. Table 9.1 gives the daunting list of some of the most important general accountability provisions by category for grants to state and local governments. Although grants received much of the administration's attention, other tools were also subject to greater scrutiny and reporting. For example, with respect to taxes, officials of the Internal Revenue Service (IRS) departed from their historic posture limiting data collection for tax programs and instituted heightened reporting for many of ARRA's fifty tax provisions. Thus, though the IRS did not collect any additional data related to the five-year net operating loss carryback for the Job Creation and Worker Assistance Act of 2002, it did collect carryback data for the Recovery Act's net operating loss provision.[15] As is discussed later in this chapter, national officials ranging from the president to IGs were engaged in ARRA accountability in unprecedented new ways that further centralized expectations. These stronger national accountability expectations posed major challenges for not only program managers but also accountability actors.

Although stimulating the economy was of course the Recovery Act's primary impetus, the act also became a veritable magnet for other policy goals and programs that had little to do with near-term economic growth. The administration chose to use ARRA to provide a down payment on longer-term programmatic investments, including high-speed rail, broadband dissemination, and health care technology. On top of this, other policy requirements— such as Buy America and Davis-Bacon wage provisions—sowed mixed messages about goals and complicated implementation. For instance, the addition of Davis-Bacon wage requirements slowed the use of weatherization funding by local communities as they waited for federal guidance on pay rates for contractors.[16]

Most critically, the premium placed by ARRA on expeditious spending to quickly stimulate the economy threatened to undermine accountability and thoughtful implementation design. The GAO observed that the Recovery Act required a large amount of federal grant funds to both be obligated and also

Table 9.1. Selected Major ARRA General Accountability Provisions

Reporting and accounting
- Requirement for recipients of ARRA funds to report on use of funds and number of jobs created each quarter
- Reporting requirement also applied to the first subrecipient of grants and contracts
- New federal website Recovery.gov established to provide open data on spending of ARRA money by program, congressional district, and other data
- Agencies and recipients required to separately account for ARRA funds with separate identifier

Audits
- Single audit applies for annual audits, with a special focus on ARRA programs
- Inspectors general are required to examine concerns expressed by the public about investments
- GAO is required to prepare bimonthly reports on the use of funds by states
- Recovery and Accountability Transparency Board created to conduct reviews and audits of ARRA, with a board membership of twelve inspectors general

Evaluations
- Council on Economic Advisers required to prepare periodic reports on the employment and economic effects of ARRA spending
- Congressional Budget Office required to periodically estimate ARRA's macroeconomic effects

State and local governments
- Certifications by the governor required, with backup acceptance by state legislature

Source: Author's analysis, drawn from Government Accountability Office, *Recovery Act: Grant Implementation Experiences Offer Lessons for Accountability and Transparency*, GAO-14-219 (Washington, DC: Government Accountability Office, 2014).

spent within nineteen months, by September 2010.[17] The tensions between the urgency of getting money out to generate new economic activity and the need for accountability and careful administration is an old story that goes back at least to the New Deal. For instance, Harold Ickes, President Franklin D. Roosevelt's adviser charged with implementing the Public Works Administration Program, built an excellent record for effective management and efficiency through his painstaking caution in allocating funds but faced unremitting criticism for being overly slow and failing to respond to the exigencies of the Great Depression's economic crisis.[18]

In truth, however, the tension between the seemingly contradictory goals of speed and accountability was not a zero-sum game. Instead, these two goals were in tension as public managers and other leaders tried to meet them simultaneously. As the following section indicates, accountability professionals significantly adapted their public reporting and related processes to expedite their findings and make them relevant in a higher-pressure environment on steroids. And government officials who were anxious to roll out programs to jump-start the economy nonetheless took pains to ensure that implementing institutions provided checks and balances.

Accountability Strategies

The administration and Congress showed that they were well aware of the potential accountability pitfalls facing ARRA as it rolled out during implementation. Some of the strategies were tailored to address specific challenges faced by particular programs. For instance, both agencies responsible for managing the broadband program worked in partnership with each other and engaged other staff to help them administer the new grant, as shown in chapter 7. The Department of Transportation created a new reporting requirement for its ARRA highway grant on top of the administration's government-wide ARRA reporting system at the urging of its congressional authorizing committee, which had sought additional program specific information. Although these agency-specific initiatives were notable, the federal agencies were bound by a strong government-wide accountability framework defined by both the administration and Congress to curb the risks of fraud and abuse and increase public transparency for ARRA across the board. Policymakers made an unprecedented investment in accountability by devoting additional funds to federal accountability and audit institutions as well as devising a unique reporting system for ARRA grant funds that was intended to facilitate public engagement and oversight from the bottom up. Perhaps most important, officials from the president on down throughout the system shifted their roles by defining higher profiles for themselves in overseeing ARRA. This enhanced attention by top national government officials was notable, signifying ARRA's heightened political significance and prompting greater centralization of decision making for these programs.

Jane Mansbridge has observed that accountability is ultimately achieved by balancing ex ante program design and provider selection decisions with ex post monitoring and sanctions. She suggests that principals can achieve a far better payoff by selecting up front the right partners and agents that have the requisite alignment of interests and capabilities to carry out national objectives. Well-conceived program designs and agent selections can reduce the need for onerous and burdensome auditing and monitoring.[19]

The administration and Congress in fact chose to emphasize the selection model as well as ex post facto audits and disclosures. The selection model was evidenced by a reliance on the institutional knowledge and shared values of existing program networks in delivering the bulk of ARRA funds. The ex post facto strategy used a combination of "police patrol" oversight, through the expansion of audits and central oversight throughout the system, and "fire alarm" oversight, which was evidenced by the commitment to transparent information to facilitate the participation of clients and communities in voicing demands and concerns about the programs and projects covered by ARRA.[20] Having first been applied to congressional oversight, police patrol and fire alarm oversight are concepts that aptly portray how the US system not only relies on direct federal agency oversight but must also engage the broader civil society of program claimants, interest groups, and other stakeholders to provide sufficient coverage of federal accountability interests.

Engaging Government "Topocrats" in Accountability

The program chapters in this book show how managers across levels of government and sectors were able to take advantage of established relationships to steer the Recovery Act's implementation. Research on the implementation of federal programs shows the important role played by networks of like-minded professionals at all levels of government who share similar goals and administrative histories.[21]

Building collaborative management of ARRA with program specialists, however, was not enough to satisfy the top-level accountability anxiety of federal officials. Although the speed of the Recovery Act's implementation put a premium on involving existing program specialists and accountability professionals, its high stakes also enticed government leaders to protect their considerable interests in its implementation by centralizing its management in unprecedented ways.

Consequently, ARRA brought about greater centralization of administrative networks by engaging and energizing the "topocrats"—central elected and appointed government officials at the federal, state, and local levels—to oversee policy design and implementation by program bureaucrats. These centralized political actors gained more control and leverage over program officials at both the federal and state levels, precipitating higher levels of conflict and tension between central actors and program specialists within governments. At the same time, the central actors established new forms of collaborative networks with one another across levels of government, in effect creating new networks of topocrats with common political stakes and interests. As Samuel Beer wrote many years ago, the alliance of topocrats in inter-governmental systems constitutes an effort by politically accountable officials to wrest control and leverage from the specialized programmatic networks for control over intergovernmental programs.[22]

Mapping the ARRA Accountability Networks

The network maps shown in figures 9.1 and 9.2 illustrate how many actors became engaged in the oversight of ARRA for federal grants, and thus how the relatively orderly world of accountability for intergovernmental programs before ARRA contrasts with that under the act. Not only did Vice President Joseph Biden, the Office of Management and Budget (OMB), and governors' offices become more engaged in ARRA than they were before, but the intensity of the relationships between these "topocrats" and program managers also increased.

The roles of important players in the intergovernmental management network underwent significant change as a result of ARRA. The following subsections discuss how these changes played out for the key actors.

The Presidency and ARRA

This emphasis on accountability was enforced by a high-profile, centralized role for central government and management officials in the White House. President Obama charged Vice President Biden with the lead responsibility for monitoring and overseeing ARRA's implementation. Biden's office worked closely with the staff of OMB, which exercised extraordinary levels of management control and oversight for this initiative.

The vice president fashioned himself as the "sheriff" who would single out federal, state, or local leaders across the federal system who were found to be wasting funds or violating mandated conditions. Rivaling the centralized authority exercised by President Lyndon Johnson during the Great Society era, the vice president's role added a new dimension of political centralization to the ordinary management of grants.

The vice president centralized authority for management both horizontally and vertically. His control over federal agencies was reinforced by a special "Recovery Cabinet" that met biweekly with key federal agencies. Reflecting the importance placed on implementation at the highest levels, the director of ARRA implementation—G. Edward DeSeve—reported to the president, the vice president, and the OMB director. The vice president's

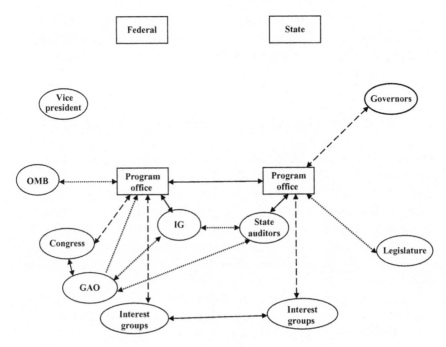

Figure 9.1. Intergovernmental Grant Accountability Network: Before ARRA

Source: Paul L. Posner.

office established regular contact with high-level officials in each government agency—usually at the deputy secretary level—whom the administration designated senior accountability officers. OMB followed up at lower levels.

With a staff of eight people, the vice president's Recovery Office conceived of its role as a network manager, bringing together groups of government officials and program managers to roll out the numerous parts that constituted ARRA. Federal agency officials recognized that, unlike collaborative networks, they were not free to develop their own goals but rather were being marshaled to support the administration's top priority at the time. Although the administration characterized its leadership strategy as collaborative network management, one observer aptly noted that one person's benign network is another's regulator.[23]

In fact, the level of centralized influence and control exercised by the vice president over federal policies and decisions under ARRA was unprecedented. The vice president's office, for instance, reviewed all grant awards as well as many contracts by agencies before the funds were released—an inter-

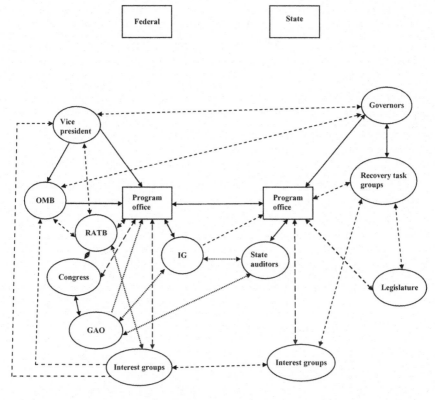

**Figure 9.2. Intergovernmental Grant Accountability Network:
Under ARRA**

Source: Paul L. Posner.

vention that represented a marked centralization of the grant process for
ARRA purposes. Even awards made under block grants were reviewed by
this office before agencies obligated funds. In the early days of ARRA, the
president issued a memo asserting that grants would be reviewed not only to
ensure their contribution to economic recovery but also to avoid "imprudent
projects."[24]

Biden took weekly trips to visit ARRA projects and called out agencies
when problems occurred. Given an adversarial media culture and polarized
congressional politics, the administration was wary that the thousands of
funding decisions made under ARRA would become grist for the proverbial
mill. Indeed, Republicans in Congress under Senator Coburn established a
recovery oversight initiative highlighting what they regarded as wasteful projects, such as turtle tunnels under an interstate in Florida and a tree census in
Las Vegas.

Although the vice president played the role of central overseer and sheriff with federal agencies, he also succeeded in articulating new collaborative relationships with state and local governments. The critical role of states and localities, as well as the urgency of implementation, forced top administration officials to reach out to their intergovernmental counterparts to gain support and resolve problems that could have compromised the speed of recovery or potentially caused performance shortfalls and accountability violations. As of 2010 the vice president had conducted fifty-seven conference calls involving governors, mayors, and county executives.[25]

The outreach began immediately following the 2008 elections, when President Obama convened the nation's governors at Philadelphia's Independence Hall, recognizing the important role that states would play in supporting his administration's recovery goals. Gubernatorial Recovery Act coordinators were invited to the White House for several conferences, featuring appearances by the president himself.[26] The vice president instituted a "24-hour rule" that required the resolution of problems brought to his office by agencies, as well as by state and local governments, within one working day.

The Office of Management and Budget

The vice president's office was assisted by OMB, which took a far more central role in developing guidance for ARRA accountability and reporting than it traditionally does for program management. OMB issued a rolling series of emergency rules and guidance governing the spending and management of ARRA funds, and it worked to actively manage agencies' implementation of these rules.

OMB issued its first guidance the day after the Recovery Act was signed into law, and it followed up with ten additional, major guidance documents during the next ten months. The guidance specified government-wide standards covering such issues as recipient reporting, agency risk assessments, budget execution, and application and review procedures for grants, contracts, and loans. Although contracting rules are traditionally standardized, the level of standardization for grants constitutes a major departure from the more generalized and often hortatory language in OMB's grant management circulars. The common reporting framework for providing data on jobs and spending provided a level of standardization and detail that is rare indeed in the world of grant management.

OMB's role under the Recovery Act was highly unusual in comparison with its traditional management roles. The agency's small size combined with congressional resistance to centralized OMB direction makes OMB ultimately dependent on agencies to implement programs. OMB is the same size as it was in 1960—five hundred staff members—even though the federal budget has grown more than sevenfold in real terms since then. The record speed of ARRA's implementation and the White House's extraordinarily strong interest made it difficult for OMB to hand off the job to agencies or to spend extensive time consulting with agencies.

Given its limited staff and urgent mandate, OMB reached out to new management partners on the ground in state and local governments. This was accomplished in part through weekly conference calls between OMB officials and governors and state budget directors. The idea was to stimulate the development of active engagement by governors and local elected officials who shared a common interest in promoting the president's economic agenda. At the same time, organizations like the National Governors' Association and the National Association of State Budget Officers worked both independently and in coordination with OMB to exchange information among their members, to prod federal agencies to issue and clarify rules, and to provide feedback on emerging problems. Their weekly conference calls and webinars were "the best advice we got," according to one state budget director.

Its budding real-time relationships with states not only helped OMB gain state support and learn from problems on the ground but also served as a feedback loop for the federal agencies themselves. Through these back channels, OMB would learn, for instance, about the parallel existence of separate federal agency reporting requirements imposed on the states. OMB's development of relationships with states complemented its traditional primary relationships with federal agencies. Consequently, for ARRA purposes, OMB's role shifted as it became a mediator and broker between the federal agencies and the states.

Federal Agencies

The management of ARRA funds posed unique management and accountability responsibilities over and above the normal tasks that federal grants and contracts demand. Complying with ARRA's accountability expectations absorbed disproportionate amounts of time and attention among federal agencies. Consistent with the heightened stakes and political attention at the center of the Obama administration, federal agencies also stepped up their administrative oversight. Program oversight, traditionally under the purview of individual program offices, was centralized within each major federal department. Operational issues—such as definitions of jobs created, rates of obligations, and other administrative matters—rose to the top of the particular department, which led to more uniform policies applying to diverse programs.

Federal program managers increased their own monitoring of implementation networks. Agencies used risk assessment to mitigate their exposure to fraud and negative audit findings. Inspections and monitoring of grantees were increased. For instance, federal highway staff used a national-level review team to visit individual states on a continual basis to monitor implementation. And the Federal Transit Administration used a risk assessment to compile ratings of potential risk for each grantee, which became the basis for the agency's identification of recipients in need of additional help or monitoring.[27]

Although using established programs helped promote more effective and expeditious implementation, accountability for regular programs suffered in the process, as scarce federal management resources were disproportionately focused on managing the new stimulus programs. One state comptroller reported that he spent more than 80 percent of his time dealing with Recovery Act issues during the first quarter following its passage, to the detriment of other pressing oversight and management concerns.[28] Off the record, one federal accountability official tartly observed that those intent on committing fraud should choose regular programs, not ARRA funds, which were swarming with attention and audits.

State and Local Governments

Similar to the federal government, the advent of ARRA prompted the fifty states' governors and their staffs to assert strong roles in monitoring and program implementation. Governors and other state officials were on the recovery hot seat, with the potential to become the scapegoat of a failed recovery effort in the same way that the nation's banks did for the financial crisis. During the US economic crisis, the high stakes associated with the Recovery Act attracted a host of overseers and potential second-guessers of state policy actions, ranging from auditors and legislators to restive public interest groups and the vice president of the United States.

The ARRA statute facilitated an expansive role for governors. For instance, in the area of education, whereas traditional programs placed funding and oversight responsibilities directly on state agencies or independently elected state chief school officers, ARRA thrust the governors into the role of certifying state programs, giving them new leverage in dealing with program specialists. For some programs, like the Education Stabilization Fund, the governor, rather than the state education agency, became the official recipient of federal funds. ARRA also promoted stronger gubernatorial and state legislative interest by virtue of the flexibility provided for a substantial portion of federal funds.

Nearly all states set up gubernatorial recovery task forces or appointed "czars" to coordinate their policies and responses to the new outpouring of federal funds and guidance. The state task forces hosted recovery websites, facilitating citizens' access to information on statewide program implementation and locations.[29] These state leaders also coordinated their agencies' implementation plans and reports to the federal government. In California, for example, the Governor's Recovery Task Force played an instrumental role in developing the state's plan for broadband by using state agencies' authority to secure rights of way and by working with private service providers to extend service to new areas. The new funds also engaged state legislative oversight—California's legislature made requests for twenty-five audits of ARRA funds by the state auditor.

The fact that the fresh infusion of new federal funds came at a time of record state deficits and budget cuts prompted officials to seek ways to use ARRA to replace funds that had been cut from priority activities. Much of the Recovery Act funding, in fact, was intended to help state and local governments finance their own policy agendas. Fortuitously, the more this aid aligned with state and local goals, the more quickly it could be used to stimulate or save jobs and boost economic growth.

The administration's most vexing intergovernmental challenge came from unprecedented levels of political polarization among the states. Mirroring trends in Congress, state and local elected officials became more strident representatives of the extreme ideological wings of their parties. The corps of pragmatic centrists was increasingly depleted, eroding the ability of such interest groups as the National Governors' Association to speak with one voice on behalf of state interests. The greater policy variability of states was manifested in states' varying responses in participating in some of ARRA's more innovative programs. Conservative states like South Carolina, Louisiana, and Alaska opted out of participation in enhanced unemployment insurance and Race to the Top programs, while governors such as John Kasich in Ohio and Rick Scott in Florida refused to apply for federal high-speed-rail funds. One study found that Republican-controlled states had less extensive Recovery Act reporting and website development than other states, reflecting their governors' efforts to downplay the importance of the stimulus initiative.[30]

These differences among states came to constitute a source of policy drag that would slow the pace of policy change and economic recovery, frustrating the policy ambitions of new federal officials. And this situation meant that national officials had to design policy tools in ways that accommodated the wider variance of policy interests and priorities among the states and localities—a familiar challenge that became more central and vexing for national policy centrists.[31]

The Prominent Role of Auditors

Auditors were significant winners under the Recovery Act. Federal auditors received augmented funding, as Congress and the administration placed hopes on them to protect the new programs from waste, fraud, and mismanagement. Although managers are ultimately responsible, auditors were viewed by the administration and Congress as providing an independent capability to assure a restive nation that the large investment would not be squandered.

The new funding provided to federal auditors was significant at a time of general austerity in federal budgets. For instance, the federal government's IG offices received $245 million in additional funds, while GAO's budget was increased by $25 million. A new federal agency—the Recovery and Accountability Transparency Board (RAT Board)—was established both to promote auditing by IGs and to establish a new ARRA reporting system. The RAT Board received $84 million to cover these costs. These funding levels dwarfed the $50 million that Congress had provided for a special IG to oversee the $700 billion bailout of the financial system, the Troubled Asset Relief Program. The asymmetrical emphasis on auditing was reflected in the fact that federal managers, for the most part, did not receive any additional funds, nor did state and local managers or auditors.

The augmented resources for GAO and the IGs not only enabled them to achieve closer coverage of ARRA funds but also facilitated shifts in their traditional roles in the administrative process so they could keep abreast of ARRA's faster clock speed for program implementation. Both GAO and the IGs felt empowered to take a far more proactive role in monitoring this implementation. Rather than waiting for the programs to accumulate a track record to audit and evaluate, both GAO and the IGs issued reports and guidance at the outset warning of potential vulnerabilities that might be expected. These reports often recommended proactive steps to be taken by managers to head off problems before they occurred. Some IGs went beyond their traditional reporting roles to issue memos to the agencies and the public providing updates on ARRA's implementation in their realms. The US Department of Transportation's IG, for instance, issued periodic monitoring bulletins about its work on ARRA—a stepped-up profile that crossed traditional boundaries with the department's operating units. IGs provided more than 2,000 training sessions to almost 139,000 individuals on the requirements of Recovery Act programs, how to prevent and report fraud, and how to manage grant and contract programs to meet legal and administrative requirements.

GAO's role was particularly noteworthy in that it was mandated by Congress to report on ARRA every two months. During this period, GAO selected sixteen states to visit for continuous monitoring and then reporting on selected issues. This study was among the most extensive in GAO's history, as was the investment of its auditing staff members' time. Reports were issued monitoring federal and state administrative rollouts of ARRA programs, containing both national data and detailed reports on the sixteen states that GAO had selected. All told, GAO issued 167 Recovery Act reports from 2009 through 2012.

Consequently, the line separating program management from the post audit began to become less defined, as auditors flexed their newfound prominence and funding to become more proactive. Federal, state, and local managers alike wondered if they were intended to take their cues from agency managers and leaders or from the newly assertive auditors who could independently pass judgment on their actions.

These higher stakes caused new fissures to undermine the prevailing accountability paradigm for federal grants—the single audit. This 1984 federal initiative promised to eliminate duplicative audits by federal, state, and local auditors by requiring each major grant recipient to arrange for one audit to cover all its federal programs—an audit that federal IGs were required to build on rather than replicate. Inspired by the expansive accountability expectations engendered by ARRA, federal IGs' audit work departed from this collaborative audit framework by launching reviews of state programs and agencies—in many cases, without first consulting their state and local auditing counterparts.

Although the heightened expectations for IGs were partly responsible, this dispersion of audit collaboration across intergovernmental actors was also caused by underlying problems in the ability of the single audit to respond to ARRA programs' faster clock speed and heightened national accountability concerns. Because the single audits had to cover the broad range of management and financial controls for the entire state or local agency administering federal grants, these reports were often characterized as a mile wide and an inch deep, sacrificing depth of coverage of individual grants for the breadth of coverage required by audit legislation and professional audit standards. The ambitious scope also slowed down the work, and thus many single audit reports were issued many months after the end of a grant year.[32]

As noted above, the high stakes associated with accountability were reflected in the establishment of an entirely new audit institution within the executive office of the president: the RAT Board. Not satisfied to use existing accountability institutions to coordinate the federal audit presence, Congress created this new organization to symbolize its commitment to accountability and the safeguarding of stimulus funds by providing for this additional layer of audit coverage. The RAT Board had a dual mission: to improve the coverage of ARRA across the federal auditing community and to establish a new federal grant-reporting system to bring more transparency to ARRA spending. In its audit role, the RAT Board collaborated with the IGs and state auditors by assisting them with their own work. And it established the Recovery Operations Center, which applied new document-matching and data-mining techniques to spotlight areas of potential fraud in such major assistance programs as Medicaid that had heretofore gone undisclosed.

The new RAT Board chair, Earl Devaney, chose to lead as the hub of a network rather than the apex of a hierarchy. He viewed the board's role as a clearinghouse and laboratory rather than a cop on the beat. The fact that the board consisted of only IGs made it far more cohesive than if it had also included agency deputy secretaries and OMB—as did its successor, the Government Accountability Board. The RAT Board was also mandated to establish a reporting system tracking the use of ARRA funds across the nation—an executive management function that is traditionally outside the scope of audit institutions. Devising a reporting system brought the board into the role of managing ARRA's government-wide implementation, which was nominally the province of OMB and the vice president's office. Originally, this reporting function was to be assigned to OMB, along with the funding—a logical choice, given that agency's critical role in ARRA oversight and accountability. However, when the proposed OMB deputy director for management failed to gain the Senate's confirmation, congressional actors moved the funding and responsibility to this new independent entity.

Questions might have been raised about the compatibility of locating a high-visibility administrative function in an audit office that had to remain independent. This required the RAT Board to balance resources between its all-consuming tasks of establishing ARRA reporting systems and its audit role.

Public Transparency

Perhaps the most significant governance legacy of ARRA will be the unprecedented public transparency provisions—a form of "fire alarm" oversight, in the terminology of Matthew McCubbins and Thomas Schwartz.[33] Ultimately, it was hoped that more transparency would prompt "citizen IGs" to track spending in their own backyards. Although transparency was trumpeted as a new technology in action, in reality fire alarm oversight is already used as the primary way that federal goals are monitored, given the inherent limits on federal oversight resources. Indeed, advocates typically monitor programs and have access to the media, the courts, and federal agencies to ring the proverbial alarm when they find problems.

Led by the RAT Board, a new reporting strategy was developed for disclosing the use of federal funds down through the system. Traditionally, federal agencies enter data based on reports received from grantees throughout the country. Under ARRA, however, federal agencies were bypassed, as grantees and contractors were required to report quarterly data directly to an online federal website covering the one-third of ARRA funds flowing from discretionary appropriations. In contrast to the traditional grant system, federal agencies had to resort to editing and correcting errors after the fact.[34] This new process produced a veritable bow wave of information that was searchable down to specific communities on electronic maps. Devaney called transparency the "force multiplier" that drives accountability. He credited heightened transparency for the low rate of fraud experienced under ARRA.

Indeed, substantial improvements became evident. Data became publicly available for oversight in a far more accessible and timely way than before. In Florida, for instance, ARRA reports were the first centralized source of information on federal grants and contracts available in the state. Local governments and subrecipients were encouraged to report more uniformly than before. Ironically, because of the emphasis on ARRA reporting, data on federal funds were far more complete in Florida—and in many other states—than are the data on the state's spending of its own funds.

The Recovery Act's website at the federal level and in many states stressed connections with the public by facilitating the use of social media. The federal Recovery.gov website could be downloaded to mobile telephones and had links to Facebook, Twitter, and other social media applications. Place-based reporting was a highlight of these initiatives, enabling the public to trace Recovery Act spending by zip code and other local identifiers.

Ultimately, transparency's success rests on whether the information disclosed is both reliable and meaningful. As Devaney noted, the public reporting of inaccurate data will set transparency back. Indeed, the first round of recipient reports showed significant problems with data reporting and quality, according to GAO. The 640,000 jobs reported included numerous inconsistencies and apparent errors caused by confusion about federal guidance, among other factors, although substantial improvements were subsequently made.[35]

Whether accurate or not, the data reported on job creation were inherently limited in three main ways. First, the reports applied only to programs funded through the discretionary portion of the budget, leaving out programs and projects funded through entitlements such as temporary assistance for needy families or Medicaid and tax subsidies. Second, data reporting followed federal funds only to the first subrecipient, not all the way down through the many layers of the US system to the ultimate service delivery point. This is understandable, given the complexity of the federal system and the lack of clarity about how many subrecipients any one program actually has. Third, federal agencies played a more limited role than usual in entering the data and were given only ten days to review the information entered by recipients before it went "live" on the website. Some in the transparency community believe that shifting reporting and data entry responsibility to recipients ultimately improved accuracy, while federal agencies felt that many subrecipients lacked the information to provide high-quality reporting.

Fourth and finally, the recipient-reported job data—even when accurate—were not able to directly address a central question about the impact of this stimulus on job creation and retention. The jobs reported by recipients were only direct jobs, not the indirect multiplier effects of creating the first tier of jobs. Moreover, the recipient-reported data cannot assess the counterfactual—in the absence of these new funds, what would have happened to jobs in various sectors? This is why one must look at the reports from the Council of Economic Advisers and the Congressional Budget Office to capture these programs' comprehensive effects on the economy.[36]

The most important transparency issue was the response of the policy-making process to this new information deluge. Various interest groups were not shy about highlighting those data that supported their views. An eager media and a vast array of blogs became preoccupied with a daily diet of fresh incidents to follow and highlight. Advocates of programs hoped that open data would promote greater appreciation for the effects that ARRA was making in their communities' lives. In addition to official federal overseers, a virtual army of nonprofit organizations sprang up as nonofficial watchdogs of the Recovery Act—including the Coalition for an Accountable Recovery, an umbrella for thirty-five nonprofit advocacy organizations, which made its presence known in monitoring ARRA guidance, reports, and websites. However, those who opposed the stimulus and specific programs were delighted to select data that suited their own biases. Senator Coburn led a congressional ARRA oversight initiative that specialized in highlighting projects that seemed on their face to be outrageous or wasteful.

The question of transparency ultimately involves how to interpret the mountains of data released from the ARRA reports. At worst, transparency constituted a "data dump" that was difficult to understand without context. Reports revealed that ARRA funds paid for cotton candy machines, interactive art exhibits featuring electric fish, and breakfast at Fuddruckers—all items that had programmatic rationales that were not readily apparent from the data excerpted by opponents.[37]

All this suggests that public confidence may not necessarily flow from transparency.[38] The public would need significant institutional knowledge and perspective to weigh and balance the statements of the many groups seeking to interpret the flood of data in an increasingly contested and contentious public space.

Conclusions: The Legacy of ARRA for Accountability

This chapter has illustrated how high-stakes public policy events with highly salient political consequences pose unique accountability challenges and issues. All the actors in the system face nearly unprecedented pressures to deliver on extraordinary public expectations, which are often provoked by government leaders themselves.

Accountability institutions and provisions had wide-ranging implications both for the Recovery Act itself and for public managers and publics in general. By the standards of its core legislative objectives, ARRA was relatively successful in achieving its ambitious and highly visible national programmatic goals. Most of the stimulus funds were spent or obligated within the specified two-year time frame, substantial numbers of jobs were created or saved, and there were remarkably few reports of major-scale waste or abuse for a program of this size. According to the Congressional Budget Office's estimates, ARRA increased the numbers of jobs at its peak year, 2010, by a range of 1 million to more than 4 million, lowering the unemployment rate by a range of 0.4 to 1.8 percentage points.[39]

The extensive focus on accountability seems to have paid substantive dividends. Given its size, ARRA would have been a tempting target for fraud and corruption if it had not been for the significant reliance on long-standing intergovernmental program delivery networks and accountability. Indeed, IGs found incidents of fraud and abuse involving ARRA funds. The Treasury IG for tax administration, for instance, found that taxpayers erroneously claimed $33 million in tax credits for the purchase of electric and other alternative motor vehicles in 2010, out of a total of $163 million in credits issued—an improper payment rate of 20 percent.[40] The Department of Health and Human Services found questionable or unsupported cost claims of nearly $100 million under ARRA programs from 2009 through 2014, the results of more than 360 audits and reviews conducted during this period.

However, these cases were small indeed and paled in comparison with initial fears of a 7 percent loss to fraud, or $55 billion.[41] The administration reported in 2014 that fewer than 1 percent of all grant awards were hit by instances of waste, fraud, or abuse.[42] The significant investment in audits and transparency may very well have created an anticipatory reaction by program officials that resulted in greater management attention to ARRA programs and less reported fraud and abuse.

Although the extraordinary institutions associated with the stimulus were largely dismantled, the accountability and management regime had a lasting legacy. Most important, federal officials paid more attention to grant management than they had in years. In the years following ARRA, OMB formed the Federal Council on Financial Assistance Reform, which consisted of federal grant-making agencies to provide more attention to grant management and reporting. The agency succeeded in updating its grant management circulars A-102 and A-87 as part of this process.[43] Congress passed the Digital Accountability and Transparency Act of 2014, aka the Data Act, which was designed to promote lasting improvements in reporting and disclosure about grants, contracts, and other federal benefits, capitalizing on social media and other innovative technologies to improve tracking and transparency.[44]

However, other innovations did not carry over. For instance, the regular consultations between top-level administration officials with state leaders did not become institutionalized. Leaders of state interest groups were rebuffed when they sought to use these same communications channels to better inform states about ongoing federal budget cuts and other actions affecting the states. Thus, in the wake of the 1995 abolition of the US Advisory Commission on Intergovernmental Relations, the United States still has no regular institution to convene and foster collaboration across levels of government in the increasingly interdependent federal system.

Beyond the consequences for ARRA itself, the experience illustrates the broader implications that the accountability imperative can have for government officials and public managers coping with high-stakes public policy issues. Recognizing the high political stakes associated with economic recovery and ARRA, the administration was enticed to centralize ARRA's management and oversight to provide leadership and steer the far-flung networks whose efforts would help determine the economic and programmatic success of ambitious initiatives. The stakes could not have been higher for the president and his young administration, which was anxious to show progress in resolving the worst economic downturn since the Great Depression. The actors involved with ARRA oversight multiplied every bit as much as accountability provisions did. These institutions made major investments in both police patrol and fire alarm oversight, crisscrossing public implementers of the Recovery Program with a welter of reports, audits, real-time data indicators, and other accountability provisions that provided grist for a contentious and high-stakes policy process.

The high-stakes accountability enterprise launched under ARRA required significant effort by and imposed substantial burdens on many administrators throughout the system. Unlike the auditors, federal managers and state and local officials were not compensated for these costs. The presence of multiple forums of accountability can also cause conflicts and deplete administrative capacity and energy. Tensions emerged among newly empowered accountability actors, such as centralized government officials, auditors, program managers, and other stakeholders. As Thomas Schillemans and Mark Bovens suggest, multiple accountabilities can be mutually reinforcing as principals gain new insight and information.[45] However, the proliferation of multiple accountability networks most likely undermined overall collaboration in implementing ARRA.

Regardless of their administrative consequences, the heightened accountability institutions under ARRA did not create political capital for the president, who was desperate to gain credit for restoring the economy. Though they were credited by most economists with staunching the loss of jobs in a free-falling economy, the complex networks and program structures encompassed by ARRA were not associated by the public with the bottom line of job reports for the national economy. In fact, the president failed to capture credit from a public that had grown skeptical of the Recovery Act's purported accomplishments. The furious efforts to protect against blame through the accountability provisions failed to earn the president or congressional Democrats the credit for the success they so desperately sought.

This paradoxical outcome is partly a reflection of the polarization of American politics. But it also reflects the deep-seated challenges associated with capturing the national results of programs whelped through the decentralized networks used to implement these initiatives. We will elaborate on these tensions in the concluding chapter.

Notes

1. Christopher Hood, *The Blame Game: Spin, Bureaucracy, and Self-Preservation in Government* (Princeton, NJ: Princeton University Press, 2010), 6.

2. Paul L. Posner, "Accountability Challenges of Third-Party Government," in *The Tools of Government*, ed. Lester Salamon (New York: Oxford University Press, 2002).

3. Laurence J. O'Toole Jr., "Networks and Networking: The Public Administration Agendas," *Public Administration Review* 75, no. 3 (May–June 2015): 363.

4. Jeffrey L. Pressman and Aaron Wildavsky, *Implementation* (Berkeley: University of California Press, 1973).

5. Beryl A. Radin and Paul L. Posner, "Policy Tools, Mandates, and Intergovernmental Relations," in *Oxford Handbook on American Bureaucracy*, ed. Robert F. Durant (New York: Oxford University Press, 2012).

6. Lester Salamon, "Training Professional Citizens: Getting beyond the Right Answer to the Wrong Question for Public Affairs Education," paper presented at the annual conference of the National Association of Schools of Public Affairs and Administration, Indianapolis, October 22, 2004.

7. Richard Elmore, "Backward Mapping," *Political Science Quarterly* 94, no. 4 (Winter 1979–80): 601–16.

8. Robert Agranoff and Michael McGuire, *Collaborative Public Management: New Strategies for Local Governments* (Washington, DC: Georgetown University Press, 2003); Kenneth J. Meier and Laurence J. O'Toole Jr., "Public Management and Educational Performance: The Impact of Managerial Networking," *Public Administration Review* 63, no. 6 (2003): 689–99.

9. Robert Stoker, *Reluctant Partners* (Pittsburgh: University of Pittsburgh Press, 1991).

10. Helen Ingram, "Policy Implementation through Bargaining: The Case of Federal Grants-in-Aid," *Public Policy* 25 (Fall 1977): 499–526.

11. Steven E. Rhoads, *The Economists' View of the World* (New York: Cambridge University Press, 1985), 53.

12. Christopher K. Lehman, "The Forgotten Fundamental: Successes and Excesses of Direct Government," in *Beyond Privatization: The Tools of Government Action*, ed. Lester Salamon (Washington, DC: Urban Institute Press, 1989), 53–92.

13. Donald Kettl, *Performance and Accountability* (Washington, DC: National Academy of Public Administration, 1989), 49.

14. Agranoff and McGuire, *Collaborative Public Management*; Jane Fountain, *Implementing Cross-Agency Collaboration: A Guide for Federal Managers* (Washington, DC: IBM Center for the Business of Government, 2013).

15. US Government Accountability Office, *Recovery Act: IRS Quickly Implemented Tax Provisions, but Reporting and Enforcement Improvements Are Needed*, GAO-10-349 (Washington, DC: US Government Accountability Office, 2010).

16. US Government Accountability Office, *Recovery Act: Funds Continue to Provide Fiscal Relief to States and Localities, While Accountability and Reporting Challenges Need to Be Fully Addressed*, GAO-09-1016 (Washington, DC: US Government Accountability Office, 2009), www.gao.gov/assets/300/295645.pdf.

17. US Government Accountability Office, *Recovery Act: Grant Implementation Experiences Offer Lessons for Accountability and Transparency*, GAO-14-219 (Washington, DC: US Government Accountability Office, 2014), 10.

18. William E. Leuchtenburg,, *Franklin D. Roosevelt and the New Deal* (New York, Harper & Row, 1963).

19. Jane Mansbridge, " A Selection Model of Political Representation," *Journal of Political Philosophy* 17, no. 4 (2009): 369–98.

20. Matthew D. McCubbins and Thomas Schwartz, "Congressional Oversight Overlooked: Police Patrols versus Fire Alarms," *American Journal of Political Science* 28, no. 1 (1984): 165–79.

21. Paul E. Peterson, Barry G. Rabe, and Kenneth K. Wong, *Making Federalism Work* (Washington, DC: Brookings Institution Press, 1986); Stoker, *Reluctant Partners*.

22. Samuel Beer, "Federalism, Nationalism and Democracy in America," *American Political Science Review* 72 (1977): 1–13.

23. This was an off-the-record comment to the author from a senior federal manager.

24. "Ensuring Responsible Spending of Recovery Act Funds," memo to heads of executive departments and agencies, White House, March 20, 2009.

25. Frank DiGiammarino, "Implementation of the American Recovery and Reinvestment Act in the United States," speech delivered to the Territorial Development Policy Committee of the Organization for Economic Cooperation and Development, Paris, December 2010.

26. Account based on interviews with vice presidential staff and report by G. Edward DeSeve, *Managing Recovery: An Insider's View* (Washington, DC: IBM Center on the Business of Government, 2011).

27. Relmond Van Daniker and Helena Sims, *Redefining Accountability: Recovery Act Practices and Opportunities* (Alexandria, VA: Association of Government Accountants, 2010).

28. Ibid., 10.

29. Good Jobs First, "States Are Making More Effective Use of Web to Inform Taxpayers about Economic Stimulus Spending," Washington, January 26, 2010.

30. Edward T. Jennings Jr., Jeremy L. Hall, and Zhiwei Zhang, "The American Recovery and Reinvestment Act and State Accountability," *Public Performance and Management Review* 35, no. 3 (March 2012): 541.

31. Timothy J. Conlan and Paul L. Posner, "Inflection Point: Federalism and the Obama Administration" *Publius* 41, no. 3 (2011): 421–46.

32. GAO urged OMB to expedite single audit reports, which led to pilots in sixteen states where reports were produced three months earlier than required. US Government Accountability Office, *Recovery Act: States' and Localities Use of Funds and Actions Needed to Address Implementation Challenges and Bolster Accountability*, GAO-10-604 (Washington, DC: US Government Accountability Office, 2010).

33. Matthew D. McCubbins and Thomas Schwartz, "Congressional Overlooked: Police Patrols vs. Fire Alarms," *American Journal of Political Science* 28, no. 1 (February 1984).

34. Tax and entitlement programs, including Medicaid, are not covered by public reporting requirements.

35. US Government Accountability Office, *Recovery Act: Recipient Reported Jobs Data Provide Some Insight into the Use of Recovery Act Funding, but Data Quality and Reporting Issues Need Attention*, GAO-10-223 (Washington, DC: US Government Accountability Office, 2009).

36. See Congressional Budget Office, *Estimated Impact of the American Recovery and Reinvestment Act on Employment and Economic Output for 2014* (Washington, DC: Congressional Budget Office, 2015); Council of Economic Advisers, *The Economic Impact of the American Recovery and Reinvestment Act Five Years Later: Final Report to Congress* (Washington, DC: Council of Economic Advisers, 2014).

37. Michael Grabell, "Stimulus for Cotton Candy, Tango and a Fish Orchestra? Wacky, or Actually Worthy?" *Pro Publica*, November 5, 2009, www.propublica.org /article/stimulus-for-cotton-candy-tango-and-a-fish-orchestra-wacky-or-actually -wort.

38. Timothy J. Conlan, *Grants and the Recovery Act: Classic Challenges, New Dilemmas, and Best Practices* (Fairfax, VA: CGI Initiative for Collaborative Government, 2009), 15.

39. Congressional Budget Office, *Estimated Impact of the American Recovery and Reinvestment Act on Employment and Economic Output* (Washington, DC: Congressional Budget Office, 2013).

40. Inspector General for Tax Administration, US Department of the Treasury, "Semiannual Report, October 2010–March 2011," 48.

41. Gregory Korte, "Five Years Since Stimulus: Many Fraud Cases, Few Losses," *USA Today*, February 16, 2014.

42. Council of Economic Advisers, *Economic Impact*.

43. See the website of the Council on Financial Assistance Reform, https://cfo.gov/cofar/.

44. This is per PL-113-101.

45. Thomas Schillemans and Mark Bovens, " The Challenge of Multiple Accountability: Does Redundancy Lead to Overload?" in *Accountable Governance: Problems and Promises*, ed. Melvin J. Dubnick and H. George Frederickson (Armonk, NY: M. E. Sharpe, 2011), 3–21.

10

Conclusions

NETWORKED GOVERNANCE UNDER STRESS

Paul L. Posner, Timothy J. Conlan, and Priscilla M. Regan

WE LIVE IN PARADOXICAL TIMES. As a nation, we have become more reliant on the federal government to resolve any number of policy problems that were heretofore the responsibilities of the private sector or state and local governments. Whether it be education, health care, or abortion, both political parties and an increasingly nonstop media deposit all sorts of issues on the federal doorstep. Yet, at the same time, public trust in government is at record lows. The two most recent presidents watched their ratings drop in the wake of numerous problems with federal agency management on their watch—the botched response to Hurricane Katrina and the troubled roll out of health reform under President Barack Obama. Many have questioned whether the federal government has the political and managerial capacity to deliver on the high expectations that the public still holds for public action. Ironically, the growth of government's role appears to have fueled cynicism and disappointment, as the higher stakes have created opportunities for political leaders and media critics to instigate a cycle of blame and disillusionment.

Against this backdrop, the American Recovery and Reinvestment Act of 2009 (the Recovery Act, or ARRA) constituted a crucial test of government's ability to deliver on major policy promises and challenges. The stakes were as high as they come for domestic policy. Facing the largest economic downturn since the Great Depression, the new president and his Democratic Congress would be held accountable for rescuing the economy from the depths of this crisis. Their response, ARRA, was a massive stimulus package that was larger and more complex than any comparable countercyclical policy since the 1930s.

We can assess the outcomes of the Recovery Act through three different lenses: economic, administrative, and political. Overall, ARRA packed an economic punch that delivered a significant and well-timed stimulus to the economy. Along with the Federal Reserve and the financial bailouts of important private firms via the Troubled Asset Relief Program, the Recovery Act was able to prevent the most significant economic downturn since the 1930s from turning into the next Great Depression, leading other nations in the magnitude and timing of the response.

Evaluating the success of ARRA's implementation and accountability regime is more complicated. The use of existing networks for many of ARRA's programs provided the institutional knowledge and trust necessary to quickly roll out programs with a minimum of fraud and abuse, and this was reinforced by the extensive investment in accountability institutions and transparency. Moreover, for an initiative of this size, complexity, and urgency, many of the Recovery Act's programs outperformed the dismal expectations of the implementation literature. However, the complex program structures and novel goals of other ARRA programs, along with conflicts between programmatic experts and highly engaged centralized government officials, made the implementation of many initiatives challenging and, at times, burdensome.

Politically, despite the economic gains and the investment in administrative management, the public largely failed to give credit to national officials for these accomplishments. Instead, a skeptical public failed to be convinced of the benefits and retained a deep and lasting cynicism about the capacity of government to solve large-scale problems.

The Economic Outcomes of the Recovery Act

The chapters in this book analyze the implementation and impact of government's response to the Great Recession. At first blush at least, the champions of government investment would appear to have been vindicated. The level of stimulus alone—$800 billion, or more than 5 percent of the gross domestic product (GDP)—made ARRA among the largest stimulus initiatives provided across the nations that belong to the Organization for Economic Cooperation and Development.[1] There was far greater reliance on fiscal policy to regain full employment than in previous postwar recessions.[2]

When viewed against the international experience, one lesson stands out—the United States' fiscal position enabled it to run up significant stimulus and high countercyclical deficits with relative impunity in the aftermath of the financial crisis. Unlike nations in Europe and elsewhere, the United States enjoys considerable freedom from external fiscal rules hampering fiscal expansion as well as market pressures that keep fiscal balances reined in. US Treasuries remain a safe haven where central banks and savers worldwide have chosen to park their money during times of global stress. This kept US interest rates low and permitted the nation to increase borrowing for a record stimulus.

Previous stimulus programs from past recessions often suffered from being too late, too poorly targeted, and too difficult to turn off when the crisis subsided. By comparison, the Recovery Act was timely, targeted, and largely temporary. Facing mounting job losses and bank failures, Congress and the Obama administration acted with near-record speed. The Recovery Act became law just one month into the new president's term and fourteen months after the recession officially began—far faster than the average twenty-seven months between the beginning of past recessions and the enactment of antirecession job creation programs.[3] The $87 billion in Medicaid funds provided by ARRA were allocated on a more targeted basis than regular Medicaid funds, using a formula based on states' relative unemployment rates. Those concerned about deficits would be pleased that the bulk of tax cuts and spending were indeed temporary and terminated on time.

Ultimately, the Recovery Act achieved its core legislative objectives. Most of the stimulus funds were spent or obligated within the specified two-year time frame, substantial numbers of jobs were created or saved, and there were remarkably few reports of major-scale waste or abuse for a program of this size. At its high point of impact in 2012, the Congressional Budget Office credited ARRA with raising GDP growth by between 1 and 4 percentage points and with lowering unemployment from 0.3 to 2 percentage points.[4]

With nearly half of all ARRA spending going to state and local governments, a good deal of its impact was achieved by reducing budget cuts that those governments would have been forced to make in its absence. Much of the aid delivered through state and local governments was provided as relatively flexible funding. One estimate concludes that ARRA funding covered 40 percent of states' deficits stemming from the recession.[5]

Contradictions of National Policy Management

Achieving these results called on public administrators at all levels of government to make strenuous—and often heroic—efforts, fashioning adaptive and ad hoc institutions in very short order in an administrative state where collaboration among and across governments was insufficiently institutionalized. Strenuous efforts were required because substantial challenges and tensions among competing goals were built into ARRA at its birth.

The Recovery Act was notable in its strong focus on accountability and transparency. Unlike many emergency programs, where the urgent trumps the important, this initiative rested on a management structure that would help avoid some of the predictable problems entailed with high-octane and high-pressure public programs. The frequent reliance on established programs and networks ensured that seasoned professionals with long-standing expertise and collaborative relationships across levels of government would be staffing the rollouts of these programs. Unlike the proverbial administrative agents who are scheming to outfox their congressional and administration principals, these agents were trusted allies and champions of these programs, much akin to John Dilulio's "principled agents."[6] Moreover, the emphasis on accountability backed by investment of additional resources for federal auditors at least helped forestall some of the obvious temptations and vulnerabilities that large dollar amounts and short time frames can induce.

The Challenges of Complexity and Fragmentation

However, managers and leaders alike struggled to overcome the burdens of complexity and fragmentation. Rather than provide assistance through a single major grant, Congress chose to carve funding up among a daunting range of programs, each with strong support among the interest groups, agencies, and congressional committees that influence legislation.[7] According to one estimate, more than 250 individual federal programs received ARRA funding.[8] The nearly 100 grants to state and local governments through ARRA equaled approximately one-fourth of all grant outlays in fiscal year 2008, the last year before ARRA. Many additional tax expenditure, loan, and contract programs also fell under ARRA's purview. The Treasury Department's inspector general, for instance, reported that more than fifty new tax provisions were enacted as part of ARRA.[9]

The reliance on existing programs had the benefit of tapping into existing program expertise and administrative infrastructures, which were vital for hitting the ground running with minimal risk of abuse. This was evident in the case of federal highway grants in particular, as Sheldon Edner and Matthew Critchfield demonstrate in chapter 4. Similarly, Timothy Conlan's analysis of the State Fiscal Stabilization Fund program in chapter 3 indicates that implementation difficulties were minimized where states were able to utilize their existing education policy networks and state aid formulas for public schools. Research on the implementation of the domestic programs shows the importance played by the presence across levels of government of networks of like-minded professionals who share similar goals and administrative histories.[10] For federal grants, the bonds between these professionals proved to be stronger than those with their nominal political overseers in executive and legislative offices. It takes years to build the necessary processes, social capital, and trust for these networks to develop the capacity to work well together on complex and demanding public policy problems.

However, these existing stovepipes also complicated public understanding of the initiative. When used to top up existing programs, ARRA funds tended to lose their political identity and potential for credit claiming by public officials—a problem to which we return later in this chapter. Capital projects in particular were only partially supported by ARRA, which made it difficult for the public to draw a line of sight from completed projects to this high-profile national stimulus program. One writer deemed ARRA to be the "invisible stimulus."[11]

Other agendas, many noble in their own time and place, were laid on top of ARRA's core objective of economic stimulus. These additional goals and agendas complicated the timely and expeditious spending of funds that was needed to save the economy. Congress insisted on adding regulations such as Buy America and Davis-Bacon that increased the costs of each job created and slowed down implementation at the local level. As Alan Abramson demonstrates in chapter 6, this was a major problem for the Weatherization Assistance Grant program in particular.

Although most of ARRA was incremental in its reliance on established federal programs as the conduit for delivering the new stimulus funding, the act's fast legislative track in Congress provided a window of opportunity for the new administration to attach several new and untried initiatives, such as expanded broadband internet access and high-speed rail. These initiatives had great potential for national leaders to claim credit, but they also raised difficult implementation challenges, as Priscilla Regan's case study of grants for broadband internet access assistance illustrates in chapter 5.

The Challenge of High Stakes

Crises, whether related to the economy or to security, traditionally have had centralizing effects on the US political system. The rapid starting up of programs and high national stakes together provide compelling incentives for national-level officials to take strong measures to drive implementation. Politically, the president and Congress were in the hot seat. Even though state and local governments shared responsibility for ARRA's administration and shortfalls, prior research suggests that the broad public would blame the president in particular, as was the case with the botched response to Hurricane Katrina.[12]

Commensurate with the high political stakes, the Obama administration and Congress established policy implementation roles, strategies, and policies that represented a significant centralization of authority for many intergovernmental and third-party programs. The unprecedented role played by the vice president and the Office of Management and Budget (OMB) had an impact on managers at all levels in the system, as program managers had to constantly be alert to the prospects of high-level directives and interventions.

High stakes also multiply the different imperatives and networks engaged with large-scale initiatives, leaving public managers conflicted between rival imperatives and the networks representing these imperatives. The tension between delivering program funds quickly and protecting against fraud and abuse was woven deeply into the legislation and the regulations for the Recovery Act. The institutionalization of auditors as prominent public officials only intensified this clash, as Paul Posner shows in chapter 9. Thus, the traditional roles played by auditors and managers became blurred as the former were given important responsibilities in the up-front design of reporting requirements in addition to their traditional responsibility for post hoc reviews of compliance. The changing relationships between these two separate communities of program managers and auditors created tensions that radiated down to the lowest-level implementers in the ARRA system. With a more proactive and public role, auditors sent signals that at times were at odds with those sent by program managers. And recipients seeking to adapt the complex array of federal programs to differing local conditions faced dilemmas about whether caution or innovation should govern their actions.

The Recovery Act also mobilized elected officeholders and central management officials to join together in "topocratic" networks, which vied with long-established networks of program specialists. The prominent role of the vice president in ARRA's implementation process served to centralize accountability, reporting, and decision making, thus placing new limits on networks of program specialists. The traditional grant programs were largely left alone to manage through vertically integrated "picket fence federalism" arrangements, but the high stakes of the Recovery Act vaulted grant administration from obscure realms of pluralist policymaking to the partisan realms of contestation and mobilization.

Thus, though networks remained the backbone for the delivery of ARRA funds, they were fundamentally transformed by the political stress test of ARRA. As a result, there was probably less collaboration overall in implementing ARRA, even while crosscutting topocratic and auditing networks proliferated and became more engaged in the project.

Constructing Special Partnerships with States

Given their critical role in implementing stimulus programs, it behooved the Obama administration to find ways to enlist states and localities in the Recovery Act as effective and engaged partners. However, doing so was a challenge because, during the past twenty-five years, Washington has stripped away its institutions of intergovernmental expertise and collaboration. These included the offices of intergovernmental management in OMB, intergovernmental relations subcommittees in Congress, and collaborative forums like the Advisory Commission on Intergovernmental Relations. Some nations, like Australia, were able to develop their stimulus plans and oversee implementation through an established intergovernmental forum—the Council of Australian Governments.[13] Lacking such a venue, American national leaders were forced to improvise by creating ad hoc consultation strategies, featuring weekly calls among top staff members to federal and state leaders and periodic meetings among intergovernmental principals.

However, bringing states into the ground floor of Recovery Act planning and management introduced yet another source of network conflict into the mix. Political polarization has spread far beyond Washington and has deeply infiltrated American state governments, ripping apart consensuses among governors over the Recovery Act partnerships with the federal government. Taking the states as they found them, the administration was forced to design workarounds to compensate for those states that opted out of such Recovery Act initiatives as high-speed rail, extended unemployment insurance, and Race to the Top education grants. The advent of intergovernmental polarization meant that federal leaders had to adopt network collaboration strategies with "variable speeds" to reflect the increasingly different priorities of the states.[14]

Variable Policy Implementation Regimes

Given the wide range of programs deployed under the ARRA umbrella, considerable variability in program management and implementation was to be expected. The vexing challenges in management and oversight discussed above can be understood in greater depth by assessing how they played out in the very different program structures under ARRA. The chapters in this book highlight some of the most important differences that were experienced in the implementation of ARRA. In effect, this study of ARRA provides a testing laboratory to assess what we know about the implementation process for public programs. It is not often that one single initiative encompasses the presence of differing networks, tools, and implementation actors. As such, ARRA provides fertile ground for drawing lessons from this natural experiment in policy management and implementation. Table 10.1 highlights how the seven ARRA programs covered in this book dealt with some of the more important dimensions relevant to implementation and accountability.[15]

As the table indicates, there were many key differences in the implementation regimes used to deliver and manage ARRA funding. Indeed, we designed

Table 10.1. An Implementation Profile of ARRA Case Studies

Program Characteristic	Education Stabilization	Race to the Top	Highways	New Markets	Weatherization	Broadband	Advanced Energy
Network Tool	Established Formula grant	Established Project grant	Established Formula grant	Established Tax expenditure	New Formula grant	New Project grant	New Tax expenditure
Primary implementation agents	States and local schools	States and local schools	States with local governments and private contractors	Private for-profit companies	State energy agencies with pass-through to local nonprofits and private contractors	States, private, and nonprofit organizations	Private for-profit companies
Federal roles	Decentralized to states through broad-based grant	Centralized	Decentralized to states, which have discretion to choose projects within broad federal guidelines	Centralized federal awards and management steering, with devolution to private networks	Federal grants to states, which deliver through nonprofit networks, with stronger federal standards and monitoring	Centralized projects funded by two federal agencies, with some additional state role	Centralized federal awards with a potential audit by the Internal Revenue Service

Congruence between federal and nonfederal goals	High, with fiscal support for state priorities	High for participating states	High, with states in charge of project selection	High, with private partners	Mixed	Low	High
Degree of change in policy (low, moderate, and high)	Low, with subsidies to existing state and local education budgets	High, with prescriptive national standards for education for participating states	Low, with additional funds to support state highway projects	Low, with ARRA funds increasing the tax credits available under the existing New Markets program	Moderate, with a significant expansion of funding and accountability	High, with new delivery responsibilities for partners with little prior engagement	Low, with tax credit funds available to support proposals initiated by private firms

our case studies to deepen our understanding of the implications of different network arrangements and funding tools for the implementation of this major national initiative. The following discussion uses the implementation profiles in table 10.1 to highlight the effects that can flow from differences in networks, tools, and implementing agents.

Institutionalization of Delivery Networks

One of the most important differences across ARRA programs was the age and experience of the networks of managers used to implement programs. The administration and Congress were well aware of the advantages that would accrue by using the wide range of existing and time-tested programs as delivery mechanisms for the new ARRA funds. In a triumph of path dependence, the fifty-year development of federal domestic programs constituted an advantage that federal leaders were able to use to promote accountability for the Recovery Act. By comparison, federal officials during the New Deal were forced to create new programs and administrative institutions from whole cloth, hurriedly building an administrative establishment and capacity to match the breathtaking new roles taken on by the federal government.[16]

Existing programs that received ARRA funding were generally advantaged by the presence of established and often robust policy implementation networks and routines.[17] As chronicled in chapter 4, the federal highway grant program received a 77 percent boost in temporary funding through the Recovery Act ($28 billion, on top of the regular $35 billion), but this was otherwise consistent with the regular highway program. Although some confusion and conflicts arose due to the unique requirements for the use of ARRA funds, including maintenance of effort and new reporting requirements for transparency and job creation, states typically funded projects that were already in the pipeline and prioritized them according to existing program standards.

The use of existing conduits and networks for tax credits also smoothed ARRA's implementation. As discussed in chapter 7, the New Markets Tax Credit Program, which brought $3 billion in additional tax credit authority, was disbursed smoothly by federal managers without complications to various hard-pressed communities, thanks to the use of existing private investment networks and rules already in place for the regular tax credit program.

This is not to say that implementing ARRA funding for established programs did not involve challenges. Agencies and states had to maintain their regular program at the same time that they implemented ARRA under an expedited timeline. They also had to come up with new data-reporting systems and maintain both new and existing reporting and monitoring systems simultaneously, typically without additional staffing or resources. And they had to deal with multiple oversight and audit efforts from inspector generals' offices and the Government Accountability Office.

Despite these challenges in existing intergovernmental programs, the contrasting experiences of new programs and networks under ARRA is instructive. As shown in chapter 6, the twenty-five-fold increase in federal Weatherization Assistance Program funds, along with new ARRA program requirements, overwhelmed the existing implementation network and led to serious delays and well-publicized problems. Subgrantee community action agencies were forced to move quickly and under great stress to hire, or contract out for, workers to do the increased work under ARRA. This led to numerous reports that many homes were not weatherized properly and that funds were not spent appropriately.

Weatherization's difficult implementation record was mirrored in programs intended to expand access to broadband internet access. Because the federal government had generally played a hands-off role regarding broadband development before ARRA, the scaling up of this new initiative caused enormous staffing problems for both the federal Rural Utility Service (RUS) in the Agriculture Department and the National Telecommunication and Information Administration (NTIA) in the Commerce Department. Both contracted with private-sector entities for assistance with evaluating applications and overseeing the implementation of the grants, including audits and site visits. NTIA also used unpaid volunteers during the first round of awards to help examine and score applications. With respect to state governments, neither NTIA nor RUS had formal, ongoing interactions with state governments on the topic of broadband. As discussed in chapter 5, there was a perception among the states that NTIA was a "black hole," reflected in a lack of feedback and paucity of information.

Tools

Lester Salamon's work illustrates how program outcomes and implementation can be critically shaped by the policy instruments used by the federal government in delivering programs.[18] Three primary tools were involved in our case studies—formula grants, project grants, and tax expenditures. The analysis in our chapters demonstrates that tools do have distinctive "political economies" that carry substantial implications for incentives and accountability across the numerous third parties involved in implementation, but only as modified by their context and networks.

Grants constituted more than $275 billion of the federal ARRA funds and were the primary tool used in five of our seven programs to provide stimulus funding through third parties—notably states, local governments, and nonprofits. The federal government gains the opportunity to attract the participation, resources, authority, and legitimacy of third parties, which are motivated to join by the presence of federal funding.[19] Thanks to their potential to gain collaboration across the boundaries of the US intergovernmental system, grants have emerged as the workhorse of domestic policy, and it is no surprise that they proved to be one of the critical mainstays of ARRA as well.

We have long known that though grants have certain overall properties, they vary considerably in the relative authority enjoyed by federal and nonfederal partners. At one end of the spectrum, block grants provide significant authority and flexibility for states, localities, and other nonfederal partners to use the funds for their own priorities and needs. Categorical project and formula grants, conversely, articulate specific and often prescriptive national requirement and goals that recipients must meet in the interest of national uniformity and goals.

The five case studies using grants illustrated this wide variation in the tool. Broad-based grants to states for education and highways became a top federal priority because they promised to jump-start the economic recovery both by preventing major cuts in state and local education and by promoting short-term jobs for shovel-ready transportation projects. The Education Stabilization Fund acted as a one-time, broad purpose grant to the states to enable them to fill their fiscal gaps and avoid layoffs of teachers and other state and local employees that would worsen the recession. As long as states satisfied federal requirements to maintain previous state levels of education spending and assure commitments to certain education reform goals, they were able to use these funds to support their existing state education programs and thus to fund local schools. In some respects, the Stabilization Fund played the role more of a funding stream than a discrete program, with a primary focus on fiscal subsidization rather than program goals and objectives.[20]

By contrast, within the same area of education, a more centralizing and prescriptive grant was used to promote educational reform. The Race to the Top program used highly competitive project grants with prescriptive federal requirements and standards intended to promote a highly specific federal educational reform agenda. Although formula grants tend to allocate funds to all eligible recipients, competitive project grants maximize federal leverage by limiting grant awards to only those applicants whose proposals best fit federal objectives. At a time when nonfederal budgets were at a crisis point, states were even more motivated to go the extra mile to satisfy these federal program funding criteria.

By far, grants and contracts constituted the major portion of ARRA, but 35 percent of the total went for individual and business tax expenditures.[21]

We have examined the implementation of two of those tax provisions—the New Market Tax Credit (chapter 7), and the Advanced Energy Tax Credit (chapter 8). The goals of the tax credits were to stimulate private investors to allocate private funds—either in pursuit of eligible investments in low-income communities or clean energy.

Tax expenditures are thus subsidies by the government to certain tax-payers to support specific activities and purposes defined by Congress. They are provided not as outlays from the US Treasury but rather by revenue losses stemming from taxpayer claims. Salamon ranks tax expenditures as among the least coercive and least direct tools in the federal arsenal.[22] Unlike other tools, there is often no formal approval by federal officials before the claiming of these subsidies by taxpayers, nor is there prior federal review of their plans. Except for the limited federal audits of general tax returns, there are typically few federal audits or evaluations of the use of specific tax expenditures.[23]

These two cases show how minimal accountability requirements for tax tools under ARRA eased the implementation of these stimulus programs, highlighting the differences between using tax credits to achieve policy objectives instead of using other tools of government, such as direct federal provision or intergovernmental grants. Unlike ARRA spending programs, the tax provisions under ARRA did not have the same accountability and transparency requirement as grants, contracts, loans, and loan guarantees. Without pressure to report job numbers on a regular basis, or the need to adhere to extra accountability requirements, an obvious source of conflict between federal managers and investors was removed. As one federal official remarked, the biggest difference between grants or contracts and tax credits is that there are not any visible federal dollars going out the door. Overall, we found that the federal government's role for both tax credit programs was more reactive than proactive; it involved steering diverse private investors toward goals that will have the greatest economic benefit and, to a lesser extent, mediating relationships among third parties.

Yet both tax credits operated in ways that involved greater federal roles in authorizing subsidies than most tax expenditures. Rather than simply letting taxpayers claim credits on an open-ended basis without overall limits on the federal commitment, federal subsidies were limited to a fixed amount for both tax credits. Similar to project grants, the federal government made awards for tax credits through a competition among competing firms for the fixed pot of federal credits. Another unusual feature was the partnership between the Internal Revenue Service (IRS) and the substantive federal program agency responsible for the aided activities. The Energy Department and Treasury Department did the ranking and scoring of applications, leaving it to the IRS to audit the projects upon completion.

Our cases thus illustrate that tools matter—but also that there is considerable variation within each tool, which can make a great difference in the impact of the policy instrument on the nation. Tools matter, in concert with their context, their use in unique program designs, and their particular networks deployed in the delivery of subsidies to ultimate beneficiaries.

Implementing Agents and Roles

The foregoing suggests that the roles and relationships among those engaged in both using tools and carrying out programs are critical ingredients for accountability and impact. Our seven case study programs cover a wide range of implementation regimes—from the relatively simple, bilateral relationship between the federal government and the states for the Education Stabilization Fund or the highway program to the far more complex and layered implementation networks that are engaged in carrying out the New Markets Tax Credit and weatherization programs. All other things being equal, networks grow in complexity when the numbers and types of actors multiply, presenting members with the challenge of multiplexity—the need to build ties and links across numerous organizations.[24] The presence of multiple actors can constitute a strength by providing opportunities to engage the unique resources possessed by different actors in the system. But they also constitute a potential source of conflict and goal slippage, particularly when the actors do not share common interests, ends, or trust. The challenge to the federal government and its partners is to find approaches to overcome fragmentation across the welter of providers, sharing some responsibility for providing services for the nation, the states, or various regions.[25]

The implementation regimes for the Education Stabilization and highway programs were the most stable and least fragmented among our case studies, centered on the bilateral relationship between the federal government and the states. As noted above, the federal ARRA grants primarily served the role of providing a funding stream to support existing state and local programs and delivery systems. The implementation regimes for substate delivery of both education and highways were, for the most part, well established and well practiced in using and accounting for federal aid for many different programs. Administrative relationships with private firms in highway planning and construction, for instance, had become institutionalized and well articulated at all levels of government for many years.

By contrast, a far broader range of state, local, nonprofit, and private for-profit implementation actors were involved in our other case studies. For these, actors faced the challenge of collaborating across a wide range of governmental, nonprofit, and private for-profit entities that had varying levels of capacity, program commitment, and priorities. The broadband program, discussed in chapter 5, featured direct grants from the federal government to many of these actors with little history in broadband development and little coordination by the federal government. Although state governments had the option of commenting on a portion of the grant proposals, this was done after proposals were submitted, which put state leaders at a disadvantage in promoting up-front strategic collaboration for broadband networks. Some governors rose to the challenge by providing coordination among state agencies and regional entities, bringing in state transportation and environmental agencies whose cooperation was instrumental to expeditious completion of these new communications systems.

Tensions occurred among the implementation actors involved in these programs. Private cable firms, for instance, eyed federal broadband initiatives with suspicion, fearing potential invasion by federally subsidized service providers into markets they had carefully groomed. The ambitious federal funding and time frames for weatherization proved to exceed the organizational, technical, and financial capacity of states, local nonprofits, and private contractors, leading to problems with both timeliness and quality. In some cases, conflicts among the actors had a beneficial result. Under the New Markets Tax Credit, private investors that were fearful of IRS penalties if the terms of the credit were abused by the community development entities managing projects exercised their own oversight for these agencies. The use of third parties to provide oversight may have enhanced incentives for accountability, but perhaps at the expense of higher transaction costs.

As the foregoing suggests, implementation regimes for tax credits had more of a private-sector cast than what is typically found in federal programs. Yet third-party roles were very different for the two tax subsidy programs in our study. The New Markets Tax Credit perennially engages a diverse set of third parties—community development entities—with highly sophisticated financial and accounting expertise to raise the necessary equity and investment for covered businesses. These organizations are the center of a complex financing network linking investors with projects for low-income areas.

By contrast, the alternate energy program featured far more limited third-party networks. Third parties, in particular industry groups and consulting firms, were involved in redistributing federal program information and, to some extent, in helping clean energy manufacturers through the application preparation process. But for the most part, the public objective (primarily to create construction and manufacturing jobs) closely aligned with the business interests of the program's targeted beneficiaries (clean energy manufacturers), obliterating the need for more complex relationships between various third parties that would have posed the kind of steering problems that federal managers otherwise encounter in more network-dependent tools and programs. The congruence between the goals of federal tax subsidies and the financial interests of market investors established more of a vertical and unmediated relationship between the IRS and the investors claiming the credit. Essentially, this tax credit functioned much like a federal block grant to states, whereby the federal policy goal and the priorities of recipients are closely aligned. Lacking the complications of goal conflict and tensions among federal objectives, these kinds of program subsidies are ideally suited for the expedited implementation of stimulus programs.

The Federal Role

The foregoing suggests some variability in the federal role for the case study programs. Although the overall management and oversight of ARRA was highly centralized, as noted in chapter 9, individual programs ranged from the highly state-centered Education Stabilization and highway programs to the centralized project grants of the Race to the Top and broadband programs. The tax credit programs had fewer administrative requirements but, surprisingly, greater up-front federal roles in awarding credits than is typical for tax expenditures.

The range of federal roles broadly corresponds to the different purposes underlying each ARRA program. Programs like Education Stabilization were primarily geared to short-term jobs recovery, and a funding stream model working through established state priorities and networks appeared to be the ideal way to implement this high federal priority. Conversely, for those programs where recovery was coupled with new investment and other policy goals, the federal government could not accept nonfederal partners as they found them. Instead, the inconsistent capacity and priorities across the nation called for a more centralized program accountability structure with greater federal prescription of standards and requirements. Table 10.1 shows that those programs largely using existing policy goals and networks for ARRA had lower federal role profiles than those that sought to institute broader changes in policy goals and networks.

Finally, the federal role can reflect the degree of anticipated congruence between federal and nonfederal interests and objectives. Don Kettl posits congruence as the critical variable affecting the successful implementation of third-party programs.[26] The presence of significant conflict in goals and interests can presage slippage and shortfalls in program implementation, as third-party implementers use different criteria and priorities to guide their management of programs. Often, the presence of long-standing networks is highly correlated with agreement among key implementation actors across the federal system. Research has indeed shown that over time, many federal programs succeed in bringing about congruence through the gradual internalization of national program norms and values by third parties.[27] Indeed, our case studies affirm the close correspondence between long-standing networks and goal agreement. Of the seven cases in this book, only two showed significant conflict across participants in implementation networks. One of these was the new broadband program, which had little or no previous federal program antecedent from which to build partnerships. The other was the weatherization program, which was laden with ambitious funding, goals, and requirements that, in effect, redefined the roles and responsibilities of nonfederal partners in significant ways. The Race to the Top program engendered considerable agreement between those states that wished to participate in the nationally defined education reform mission; but it also inspired other, more conservative states that did not share these priorities to choose not to participate. The decision by states to opt out of programs with significant federal funding is a marked departure for the US federal aid system and reflects the deepening polarization between federal priorities and those of some states.[28]

The congruence between federal and nonfederal roles for ARRA is a reflection of the underlying policy ambition of each covered program. As table 10.1 illustrates, programs such as those for highways and education stabilization largely ratified existing arrangements with states and other providers, with relatively little expectations for changes in providers or their priorities. It is not surprising that programs with limited expectations for policy change achieved greater congruence between federal and nonfederal goals. Conversely, programs such as those for broadband and weatherization had ambitious federal policy goals that pushed state and local providers beyond their comfort zone. Accordingly, these programs had low congruence between national and subnational goals.

Unrequited Presidential Leadership: The Politics of National Policy in a Network Regime

The contradictions of national policy implementation were felt most acutely by the president himself. Although the stakes could not have been higher for him, his success rested on the performance of far-flung, decentralized networks that were neither commanded by nor beholden to the federal government. The tensions between centralized political accountability and noncentralized management responsibility were placed in sharp relief by the economic crisis and the implementation of the Recovery Act.

Deep-seated tensions exist between decentralizing management imperatives and centralizing political imperatives. Expediting effective stimulus programs ideally calls for managing through networks. Efficiency and speed alone dictated the reliance on long-standing networks and existing programs where trusting relationships had been established. Perhaps the most efficient stimulus is that which merely augments existing grant programs to states with a minimum of additional policy overlays and administrative layers.[29]

However, relying on existing networks presented asymmetrical political challenges to national elected officials. On one hand, credit is diffused throughout the system. Indeed, most governors—Republicans and Democrats alike—were only too happy to take credit for managing their state's finances during these troubled times while giving little recognition to the federal government's role in limiting the need for even more drastic budget cuts and tax increases.[30] On the other hand, blame remains centralized, as numerous political actors were ready to pin any misstep on the president himself. The president needed all the credit he could muster, facing a deeply conflicted and skeptical political culture both inside and outside Washington.

Notwithstanding the positive effects that the Recovery Act had on the economy, the public remained skeptical and opposed. Part of this hostility stemmed from the polarization of party elites vis-à-vis the Recovery Act; thus, not a single House Republican voted for the bill.[31] Ironically, part of the opposition stemmed from the unprecedented transparency introduced by the administration—transparency that radiated granular information on local spending, which was usable by friend and foe alike. In today's polarized political system, opponents were as well organized as the White House, and thus they were ready to pounce on new information to use it to blame the administration in their persistent campaign to delegitimize this large government initiative. These campaigns took root among a more ideologically divided public, offsetting much of the hard work done by the administration to insulate these programs from blame through more rigorous accountability provisions. The accountability frameworks deployed to insulate the Recovery Act initiative against blame and mismanagement seemed to have had little if any impact on a questioning public that was primed to oppose such a large government investment.

A look back at the New Deal may help explain the disconnect between the positive economic results of this stimulus and its dispiriting political report card. The New Deal job creation programs—the Works Progress Administration, the Public Works Administration, and the Civilian Conservation Corps, among others—enjoyed tremendous popular support, which benefited President Franklin Roosevelt. Each of these programs was newly developed to meet the challenges of the Great Depression and generated a strong political following, both among grateful clients and prospective clients, who identified the programs as a safe harbor in a horrible economic storm. Strong support for President Roosevelt, and a far deeper and longer Depression, primed the public to support stronger government intervention. By contrast, President Obama, and most postwar presidents, have more difficulty gaining support from a more ideological and polarized Congress and public.

Beyond these obvious political differences, it was critically important that the jobs initiatives of the New Deal were primarily direct federal programs whose resources and benefits were largely distributed by federal officials, who were often the president's political appointees. The millions of grateful clients of these programs, as well as many others seeking relief, learned to train their hopes on the White House for deliverance. President Roosevelt was not only able to take credit for the millions of jobs produced but he also was able to steer benefits to reward political allies and punish his opposition, as Washington agencies often controlled the projects to be funded, the wages to be paid, and the eligibility for benefits.

By contrast, the Obama administration relied on third-party networks of state, local, nonprofit, and private actors to deliver this stimulus. Although efficacious as a governing strategy, networked governance carried distinct political downsides for President Obama by dissipating the political credit that the president and other national officials could take for these results. In the first quarter of the Recovery Act, more than 130,000 state and local governments, nonprofits, and private firms reported receiving stimulus funds under federal grants, contracts, and loans—a figure that excludes thousands of others playing a role in delivering entitlements and tax programs. In many cases, federal Recovery Act funds passed down through several layers before reaching the ultimate recipients. There was no clear line of sight for the public to attribute credit to the president at the same time that governors, mayors, and other political actors could share in the management and claiming credit. Public confusion can easily set in when so many hands are stirring the pot.

In theory, the decentralized networks used in the Recovery Act could have been viewed as ideal ways to devolve blame to others for problems experienced during implementation. Christopher Hood argues that political leaders have an asymmetrical preference for blame avoidance, even if it diminishes their opportunity to claim credit. He argues that loss aversion has a more compelling influence on officials, who seek above all to limit their downside political risks.[32] This may be the case in the short term, but the inability to claim credit can be politically crippling as well. Moreover, the president's strong imprimatur on the stimulus would have made it difficult for him to off-load problems onto other actors in any case.

Thus, the disappointing public perception of the Recovery Act had complex causes, but its complex and confusing implementation structure played no small part. When the president and Republican governors both claimed credit for creating the same jobs, it is no wonder that the public was destined to be confused, diminishing the link between the president and the policy outcomes.

Ultimately, the pushback to the stimulus was not, as many have alleged, that President Obama centralized too much power at the national level. Rather, his greatest political vulnerability was the combination of invoking high expectations while using a highly decentralized governance regime that dispersed credit throughout a decentralized system.

The Recovery Act was not a singular event but rather a pattern that is destined to be repeated in ways that will make national leadership more difficult and complex. Presidents, the media, and the public conspire together to raise expectations to dizzying heights. Candidates campaign in primary states by giving voice to grand, new national visions, all the while ignoring the states where they are standing. Once elected, however, our national ambivalence about federal power returns with a vengeance, consigning presidents to fulfill these bold promises by working with, not around, state and local governments, nonprofits, and private leaders. Former president George W. Bush learned this lesson when recalcitrant states jeopardized his No Child Left Behind program and his Real ID mandate to establish secure driver's licenses. President Obama encountered it with both his stimulus program and health insurance reform legislation.

Roosevelt may have been the last of our presidents who was able to stride across the national stage relatively unencumbered by the centrifugal forces of our pluralistic third-party state. Yet even he was reminded of his limited powers as resentment grew over his centralized governing style, whether it be trying to pack the Supreme Court or micromanaging the New Deal jobs programs. Elected as national champions, contemporary presidents must quickly learn how to govern through collaboration with the wide range of dispersed powers in our system. Presidents and their allies chafe at the limits and compromises that must be made in this process. However, the nation is often better off through a third-party governance approach because the complex, wicked problems of our time are perhaps best addressed by multiple actors deploying approaches tailored to particular areas and publics.

Ultimately, regardless of the relative efficacy of third-party government to solve national problems, such indirect governance strategies are rooted in the widespread public ambivalence about the role of government. With broad public support for government benefits but not government bureaucrats, the turn to third-party government has deep roots in the political culture of the nation. Although particular presidents may have had sufficient political capital to govern more unilaterally for a brief time, those episodes are destined to be short-term events in the US system.

Over the longer term, the reliance on increasingly complex networks and more indirect governance tools can exact a cost in public support for government. Suzanne Mettler details the lack of transparency and public understanding of government benefits delivered through tax expenditures, loan guarantees, and other instruments of third-party governance in her insightful work on the "submerged state."[33] It is ironic indeed that a model of governance with roots in public distrust and disenchantment with government may end up exacerbating those very same beliefs.

Preparing for the Next Time

ARRA, of course, did not repeal the business cycle. The next time the United States needs to deploy a stimulus, it is unlikely that its system will fundamentally change its stripes and return to the days of the New Deal. Rather, it is safer to predict that many of the same constraints on ARRA will be carried into any new initiative. Leaders will face continued polarization and political accountability for national results while being consigned to work within decentralized implementation networks that are both far flung and independent. The system will continue to be challenged to balance speed in program implementation with accountability and planning for longer-term outcomes. A complex congressional politics will continue to dissipate funds across numerous programs and governance tools. State and local governments will be vital partners even while such collaborations continue to be situational and evanescent in nature. The public itself will continue to be ambivalent, crosspressured between a desire to rein in the federal government and an attachment to specific program benefits during hard times.[34]

Given these continuing constraints, lessons can be drawn from the ARRA experience that could enable greater capacity and collaboration to be exercised during the response to the next economic downturn. Most important, we should devote time while the economic sun is shining to strengthen institutions and insight about implementation well before the crisis is upon us. Federal and state governments together can engage in the following common reforms that could collectively enhance their joint capacity to govern:

- Engage all agencies of government in an initiative to better understand the capacity, priorities, and effects of networks of program implementers— public, nonprofit, and private—which will vitally affect ultimate program outcomes;

- Create a government-wide initiative led by central management and budget offices to assess the implications of using different tools such as grants, tax expenditures, loans, and contracts for program implementation;
- Strengthen data collection for the financing and performance of federal programs, building on the Data Act of 2014;
- Establish institutional forums for collaboration and joint policymaking between federal, state, and local officials, as well as with the nonprofit and private sectors;
- Build greater stewardship by upgrading the capabilities of both managers and auditors and evaluators to perform oversight of complex intergovernmental and intersectoral programs.

None of these initiatives can solve the vexing political dilemmas facing public officials as they seek to mount effective stimulus programs in polarized and contentious political environments. However, they can strengthen the capacity to govern in hard times and, perhaps, improve the public's confidence in government over the longer term. At a time when more demands are being placed on government, reversing the public's flagging trust in government performance is perhaps the most important task facing the nation.

Notes

1. Ben Ansell, "Crisis as Political Opportunity," in *Coping with Crisis: Government Reactions to the Great Recession*, ed. Nancy Bermoe and Jonas Pontusson (New York: Russell Sage, 2012), 336.

2. Nancy Bermeo and Jonas Pontusson, "Coping with Crisis: An Introduction," in *Coping with Crisis*, ed. Bermoe and Pontusson, 10.

3. Pamela Prah, "Promise and Peril," *Stateline.org*, March 20, 2009.

4. See, e.g., Congressional Budget Office, *Estimated Impact of the American Recovery and Reinvestment Act on Employment and Economic Output from January 2011 through March 2011* (Washington, DC: Congressional Budget Office, 2011).

5. Organization for Economic Cooperation and Development, *Fiscal Policy across Levels of Government in Times of Crisis* (Paris: Organization for Economic Cooperation and Development, 2010).

6. John D. Dilulio and John T. Dilulio, "Principled Agents: The Cultural Bases of Behavior in the Federal Bureaucracy," *Journal of Public Administration Research and Theory* 3, no. 4 (July 1994): 271–318.

7. The Office of Management and Budget estimated that three hundred programs were subject to the public reporting provisions of ARRA, section 1512.

8. G. Edward DeSeve, *Managing Recovery: An Insider's View* (Washington, DC: IBM Center for the Business of Government, 2011).

9. Treasury inspector general for tax administration, "Semiannual Report to Congress, April 1, 2013–September 30, 2013," 57.

10. Paul E. Peterson, Barry G. Rabe, and Kenneth K. Wong, *Making Federalism Work* (Washington, DC: Brookings Institution Press, 1986); Robert Stoker, *Reluctant Partners: Implementing Federal Policy* (Pittsburgh: University of Pittsburgh Press, 1991).

11. Chad Ress, "The Invisible Stimulus: In Search of What Obama Built," *Harper's Magazine*, November 2012.

12. Charles D. Maestas, Lonna Rae Atkeson, Cherie D. Maestas, Thomas Croom, and Lisa A. Bryant, "Shifting the Blame: Federalism, Media and Public Assignment of Blame Following Hurricane Katrina," *Publius* 38, no. 4 (2008): 609–32.

13. Organization for Economic Cooperation and Development, *Making the Most of Public Investment in a Tight Fiscal Environment* (Paris: Organization for Economic Cooperation and Development, 2011), 86.

14. Timothy J. Conlan, Young Sung Kim, Mariely Lopez-Santana, and Paul Posner, "Unsafe at Any Speed: The Emergence of Variable-Speed Federalism in the United States and the European Union," paper presented at the annual meeting of the American Political Science Association, Washington, September 1, 2014.

15. Some of these dimensions are derived from the discussion by Paul Sabatier and Daniel Mazmanian, "The Conditions of Effective Implementation: A Guide to Accomplishing Policy Objectives," *Policy Analysis* 5, no. 4 (Fall 1979): 481–504.

16. James T. Patterson, *The New Deal and the States* (Princeton, NJ: Princeton University Press, 1969).

17. This discussion of program implementation draws on George Mason University, "Networks under Stress: The American Recovery and Reinvestment Act of 2009," February 2013.

18. Lester Salamon, ed., *The Tools of Government: A Guide to the New Governance* (New York: Oxford University Press, 2002).

19. David R. Beam and Timothy J. Conlan, "Grants," in *Tools of Government*, ed. Salamon, 340–80.

20. Susan S. Westin, "Balancing Flexibility and Accountability: Grant Program Design in Education and Other Program Areas," Testimony before the Education Task Force, Senate Budget Committee, Government Accountability Office, GAO/GGD/HEHS-98-94, February 11, 1998.

21. US Government Accountability Office, "Recovery Act: IRS Quickly Implemented Tax Provisions, but Reporting and Enforcement Improvements Are Needed," GAO-10-349, February 2010.

22. Salamon, *Tools of Government*, 24–32.

23. Government Accountability Office, "Performance and Accountability: Tax Expenditures Represent a Substantial Federal Commitment and Need to Be Reexamined," GAO-05-690, September 2005.

24. Keith G. Provan, Mark A. Veazie, Lisa K. Staten, and Nicolette I. Teufel-Shone, "The Use of Network Analysis Strengthen Community Partnerships," *Public Administration Review* 65, no. 5 (September–October 2005): 603–13.

25. Jungae Bae and Richard C. Feiock, "Managing Multiplexity: Coordinating Multiple Services at the Regional Level," *State and Local Government Review* 44, no. 2 (June 2012): 162–68.

26. Donald Kettl, *Government by Proxy* (Washington, DC: Congressional Quarterly Press, 1988), 16.

27. Peterson, Rabe, and Wong, *Making Federalism Work*.

28. Timothy J. Conlan and Paul L. Posner, "Inflection Point? Federalism and the Obama Administration," *Publius: The Journal of Federalism* 41, no. 3 (2011): 421–46.

29. For a useful review of the literature on this, see Chad Stone and Kris Cox, *Principles for Fiscal Stimulus: Economic Policy in a Weakening Economy* (Washington, DC: Center for Budget and Policy Priorities, 2008), www.cbpp.org/research/principles-for-fiscal-stimulus-economic-policy-in-a-weakening-economy.

30. One notable exception to this was Florida governor Charlie Crist's famous embrace of President Obama for his help during the fiscal crisis—a symbolic hug that ended his career in the Republican Party. Much more common were the many Republican governors who denounced the Recovery Act as wasteful spending and symbolically rejected modest grants for high-speed rail or extended unemployment benefits while silently accepting the great bulk of their state's federal stimulus funds. For other instances, see Steve Benen, "Political Animal: Republican Governors Love/Hate the Stimulus Too," *Washington Monthly*, February 16, 2010, www.washingtonmonthly.com/archives/individual/2010_02/022433.php.

31. Nolan McCarty, "The Politics of Pop: The US Response to the Financial Crisis and the Great Recession" in *Coping with Crisis*, ed. Bermoe and Pontusson, 201–32.

32. Christopher Hood, *The Blame Game: Spin, Bureaucracy, and Self-Preservation in Government* (Princeton, NJ: Princeton University Press, 2011), 73.

33. Suzanne Mettler, *The Submerged State* (Chicago: University of Chicago Press, 2011).

34. Albert H. Cantril and Susan Davis Cantril, *Reading Mixed Signals: Ambivalence in American Public Opinion about Government* (Washington, DC: Woodrow Wilson Center Press, 1999).

SELECTED BIBLIOGRAPHY

Books and Articles

Agranoff, Robert. *Managing within Networks: Adding Value to Public Organizations.* Washington, DC: Georgetown University Press, 2007.

Agranoff, Robert, and Michael McGuire. *Collaborative Public Management: New Strategies for Local Government.* Washington, DC: Georgetown University Press, 2003.

Aldy, Joseph. "A Preliminary Assessment of the American Recovery and Reinvestment Act's Clean Energy Package." *Review of Environmental Economics* 7, no. 1 (2003): 136–55.

Ansell, Ben. "Crisis as Political Opportunity." In *Coping with Crisis: Government Reactions to the Great Recession,* edited by Nancy Bermoe and Jonas Pontusson. New York: Russell Sage, 2012.

Bae, Jungae, and Richard C. Feiock. "Managing Multiplexity: Coordinating Multiple Services at the Regional Level." *State and Local Government Review* 44, no. 2 (2012): 162–68.

Beam, David R., and Timothy J. Conlan. "Grants." In *The Tools of Government,* edited by Lester Salamon. New York: Oxford University Press, 2002.

Beer, Samuel. "Federalism, Nationalism and Democracy in America." *American Political Science Review* 72 (1977): 1–13.

Bermeo, Nancy, and Jonas Pontusson. "Coping with Crisis: An Introduction." In *Coping with Crisis: Government Reactions to the Great Recession,* edited by Nancy Bermoe and Jonas Pontusson. New York: Russell Sage Foundation, 2012.

Bernanke, Ben. *The Courage to Act: A Memoir of a Crisis and Its Aftermath.* New York: W. W. Norton, 2015.

Blinder, Alan S., and Mark Zandi. "How the Great Recession Was Brought to an End." July 27, 2010. www.economy.com/mark-zandi/documents/End-of-Great -Recession.pdf.

Boyd, Donald J., and Lucy Dadayan. "State Tax Decline in Early 2009 Was the Sharpest on Record." *State Revenue Report* (Rockefeller Institute), 2009.

Brito, Jerry, and Veronique de Rugy. "Stimulus Facts." Working Paper 09-46. Fairfax, VA: Mercatus Center at George Mason University, 2009.

Burtless, Gary, and Tracy Gordon. "The Federal Stimulus Programs and Their Effects." In *The Great Recession*, edited by David B. Grusky, Bruce Western, and Christopher Wimer. New York: Russell Sage Foundation, 2011.

Callahan, Richard, Sandra O. Archibald, Kay A. Sterner, and H. Brinton Milward. *Key Actions That Contribute to Successful Program Implementation: Lessons from the Recovery Act*. Washington, DC: IBM Center for the Business of Government, 2012.

Cantril, Albert H., and Susan Davis Cantril. *Reading Mixed Signals: Ambivalence in American Public Opinion about Government*. Washington, DC: Woodrow Wilson Center Press, 1999.

Center for Education Policy. *An Early Look at the Economic Stimulus Package and the Public Schools: Perspectives from State Leaders*. Washington, DC: Center for Education Policy, 2009.

———. *More to Do but Less Capacity to Do It: States' Progress in Implementing the Recovery Act Education Reforms*. Washington, DC: Center for Education Policy, 2011.

———. *Teaching Jobs Saved in 2009–10, but Teacher Layoffs Loom for Next School Year*. Washington, DC: Center for Education Policy, 2010.

Chodorow-Reich, Gabriel, Laura Feiveson, Zachary Liscow, William Woolston, and William Gui. "Does State Fiscal Relief during Recessions Increase Employment? Evidence from the American Recovery and Reinvestment Act." *American Economic Journal: Economic Policy* 4, no. 3 (2012): 121.

Conlan, Timothy J. *Grants and the Recovery Act: Classic Challenges, New Dilemmas, and Best Practices*. Fairfax, VA: CGI Initiative for Collaborative Governance, 2009.

Conlan, Timothy J., and Paul L. Posner. "Inflection Point: Federalism and the Obama Administration." *Publius: The Journal of Federalism* 41, no. 3 (2011): 421–46.

Conlan, Timothy J., Paul L. Posner, and David R. Beam. *Pathways of Power: The Dynamics of National Policy Making*. Washington, DC: Georgetown University Press, 2013.

Conlan, Timothy J., Young Sung Kim, Mariely Lopez-Santana, and Paul Posner. "Unsafe at Any Speed: The Emergence of Variable-Speed Federalism in the United States and the European Union." Paper presented at the annual meeting of the American Political Science Association, Washington, September 1, 2014.

Derthick, Martha. *New Towns In-Town*. Washington, DC: Brookings Institution Press, 1972.

DeSeve, G. Edward. *Managing Recovery: An Insider's View*. Washington, DC: IBM Center for the Business of Government, 2011.

DiGiammarino, Frank. "Implementation of the American Recovery and Reinvestment Act in the United States." Speech to the Territorial Development Policy Committee of the Organization for Economic Cooperation and Development, Paris, December 2010.

Dilulio, John D., and John T. Dilulio. "Principled Agents: The Cultural Bases of Behavior in the Federal Bureaucracy." *Journal of Public Administration Research and Theory* nos. 3–4 (1994): 271–318.

Donahue, John, and Richard Zeckhauser. *Collaborative Governance*. Princeton, NJ: Princeton University Press, 2011.

Feyrer, James, and Bruce Sacerdote. "Did the Stimulus Stimulate? Real Time Estimates of the Effects of the American Recovery and Reinvestment Act." NBER Working Paper 16759. Cambridge, MA: National Bureau of Economic Research, 2011. www.nber.org/papers/w16759.

Fountain, Jane. *Implementing Cross-Agency Collaboration: A Guide for Federal Managers*. Washington, DC: IBM Center for the Business of Government, 2013.

George Mason University Centers on the Public Service. *The Implementation of the Recovery Act: Networks Under Stress*. Fairfax, VA: George Mason University, 2013. http://psc.gmu.edu/wp-content/uploads/ARRA_Overview_Mar_13.pdf.

Goggin, Malcolm L., Ann Bowman, James Lester, and Laurence O'Toole. *Implementation Theory and Practice: Toward a Third Generation*. New York: Scott Foresman, 1990.

Goldsmith, Stephen, and William Eggers. *Governing by Network: The New Shape of the Public Sector*. Washington, DC: Brookings Institution Press, 2004.

Goldsmith, Stephen, and Donald Kettl, eds. *Unlocking the Power of Networks*. Washington, DC: Brookings Institution Press, 2009.

Grabell, Michael. *Money Well Spent? The Truth behind the Trillion-Dollar Stimulus, the Biggest Economic Recovery Plan in History*. New York: PublicAffairs, 2012.

———. "Stimulus for Cotton Candy, Tango and a Fish Orchestra? Wacky, or Actually Worthy?" *Pro Publica*, November 5, 2009. www.propublica.org/article/stimulus-for-cotton-candy-tango-and-a-fish-orchestra-wacky-or-actually-wort.

Grunwald, Michael. *The New New Deal: The Hidden Story of Change in the Obama Era*. New York: Simon & Schuster, 2012.

Hood, Christopher. *The Blame Game: Spin, Bureaucracy, and Self-Preservation in Government*. Princeton, NJ: Princeton University Press, 2010.

Howard, Christopher. "Tax Expenditures." In *The Tools of Government: A Guide to the New Governance*, edited by Lester Salamon. New York: Oxford University Press, 2002.

Ingram, Helen. "Policy Implementation through Bargaining: The Case of Federal Grants-in-Aid." *Public Policy* 25 (Fall 1977): 499–526.

Jennings, Edward T., Jr., Jeremy L. Hall, and Zhiwei Zhang. "The American Recovery and Reinvestment Act and State Accountability." *Public Performance and Management Review* 35, no. 3 (2012): 541.

Kettl, Donald. *Government by Proxy*. Washington, DC: Congressional Quarterly Press, 1988.

———. *Performance and Accountability*. Washington, DC: National Academy of Public Administration, 1989.

Kingdon, John. *Agendas, Alternatives, and Public Policy*. New York: Longman, 1995.

Leduc, Sylvan, and Daniel Wilson. "Roads to Prosperity or Bridges to Nowhere? Theory and Evidence on the Impact of Public Infrastructure Investment." *NBER Macroeconomics Annual* 27, no. 1 (2012): 89–142.

Light, Paul C. *A Cascade of Failures: Why Government Fails, and How to Stop It*. Washington, DC: Brookings Institution Press, 2014.

Manna, Paul. *Collision Course: Federal Education Policy Meets State and Local Realities*. Washington, DC: CQ Press, 2011.

Manna, Paul, and Laura L. Ryan. "Competitive Grants and Educational Federalism: President Obama's Race to the Top Program in Theory and Practice." *Publius: The Journal of Federalism* 41, no. 3 (2011): 522–46.

Mansbridge, Jane. "A Selection Model of Political Representation." *Journal of Political Philosophy* 17, no. 4 (2009): 369–98.

Matthews, Dylan. "Did the Stimulus Work? A Review of the Nine Best Studies on the Subject." *Washington Post*, August 11, 2011. www.washingtonpost.com/blogs

/wonkblog/post/did-the-stimulus-work-a-review-of-the-nine-best-studies-on
-thesubject/2011/08/16/gIQAThbibJ_blog.html.

Mazmanian, Daniel A., and Paul A. Sabatier. *Implementation and Public Policy*. Lanham, MD: University Press of America, 1999.

McCarty, Nolan. "The Politics of the Pop: The US Response to the Financial Crisis and the Great Recession." In *Coping with Crisis: Government Reactions to the Great Recession*, edited by Nancy Bermoe and Jonas Pontusson. New York: Russell Sage Foundation, 2012.

McCubbins, Matthew D., and Thomas Schwartz. "Congressional Overlooked: Police Patrols vs. Fire Alarms." *American Journal of Political Science* 28, no. 1 (1984): 165–79.

McGuinn, Patrick. "Stimulating Reform: Race to the Top, Competitive Grants and the Obama Education Agenda." *Educational Policy* 26, no. 1 (2011): 46–147.

Meier, Kenneth J., and Laurence J. O'Toole Jr. "Public Management and Educational Performance: The Impact of Managerial Networking." *Public Administration Review* 63, no. 6 (2003): 689–99.

Mettler, Suzanne. *The Submerged State: How Invisible Government Policies Undermine American Democracy*. Chicago: University of Chicago Press, 2011.

Milward, H. Brinton, and Keith G. Provan. *A Manager's Guide to Choosing and Using Collaborative Networks*. Washington, DC: IBM Center for Business of Government, 2006.

———. "A Preliminary Theory of Network Effectiveness: A Comparative Study of Four Mental Health Systems." *Administrative Science Quarterly* 40, no. 1 (1995): 1–33.

Moynihan, Donald P. *From Forest Fires to Hurricane Katrina: Case Studies of Incident Command Systems*. Washington, DC: IBM Center for the Business of Government, 2007.

Mundaca, Luis, and Jessika Luth Richter. "Assessing 'Green Energy Economy' Stimulus Packages: Evidence from the US Programs Targeting Renewable Energy." International Institute for Industrial Environmental Economics, Lund University, 2014. doi:10.1016/j.rser.2014.10.060.

Nathan, Richard P. "The Methodology for Field Network Evaluation Studies." In *Studying Implementation: Methodological and Administrative Issues*, edited by Walter Williams. Chatham, NJ: Chatham House, 1982.

Nelson, Rebecca R., and Ben Geman. "Obama Reaches for Green Legacy, but Will History Books Agree?" *National Journal*, August 2015. www.nationaljournal.com /s/70708/obama-reaches-green-legacy-will-history-books-agree.

O'Leary, Rosemary, Lisa Blomgren Bingham, and Catherine Gerard, eds. "Special Issue on Collaborative Public Management." *Public Administration Review* 66, supplement (December 2006).

Oliff, Phil, and Michael Leachman. *New School Year Brings Steep Cuts in State Funding for Schools*. Washington, DC: Center for Budget and Policy Priorities, 2011.

O'Toole, Lawrence J., Jr. "Networks and Networking: The Public Administration Agendas." *Public Administration Review* 75, no. 3 (2015): 363.

Patterson, James T. *The New Deal and the States*. Princeton, NJ: Princeton University Press, 1969.

Peterson, Paul E., Barry G. Rabe, and Kenneth K. Wong. *Making Federalism Work*. Washington, DC: Brookings Institution Press, 1986.

Pew Research Center for the People and the Press. "Republicans Draw Even with Democrats on Most Issues: Pessimistic Public Doubts Effectiveness of Stimulus, TARP." 2010.

———. "Stimulus News Seen as More Negative Than Positive." Press release, February 2009. www.people-press.org/2009/02/11/stimulus-news-seen-as-more-negative-than-positive.

Posner, Paul L. "Accountability Challenges of Third-Party Government." In *The Tools of Government*, edited by Lester Salamon. New York: Oxford University Press, 2002.

———. "The Political Reality of the Stimulus." *Governing*, February 2013. www.governing.com/columns/mgmt-insights/col-political-reality-economic-stimulus-obama-roosevelt-decentralized-government.html.

Pressman, Jeffrey L., and Aaron B. Wildavsky. *Implementation: How Great Expectations in Washington Are "Dashed" in Oakland: Or, Why It's Amazing That Federal Programs Work at All, This Being a Saga of the Economic Development Administration as Told by Two Sympathetic Observers Who Seek to Build Morals on a Foundation of Ruined Hopes*. Berkeley: University of California Press, 1984.

Provan, Keith G., Mark A. Veazie, Lisa K. Staten, and Nicolette I. Teufel-Shone. "The Use of Network Analysis Strengthen Community Partnerships." *Public Administration Review* 65, no. 5 (2005): 603–13.

Raab, Jörg, and H. Brinton Milward. "Dark Networks as Problems." *Journal of Public Administration Research and Theory* 13, no. 4 (2003): 413–39.

Radin, Beryl A., and Paul L. Posner. "Policy Tools, Mandates, and Intergovernmental Relations." In *Oxford Handbook on American Bureaucracy*, edited by Robert F. Durant. New York: Oxford University Press, 2012.

Reifler, Jason, and Jeffrey Lazarus. "Partisanship and Policy Priorities in the Distribution of Economic Stimulus Funds." Working Paper. Rochester: Social Science Research Network, 2010. http://papers.ssrn.com/sol3/papers.cfm?abstract_id=1670161.

Ress, Chad. "The Invisible Stimulus: In Search of What Obama Built." *Harper's Magazine*, November 2012. http://harpers.org/archive/2012/11/the-invisible-stimulus/.

Romm, Tony. "Wired to Fail: How a Little-Known Agency Mishandled Several Billion Dollars of Stimulus Money Trying to Expand Broadband Coverage to Rural Communities." *Politico*, July 28, 2015. www.politico.com/story/2015/07/broadband-coverage-rural-area-fund-mishandled-120601#ixzz3v9PcppPq.

Sabatier, Paul, and Daniel Mazmanian. "The Conditions of Effective Implementation: A Guide to Accomplishing Policy Objectives." *Policy Analysis* 5, no. 4 (1979): 481–504.

Salamon, Lester, ed. *Tools of Government. A Guide to the New Governance*. New York: Oxford University Press, 2002.

Schillemans, Thomas, and Mark Bovens. "The Challenge of Multiple Accountability: Does Redundancy Lead to Overload?" In *Accountable Governance: Problems and Promises*, edited by Melvin J. Dubnick and H. George Frederickson. Armonk, NY: M. E. Sharpe, 2011.

Shapiro, Matthew, and Joel Slemrod. "Did the 2008 Tax Rebates Stimulate Spending?" NBER Working Paper 14753. Cambridge, MA: National Bureau of Economic Research, 2009. www.nber.org/papers/w14753.

Silver, Nate. "Study Claiming Link between Stimulus Funding and Partisanship Is Manifestly Flawed." *FiveThirtyEight*, April 2010. http://fivethirtyeight.com/features/study-claiming-link-between-stimulus.

Sinclair, Barbara. *Unorthodox Lawmaking: New Legislative Processes in the US Congress*, 4th ed. Washington, DC: CQ Press, 2012.

Smith, James Scott. *Building New Deal Liberalism: The Political Economy of Public Works*. New York: Cambridge University Press, 2006.

Stoker, Robert. *Reluctant Partners: Implementing Federal Policy*. Pittsburgh: University of Pittsburgh Press, 1991.

Stone, Chad, and Kris Cox. *Principles for Fiscal Stimulus: Economic Policy in a Weakening Economy*. Washington, DC: Center for Budget and Policy Priorities, 2008. www.cbpp.org/research/principles-for-fiscal-stimulus-economic-policy-in-a -weakening-economy.

Summers, Lawrence. "Fiscal Stimulus Issues: Testimony before the Joint Economic Committee, January 16, 2008." www.hks.harvard.edu/news-events/news/testi monies/lawrence-summers-testifies-before-joint-economic-committee.

Van Daniker, Relmond, and Helena Sims. *Redefining Accountability: Recovery Act Practices and Opportunities*. Alexandria, VA: Association of Government Accountants, 2010.

Wilson, Daniel J. "Fiscal Spending Jobs Multipliers: Evidence from the 2009 American Recovery and Reinvestment Act." *American Economic Journal: Economic Policy* 4, no. 3 (2012): 278.

Wolfers, Justin. "What Debate? Economists Agree the Stimulus Lifted the Economy." *New York Times*, July 30, 2014. www.nytimes.com/2014/07/30/upshot/what -debate-economists-agree-the-stimulus-lifted-the-economy.html.

Wolman, Harold. *National Fiscal Policy and Local Government during the Economic Crisis*. Washington, DC: German Marshall Fund, 2014.

Government Documents and Reports

Congressional Budget Office. *Estimated Impact of the American Recovery and Reinvestment Act on Employment and Economic Output from January 2011 through March 20*. Washington, DC: Congressional Budget Office, 2011.

———. *Estimated Impact of the American Recovery and Reinvestment Act on Employment and Economic Output in 2013*. Washington, DC: Congressional Budget Office, 2013.

———. *Estimated Impact of the American Recovery and Reinvestment Act on Employment and Economic Output for 2014*. Washington, DC: Congressional Budget Office, February 2015.

———. *Report on the Troubled Asset Relief Program, March 2015*. Washington, DC: Congressional Budget Office, 2015.

Council of Economic Advisers. *The Economic Impact of the American Recovery and Reinvestment Act Five Years Later: Final Report to Congress*. Washington, DC: Council of Economic Advisers, 2014. www.whitehouse.gov/sites/default/files/docs/cea_arra _report.pdf.

Federal Communications Commission. *Connecting America: The National Broadband Plan*. Washington, DC: US Government Printing Office, 2010.

———. "Policy Statement on Broadband Internet Access FCC 05-151." August 5, 2005. http://hraunfoss.fcc.gov/edocs_public/attachmatch/FCC-05-151A1.pdf.

Internal Revenue Service. "Notice 2009-72: Qualifying Advanced Energy Project Credit." *Internal Revenue Bulletin 2009-37*, September 14, 2009. www.irs.gov/irb /2009-37_IRB/ar06.html.

———. "Qualifying Advanced Energy Project Credit." www.irs.gov/pub/irs-drop/n
-13-12.pdf.

Kruger, Lennard G. "Background and Issues for Congressional Oversight of ARRA
Broadband Awards." Congressional Research Service Report R41775. March 14,
2012; May 17, 2013; and August 4, 2015.

———. "Broadband Infrastructure Programs in the American Recovery and Reinvestment Act." Congressional Research Service Report R40436. January 4, 2011.

———. "Broadband Loan and Grant Programs in the USDA's Rural Utilities Service." Congressional Research Service Report RL33816. January 4, 2011.

———. "Distribution of Broadband Stimulus Grants and Loans: Applications and
Awards." Congressional Research Service Report R41164. September 9, 2010, and
January 4, 2011.

Marples, Donald, J. "The New Markets Tax Credit: An Introduction." Congressional Research Service Report RS22680. June 19, 2007.

Office of Management and Budget. "Initial Recovery Act Implementing Guidance."
February 18, 2009.

Organization for Economic Cooperation and Development. *Fiscal Policy across Levels
of Government in Times of Crisis.* Paris: Organization for Economic Cooperation
and Development, 2010.

———. *Making the Most of Public Investment in a Tight Fiscal Environment.* Paris: Organization for Economic Cooperation and Development, 2011.

Sissine, Fred. "DOE Weatherization Program: A Review of Funding, Performance,
and Cost-Effectiveness Studies." Congressional Research Service, January 11,
2012.

US Bureau of the Census. *2010 Census of the Population.* "Urban and Rural Population
by State, 2010." www.census.gov/geo/www/ua/2010urbanruralclass.html.

———. *2014 Population Estimates.* "American FactFinder: Annual Estimates of the
Resident Population, April 1, 2010, to July 1, 2014." http://factfinder.census.gov
/faces/tableservices/jsf/pages/productview.xhtml?src=bkmk.

US Congress, House. *American Recovery and Reinvestment Act of 2009,* PL 111-5. www
.congress.gov/bill/111th-congress/house-bill/1.

———. "Broadband Loans and Grants." Hearings before the Committee on Energy
and Commerce, Subcommittee on Communications and Technology, 112th
Cong., 2nd sess., May 16, 2012.

———. "Oversight of the Department of Energy's Stimulus Spending." Hearings
before the Committee on Oversight and Government Reform, 112th Cong., 2nd
sess., March 20, 2012. http://oversight.house.gov/wp-content/uploads/2012/09
/2012-03-20-Ser.-No.-112-136-FC-Oversight-of-the-Department-of-Energys
-Stimuls-Spending.pdf.

———. "Preventing Stimulus Waste and Fraud: Who Are the Watchdogs?" Hearings before the Committee on Oversight and Government Reform, 111th Cong.,
1st sess., March 19, 2009.

US Congress, Senate. "Clean Technology Manufacturing Competitiveness: The Role
of Tax Incentives." Hearings before the Committee on Finance, Subcommittee on
Energy, Natural Resources, and Infrastructure, 111th Cong., 2nd sess., May 20, 2010.

US Department of Agriculture. "American Recovery and Reinvestment Act of 2009:
Broadband Initiatives Program—Pre-Approval Controls." Audit Report 09703-
001-32, March 2013. www.usda.gov/oig/webdocs/09703-0001-32.pdf

US Department of Agriculture, Office of Inspector General, Southwest Region. "Audit Report: Rural Utilities Service Broadband Grant and Loan Programs." Audit Report 09601-4-Te, September 2005. www.usda.gov/oig/webdocs/09601-04 -TE.pdf.

US Department of Agriculture, Rural Utilities Service. "Broadband Initiatives Program Quarterly Report," March 31, 2015. www.rd.usda.gov/files/reports/utpBroad bandInitiativesProgramReportMarch2015.pdf.

US Department of Agriculture, Rural Utilities Service, and US Department of Commerce, National Telecommunications and Information Administration. "Broadband Initiatives Program and Broadband Technology Opportunities Program." 74 *Federal Register* 58940–58944, November 16, 2009.

US Department of Commerce, Office of Inspector General. "Broadband Program Faces Uncertain Funding, and NTIA Needs to Strengthen Its Post-Award Operations." November 4, 2010, OIG-11-005-A.

———. "Misrepresentation Regarding Project Readiness, Governance Structure Put at Risk the Success of the San Francisco Bay Area Wireless Enhanced Broadband (BayWEB) Project." January 10, 2012. www.oig.doc.gov/Pages/Misrepresentations -Put-at-Risk-Success-of-San-Francisco-BayWEB-Project.aspx.

———. "NTIA Has an Established Foundation to Oversee BTOP Awards, but Better Execution of Monitoring Is Needed." OIG-12-013-A, November 17, 2011.

———. "NTIA Must Continue to Improve Its Program Management and Pre-Award Process for Its Broadband Grants Program. ARR-19842-1, April 2010.

US Department of Education. "Clarifying Guidance on the American Recovery and Reinvestment Act of 2009." August 26, 2010. www2.ed.gov/policy/gen/leg/recovery /section-1512.html.

———. "Guidance on the Maintenance-of-Effort Requirements in the State Fiscal Stabilization Fund Program." OMB 1810-069, January 10, 2010. www2.ed.gov /policy/gen/leg/recovery/statutory/moe-guidance.pdf.

———. "Guidance on the State Fiscal Stabilization Fund Program." April 2009.

———. "Overview Information; Race to the Top Fund; Notice Inviting Applications for New Awards for Fiscal Year 2010. *Federal Register* 75, no. 71 (April 14, 2010): 19510.

———. "State Fiscal Stabilization Fund: 2011 Updates." Unpublished webinar, February 1, 2011.

———. "State Grants under the State Fiscal Stabilization Fund." www2.ed.gov /programs/statestabilization/resources.html.

US Department of Education, Office of Inspector General. *American Recovery and Reinvestment Act of 2009: The Department's Implementation of the State Fiscal Stabilization Fund Program—Final Audit Report.* ED-OIG A19J0001. Washington, DC: US Government Printing Office, 2010.

———. *American Recovery and Reinvestment Act: Virginia—Use of Funds and Data Quality for Selected American Recovery and Reinvestment Act Programs, Final Audit Report.* ED-OIG A03K0008 Washington, DC: US Government Printing Office, 2011.

US Department of Energy. "History of the Weatherization Program." June 21, 2012. www1.eere.energy.gov/wip/wap_history.html.

———. "Secretary Chu's Remarks at the World Renewable Energy Forum Press Availability—as Prepared for Delivery." May 16, 2012. www.energy.gov/articles

/secretary-chus-remarks-world-renewable-energy-forum-press-availability-prepared-delivery.

———. "Weatherization Assistance Program Allocation Formula." http://energy.gov/eere/wipo/weatherization-assistance-program-allocation-formula.

US Department of Energy, Office of Inspector General. "Audit Report: The State of Illinois Weatherization Assistance Program." October 2010.

———. "Progress in Implementing the Department of Energy's Weatherization Assistance Program under the American Recovery and Reinvestment Act." February 2010.

US Department of Energy, Office of Weatherization and Intergovernmental Programs. "Weatherization Assistance Program: National Evaluations: Summary of Results." December 14, 2015. http://weatherization.ornl.gov/WAP_NationalEvaluation_WxWorks_v14_blue_8%205%2015.pdf.

US Department of Treasury, Office of Inspector General for Tax Administration. "Assessment of the Internal Revenue Service's Interpretation of Section 1302 of the Recovery Act: Qualifying Advanced Energy Project Credit." Report 2013-40-029, March 21, 2013. www.treasury.gov/tigta/auditreports/2013reports/201340029fr.html.

———. *Processes for Ensuring Compliance with Qualifying Advanced Energy Project Credit Requirements Can Be Strengthened.* Report 2014-40-011. Washington, DC: US Government Printing Office, 2014.

US Government Accountability Office. *Broadband Deployment Is Extensive throughout the United States, but It Is Difficult to Assess the Extent of Deployment Gaps in Rural Areas.* Report GAO-06-426. Washington, DC: Government Accountability Office, 2006. www.gao.gov/new.items/d06426.pdf.

———. *Federal Assistance: Temporary State Fiscal Relief.* Report GAO-04-736. Washington, DC: Government Accountability Office, 2004.

———. *Funds Continue to Provide Fiscal Relief to States and Localities, While Accountability and Reporting Challenges Need to Be Fully Addressed.* Report GAO-09-1016. Washington, DC: Government Accountability Office, 2009.

———. *High-Risk Series: An Update.* Report GAO-15-290. Washington, DC: Government Accountability Office, 2015.

———. *Medicaid: Strategies to Help States Address Increased Expenditures during Economic Downturns.* Report GAO-07-97. Washington, DC: Government Accountability Office, 2006.

———. *Recovery Act: Further Opportunities Exist to Strengthen Oversight of Broadband Stimulus Programs.* Report GAO-10-823. Washington, DC: Government Accountability Office, 2010.

———. *Recovery Act: Grant Implementation Experiences Offer Lessons for Accountability and Transparency.* Report GAO-14-219. Washington, DC: Government Accountability Office, 2014.

———. *Recovery Act: IRS Quickly Implemented Tax Provisions, but Reporting and Enforcement Improvements Are Needed.* Report GAO-10-349. Washington, DC: Government Accountability Office, 2010.

———. *Recovery Act: One Year Later, State Uses of Funds and Opportunities to Strengthen Accountability.* Report GAO-10-437. Washington, DC: Government Accountability Office, 2010.

————. *Recovery Act: Progress and Challenges in Spending Weatherization Funds.* Washington, DC: Government Accountability Office, 2011.

————. *Recovery Act: Recipient-Reported Jobs Data Provide Some Insight into Use of Recovery Act Funding, but Data Quality and Reporting Issues Need Attention.* Report GAO-10-223. Washington, DC: Government Accountability Office, 2009.

————. *Recovery Act: States' and Localities Use of Funds and Actions Needed to Address Implementation Challenges and Bolster Accountability.* Report GAO-10-604. Washington, DC: Government Accountability Office, 2010.

————. *Recovery Act: USDA Should Include Broadband Program's Impact in Annual Performance Reports.* Report GAO-14-511. Washington, DC: Government Accountability Office, 2014.

White House. "The Race to the Top: Promoting Innovation, Reform, and Excellence in America's Public Schools." Fact sheet, November 4, 2009. www.whitehouse.gov /the-press-office/fact-sheet-race-top.

CONTRIBUTORS

Alan J. Abramson is a professor of government and politics in the Schar School of Policy and Government at George Mason University, and director of George Mason's Center for Nonprofit Management, Philanthropy, and Policy. He is also a senior fellow at the Aspen Institute and an affiliated scholar at the Urban Institute. Previously, he directed the Aspen Institute's Nonprofit Program. He is the author or coauthor of numerous books and articles, and his work has twice won awards from the American Political Science Association. For 2015–16, he is president of the Association for Research on Nonprofit Organizations and Voluntary Action, the nation's premier association of university-based and other nonprofit researchers.

Lehn M. Benjamin is associate professor at the Indiana University School of Philanthropy, where she also serves as the director of the Doctoral Program. Before joining the faculty at the school, she spent ten years on the faculty at George Mason University. Her research examines issues of accountability and effectiveness in the nonprofit sector. She also worked in South Africa during the democratic transition, for the US Senate Banking Committee's Subcommittee for Housing and Urban Development, and for the US Department of the Treasury's Community Development Financial Institutions Fund.

Timothy J. Conlan is University Professor of Government at George Mason University. Before joining the George Mason faculty in 1987, he served as a senior research analyst with the US Advisory Commission on Intergovernmental Relations and as the assistant staff director of the US Senate Subcommittee on Intergovernmental Relations. He is the author of many books, articles, and research monographs in the areas of federalism, intergovernmental relations, and public policy. His books include *Pathways of Power: The Dynamics of National Policymaking*; *Intergovernmental Management for the 21st Century*; and *From New Federalism to Devolution: Twenty-Five Years of Intergovernmental Reform*. He is a fellow of the National Academy of Public Administration. In 2002 he received the Daniel J. Elazar Distinguished Federalism Scholar Award from the American Political Science Association.

Matthew J. Critchfield was a graduate research assistant with the Centers for Public Service in the Schar School of Policy and Government at George Mason University during the academic years 2010–12. He is currently employed by the US Department of Homeland Security.

Sheldon M. Edner is on the faculty of the Schar School of Policy and Government at George Mason University. In May 2010 he retired from the US Department of Transportation as associate director for financial management in the Office of the Secretary. From 2008 to 2010 he staffed the position of senior accountable official for the implementation of the American Reinvestment and Recovery Act. From 1976 to 1991, he was a professor of public administration and chair of the Public Administration Department at Portland State University.

Paul L. Posner is the director of the Graduate Public Administration Program at George Mason University and leads the university's Centers on the Public Service. He is past president of the American Society for Public Administration and is the chairman of the Board of the National Academy of Public Administration. His most recent book, *The Pathways to Power*, with his colleague Timothy Conlan, caps years of work on national policymaking processes. His work on federalism includes his book *The Politics of Unfunded Mandates*, which won the Martha Derthick Award from the American Political Science Association's Federalism Section. He consults with the senior budget officials of the Organization for Economic Cooperation and Development, has worked with federal budget commissions, and is currently cochair of the National Budget Roundtable. He was formerly with the US Government Accountability Office, where he led its federal budget and intergovernmental work for fourteen years.

Priscilla M. Regan is a professor in the Schar School of Policy and Government at George Mason University. Before joining this faculty in 1989, she was a senior analyst in the Congressional Office of Technology Assessment (1984–89) and an assistant professor of politics and government at the University of Puget Sound (1979–84). Her books include *Legislating Privacy: Technology, Social Values, and Public Policy*; and *Transparency and Surveillance as Sociotechnical Accountability: A House of Mirrors* (with Deborah G. Johnson). She has been a member of the National Academy of Sciences, Committee on Authentication Technologies and Their Privacy Implications, and she is a fellow of the National Academy of Public Administration.

Matthew Sommerfeld is a doctoral student in political science in George Mason University's Schar School of Policy and Government. He coauthored the article "The Politics of Fiscal Austerity: Implications for the United States" with Paul Posner, which was published in the *Journal of Public Budgeting and Finance* and which won the Jesse Burkhead Award for the best article of the year.

Stefan Toepler is associate professor of nonprofit studies in the Schar School of Policy and Government at George Mason University. Before joining George Mason in 2002, he was on the faculty of the Institute of Policy Studies at Johns Hopkins University. Currently, he is also affiliated with the International Laboratory of Nonprofit Sector Research at the NRU Higher School of Economics in Moscow. He is the contributing coeditor to *Private Funds, Public Purpose: Philanthropic Foundations in International Perspective*; *Global Civil Society: Dimensions of the Nonprofit Sector*; and *The Legitimacy of Philanthropic Foundations: US and European Perspectives*. Most recently, he served as editor in chief (with Helmut Anheier) of the *International Encyclopedia of Civil Society*.

INDEX

9 781626 163706